GRASSLAND SETTLERS

CANADIAN PLAINS RESEARCH CENTER
UNIVERSITY OF REGINA
1975

GRASSLAND SETTLERS:

THE SWIFT CURRENT REGION DURING THE ERA OF THE RANCHING FRONTIER

Don C. McGowan

FOREWORD

It is difficult to define local history. For that matter, it is difficult to define history. No one today accepts the old definition of history as "past politics". History is concerned with everything in the past which is part of the human story, humanity in the world, in the region and in the locality. That is why we have, in addition to the familiar, traditional political history, social, economic, military, constitutional, ecclesiastical, scientific, artistic, literary and, of course, regional and local history.

Local history, and I include in this generalization regional history as well, has not always enjoyed the respect of academic historians in Canada, Great Britain or in the United States. Behind this peevishness has been a certain professional snobbishness, even jealousy, if only because local history has invariably been the work of amateurs. And yet there was some justification for this attitude. Local histories were too frequently dull, genealogical, antiquarian efforts, undertaken merely for the sake of recreation, to promote local pride or to throw light on one's ancestry. That is why one academic historian wrote in 1914 that local history books were just "so much dead weight on library shelves; vexatious to the student because of their disorderliness and wordiness; lacking most of what histories should contain; and containing much that histories should omit". I think that basically the unpopularity of local history among academic historians was owing to the fact that local history was sub-national in character in an era when university history appeared to be little more than meaningless anti-quarianism of no real importance to the nation.

Today this attitude has changed. The feeling is now prevalent in our universities that historians have occupied themselves too exclusively with the fortunes and misfortunes of the national state. Academic historians have come to see local history as "an intelligible field of study", because they recognize that our rural and urban communities have, each in their own way, contributed to the main currents of our national life. Local histories are the "articulation", the word is Toynbee's, of the national state. There are few Canadians who will not admit that for generations our political behavior has been determined primarily by the situations existing in the local constituencies. That will explain why, since the Second World War, our universities and colleges have devoted more and more attention to local history. It is not unreasonable to say that local history is now well in the mainstream of historical writing in Canada.

The local historian's task is to portray, for his readers, the origin, development and growth to maturity of the community in which he is interested. And this is just what Donald McGowan has done so competently in this book. He has traced the story of Swift Current and its environs from its original establishment in south western Saskatchewan, on the main line of the Canadian Pacific Railway, through its early days of tented buildings and false-fronted stores, its exciting months as a military base during the North West Rebellion, its brief period of trail-freighting, its years as a ranching area both for cattle and sheep, to the coming of the sodbusters, and the incorporation of Swift Current as a town in 1907. Like any good historian, academic or otherwise, Mr. McGowan plays the role of geographer as he explains how the land around Swift Current was subdued to human purposes, and of an economist as he outlines the various means by which men earned their livelihood in the early years of settlement. As for his historical techniques, well, what difference is there between the techniques of the local historian and those of the national historian? Surely historical method is not much more than the application of common sense.

One more word about local history. As an academic historian, I am thoroughly convinced that the best approach to teaching Canadian history in our schools is by using local materials, provided those local materials have some familiarity and relevance to the pupil and to his experience. It seems particularly pertinent in these days of instant communications that Canadian students should understand that, in the days before the daily press, the telephone, the radio and the television, almost all human experience in this country was localized; that it was the villages and the small towns that shaped our lives; that government and public administration were close to the people; and that municipalities, townships and counties played the dominant role in people's lives. It is an error to ask the schoolboy to grapple with the kind of problems that baffled statesmen in earlier ages in Europe and North America, before giving him an understanding of the meaning and relevance of history by acquainting him with the history of his own neighborhood. Such errors have all too often led to a lack of appreciation of the discipline required of the historian, even to a positive dislike of the subject itself. And that, I think, is unfortunate. More books like this one would go far towards helping students realize that they, their fathers and their grandfathers and the whole community in which they live, are part of the human story. And that is what history is all about.

George F. G. Stanley,
Director of Canadian Studies,
Mount Allison University.

Sackville,
New Brunswick,
May 2, 1975.

AUTHOR'S PREFACE
AND ACKNOWLEDGEMENTS

This book is a regional history describing the general development of Swift Current and its surrounding region during the years up to the spring of 1907. By that time Swift Current had achieved the status of an incorporated town, and a substantial farm settlement had begun around it. Before this, and ending early in 1907, the district was a typical part of the ranching frontier of the semi-arid region within the Canadian prairie West.

There is no single consistent explanation why the Swift Current region developed as it did. While economic and environmental forces appear to have been most important in regulating the development of the community, such transplanted and assimilative institutions as law, politics, government, church and school, either singly or in concert, also played a pervasive role. All history is a seamless garment woven on the loom of time from a variety of threads.

Several people helped me in the preparation of this book. The idea of writing a book on the early history of the Swift Current region first occurred to me in 1967 while attending a Centennial Conference on the history of the Canadian West held in Banff. Shortly before this, I had written an essay on Swift Current's early years for a university course. No one had previously attempted to research and write a general history of this area, and almost nothing was known about the years of exploration, early settlement and development of this important region of the prairies. Feeling that such a history was needed, I responded to the challenge by choosing this topic for a history thesis which I completed in 1971 for the University of Saskatchewan (Regina Campus), under the supervision of Professor A. Richard Allen. His willing help, guidance and encouragement is gratefully acknowledged. The manuscript, in thesis form, benefited from the constructive criticism of the following members of the thesis examination committee: Allan R. Turner (now the Provincial Archivist of British Columbia), C. B. Koester, and F. W. Anderson. In revising and enlarging the thesis manuscript into its present form, the writer profited from the counsel of two acknowledged authorities on the history of the prairie West during the Territorial period — Lewis H. Thomas (University of Alberta, Edmonton) and George F. G. Stanley (Mont Allison University, Sackville) both of whom carefully examined the entire manuscript. A special debt of gratitude is hereby acknowledged to Professor Thomas, who first inspired me to study history while I was his student at university in Regina. Professor Stanley's remarks in the Foreword of this book further increase the author's debt to this distinguished scholar. Nevertheless, any errors or omissions which remain in the book are my sole responsibility. The final stylistic revision of this history, and the indexing, were done with the assistance of Miss Ellen M. Ross, whose generous help is also gratefully acknowledged. Finally, the writer wishes to express his deep appreciation to his wife, who read the several drafts of this history, and offered helpful advice and encouragement at times when it was most needed. No man — especially a historian — is an island.

This book has been published with the help of a grant from the Social Science Research Council of Canada, using funds provided by the Canada Council.

TABLE OF CONTENTS

MAPS AND TABLES

ILLUSTRATIONS

MAP 1

Swift Current and Surrounding Region During The Territorial Period.

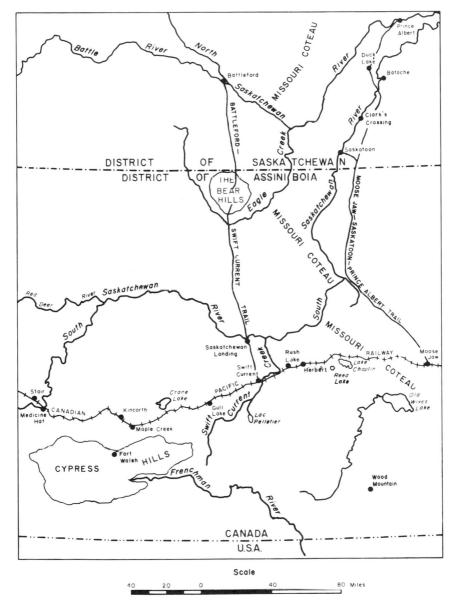

Scale

40   20   0   40   80 Miles

THE SETTING

1883-1905

Chapter I

THE LAND

The métis scout halted on a hill bordering a broad valley and, from the back of his stallion, gazed hopefully at the winding creek below. Then he scanned the parched prairie to the horizon in search of the great shaggy beasts. He was worried. His hunting party had travelled hundreds of miles since leaving home on the Red River. One more day would make five weeks of searching ever farther west. The gnawing in his stomach reminded him that the men and women were weakening and the children crying from hunger. Never had they been forced to travel so far nor endure so much on their annual hunts. Constantly they had risked attack from Sioux war parties. Now, they had entered the hunting grounds of the fierce Blackfeet.

A sudden movement among a patch of willows along the creek caught his attention. He shaded his eyes from the afternoon sun for a better look. Buffaloes! But it was only a small roving band. Disappointed, he searched the landscape again for a glimpse of the countless thousands of buffaloes they sought.

Shimmering heat waves rose from the sun-cracked plains. The hot July winds had wilted the vegetation, parching the stunted grass prematurely to a yellowish hue. White alkali, pitted black by the hooves of thirsty buffalo, glistened from a dry slough bottom. As far as his eye could see, the only greenery was along the banks of the almost dry watercourse. Here he could make out clumps of saskatoons and chokecherries, rosebushes and willows, along with a few cottonwoods and poplars that gave shade to a score of buffaloes. Beyond the creek, a small whirlwind was forming a dust funnel that twisted along its erratic course through the withered grass and sagebrush. Everywhere he could see bleached bones, a mocking reminder to him of the great herd which he had hoped to find.

Wheeling his horse back towards the hunting party, the scout reflected worriedly. Even if his people could slaughter all of the animals that he had seen by the creek, it would only ease their hunger for a few days. They needed more than a thousand prime buffalo or they would know great hardship and starvation during the coming winter. Clearly, the main herd had deserted the sun-scorched plain to pasture on the unfailing grasses of the Cypress Hills — three days farther over the western horizon. The hunt must go on to the Hills.

That frustrated scout was an imaginary member of a very real band — the first band of métis ever reported to have extended their buffalo hunts

1

into the Cypress Hills.[1] The year was 1859. The arid prairie landscape scanned in vain by our scout that afternoon is the heart of an area in southwestern Saskatchewan which is now known as the Swift Current district — the region with which this history is concerned. The winding creek — named by early métis hunters *Rivière au Courant* — is the present Swift Current Creek which has its source in the Cypress Hills. To gain a clear picture of the setting of the area we, like that band of hunters, must go on to the Hills.

The unique land formation known as Cypress Hills is an important watershed in the prairie region of southwestern Saskatchewan. From here streams originating from the underground springs and melting snows of the forested hills flow to different ends of the continent. Those that run in a southerly direction join the Missouri and Mississippi river systems, thus mixing eventually with the warm waters of the Gulf of Mexico. Other waters flowing from these towering hills finally reach icy Hudson Bay. Part of this latter network of streams forms the hundred-mile long Swift Current Creek which flows first northeasterly and then aburptly northwesterly through the rolling plains before discharging into the muddy South Saskatchewan River.

Our story centres upon a spot in a broad valley, once an ancient riverbed, through which this creek winds. At this place, late in 1882, the construction crews of the Canadian Pacific Railway (C.P.R.), who were forging westward to the Pacific Ocean, bridged the creek and began to establish the railway divisional point of Swift Current. Those unfamiliar with the Canadian prairies can easily find the location on a map. It lies eighty-nine miles due north of the Canada-United States boundary and ninety-seven miles due east of the Saskatchewan-Alberta border. Here, the small but thriving city of Swift Current now stands, while in the surrounding region are several towns and villages. All these points are engaged in serving the needs of the productive agricultural and petroleum industry in this area.

The transformation of this region from a buffalo ground to its present diversified agricultural economy is a long and complex story. The present study focusses upon the earliest period of white settlement, from the early 1880's to 1907 — the years characterized by the ranching frontier.

For centuries before the coming of the railway and the beginning of white settlement, today's southwestern Saskatchewan was little more than a great buffalo pasture. Other species of wild game were also plentiful: moose, elk, deer, antelope, grizzly and black bear, cougar, wolf, and smaller fur-bearing animals. Waterfowl and fish were likewise abundant. But both the prairie Indians' hunting skill and their way of life focussed upon the buffalo hunt. Most of what they needed the buffalo provided. In Cypress Hills and over the surrounding grasslands, hunting parties of Cree, Assiniboine, Sioux, Saulteaux and Blackfeet roamed in search of buffalo. They must have stopped by the Swift Current Creek for water and

2

firewood, to search for game, or, at times, to pick wild chokecherries and saskatoon berries which grew along its banks. On nearby Lac Pelletier Creek, a small tributary to the Swift Current, the Indians and, later, the métis buffalo hunters had a favorite winter campsite. It was located in the valley beside a small, deep, fish-filled lake which the métis named Lac Pelletier. This French name alone survived the later trend of Anglicization which was to begin with the entry of the Mounties and land surveyors into the district and the departure of the métis.

By 1860, the Cypress Hills-Swift Current Creek region was the centre of the last good prairie hunting ground on British territory. Elsewhere, the westward advance of white civilization in North America had quickly led to the slaughtering of most of the countless million buffaloes. Here, for a few more years, were still to be found the remnants of the once-great buffalo herds. Because of this, the region was claimed and fiercely fought over by rival tribes of increasingly desperate Indians. The Blackfeet nation to the west and their traditional enemies, the Cree and Assiniboine Indians to the east, all dependent for life itself upon the vanishing buffalo, struggled to control this highly-prized buffalo pasture. The Blackfeet, in particular, until the Mounties brought peace into the region in 1874, were likely to attack without warning any intruders into this territory. No other Indian tribes, not even the well-armed métis from the far off Red River area, ever entered this prized and disputed area unless in large bands organized with watchful scouts, guards, and pickets. With the arrival of white men who hunted, policed, and finally settled in the region, the almost extinct buffalo disappeared entirely from the district. When this happened, it was only a matter of a few years until the local Indians had either died of starvation or quit the area. Like the buffaloes, they left little but their bones to mark their passing.

With the coming of the C.P.R. in 1882, geographic and economic forces combined in establishing the trading area known as the Swift Current district. During the time span of this history, when it was predominantly a ranching frontier, this district extended outward from the railway point called Swift Current in distances varying from thirty to fifty miles. The boundaries of its hinterland were fairly precise and constant, conforming closely to those shown on Map 2 on page 4.

Topographical features partly defined the district. About thirty miles to the north of Swift Current, the broad South Saskatchewan River, with its steep banks and bordering coulees, largely confined the district in that direction up to the year 1907, as, to a lesser degree, did the southern slope of the Swift Current Creek Plateau which follows a line running roughly parallel to and thirty miles south of the main line of the C.P.R. The Cypress Hills, almost fifty miles due southwest along the creek, just west of the spot where its north and south forks unite, form the last physical boundary of the region.

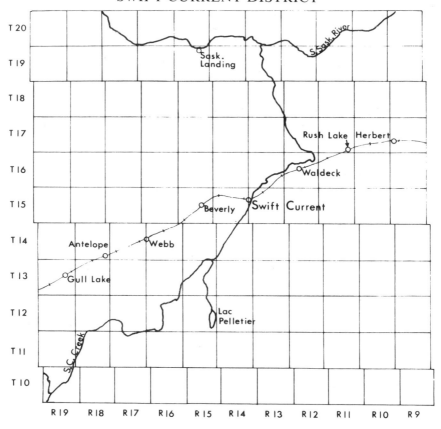

MAP 2
TOWNSHIP MAP DELINEATING THE
SWIFT CURRENT DISTRICT

Ranges are numbered from east to west.
Townships are numbered from south to north.

To a great extent, the waterways of the region were to mark the limits of early settlement. Ranchers required for their herds a water supply that was not only plentiful and reliable, but also close to shelter and good grazing land. In all respects the South Saskatchewan River, with its treed coulees and adjacent grasslands, as well as the range along the creeks in the district, was well suited to ranching. Consequently, the range of every stockman in the district during those early years bordered either upon the river's banks or on one of the local creeks. Farm settlement, which began in earnest early in the twentieth century, was likewise limited by the river, unbridged and unfordable. All early farmers of the district felt obliged to settle to the south of it. However, since farmers could settle on the open plains and meet their more modest water requirements from wells or sloughs, they were not as dependent upon waterways as were the ranchers.

4

Transportation was another important limiting factor in early settlement, and in this regard the rancher had the advantage over the farmer. The rancher could herd his livestock to the railway for shipment to market much more easily and cheaply than the farmer could haul his grain there. Yet both ranchers and farmers preferred to be close enough to a trading centre to secure conveniently the goods and other amenities of life which they desired. As a result, in 1907, when the period of the ranching frontier ended, agricultural settlement had nowhere spread out more than thirty miles on either side of the single railway line.

During this first quarter-century of the district's history, economic forces limited the extent of its hinterland even more sharply than did its topography. There were two other competing trading centres — Maple Creek, just over eighty miles to the west along the C.P.R. mainline, and Moose Jaw, the next railway divisional town, some one hundred miles to the east. Their presence limited Swift Current's hinterland to an area which extended only about forty miles both east and west. Expansion in other directions was hampered by the lack of rail transportation, for during those years there were no branch lines of the C.P.R. out of Swift Current. Had there been, or had a rival railway been built there, the hamlet's hinterland would have expanded.

Until the railway fostered settlement, there was neither fur trade, mission, nor police post within the Swift Current district. There were simply too few permanently-resident native peoples or fur-bearing animals to justify their presence. Some whisky traders and fur trade posts put in an appearance, but only briefly, in the nearby Cypress Hills. A few white explorers and fur traders had paddled by canoe along the South Saskatchewan, but none, apparently, bothered to enter the Swift Current Creek or to explore the lands along its banks. The first white man known to have set foot within the district was Isaac Cowie, a Hudson's Bay Company trader, who in June of 1868 set out from Qu'Appelle with a well-armed métis and Indian hunting party and crossed the northern part of the district in search of the now-elusive buffaloes.[2] In the pre-railway period only a handful of local white men knew anything about the Swift Current district.

Indeed, before the local railway surveys were made in 1880, only general information, and little of that, was available about the entire area now comprising southwest Saskatchewan. True, in June 1857, a British expedition led by Captain John Palliser began a three year survey of the North-West and Rupert's Land, with instructions to obtain both general and scientific knowledge of the British-owned territory lying between the Red River and the Rocky Mountains. During these three years this expedition covered thousands of miles in the west, but it skirted the Swift Current district both to the west and east. Meanwhile, a few politicians in the colony of Canada were beginning to think that this region should be secured for Canada before it, like the Oregon Territory, was lost to the United States. So, in August 1857, an expedition dispatched by the land-hungry Province of Canada and led by H. Y. Hind and S. J. Dawson also set out to make a general survey of part of the same region. A year later this Canadian party was instructed to study an additional area extending westward to the South Saskatchewan River. Like the British expedition, however, they failed to enter the Swift Current district. Their half-breed guides flatly refused to venture closer than the Elbow of the South Saskatchewan to this perilous country then fought over by rival Indian tribes. The subsequent reports made by both expeditions merely describe a large, somewhat triangular shaped region of the prairies, with the Swift Current district near its centre, as being too arid to be fit for agricultural settlement.[3] Thus, a damaging sentence was passed upon the farming potential of the district without a proper trial.

No further survey of the region surrounding the Swift Current Creek was undertaken until after Canada acquired the North-West and Rupert's Land from Britain and the Hudson's Bay Company in 1870. Despite the fact that local Indian tribes still had not made a treaty with the young Dominion to cover this region, the 1873-74 period saw two additional survey parties work fairly close to the Swift Current district. The first party, a small Canadian geological expedition led by Robert Bell, reached a point about forty-five miles northeast of the district's centre, some five miles north of present-day Ernfold, before being turned back by unfriendly Indians.[4] These Indians, probably Crees, were as determined as the métis of Red River had been in 1869 to stop unauthorized Canadian survey parties from encroaching on their land. The second group, a large, well-armed international commission surveying the boundary along the forty-ninth parallel, had the diminutive Canadian geologist, George M. Dawson, as one of its surveyors. Though Dawson, at times, extended his explorations as much as sixty miles north of the Canada-United States border and compiled much reliable scientific information, nonetheless, like his predecessors, he did not attempt to explore the dangerous area drained by the Swift Current Creek. Only with the arrival of the newly-formed North-West Mounted Police in 1874 and the conclusion later that year of Treaty Number 4 with most of the Cree and Assiniboine bands in the district, did the area become safe for peaceful surveys. And six years were to pass before such a survey was undertaken. During those years, however, the Mounties and others who travelled the several prairie trails between eastern points and Fort Walsh in Cypress Hills, became acquainted to some extent with the Swift Current region. In particular, the Mounties, bringing Canadian law and order to the prairie west, prepared the region for white settlement.

The North-West Mounted Police first entered the area in 1874 on their arduous march from Dufferin, Manitoba, en route to the Cypress Hills and infamous Fort Whoop-Up. It was on August 24th of that year that the Mounties reached the banks of *Rivière au Courant,* as Swift Current Creek was then called, some twenty miles to the south of the present-day city of

6

Swift Current. They had to camp by the creek and spend an entire day grading its steep banks in order to provide passage across it for their supply wagons.[5] Meanwhile, their half-breed scouts shot some buffalo in the district to provide the weary police force with a welcome change from salt pork.

When the N.W.M.P. rode on patrol through this district and first saw the great rolling plains, there were no fences, no plowed furrows, no houses, and no roads except for two faint trails.[6] There were, however, numerous shallow foot-wide paths cut into the brown prairie sod by the countless hooves of the quickly vanishing herds of buffalo. Spreading out before the lawmen was the grey-green bunch grass and short "prairie wool" interspersed with silver sagebrush. The expanse of prairie hills and the immense sky with soaring, white, flat-bottomed clouds must have caused them to marvel at the vastness and wild beauty of these plains. At times while on patrol they would detect the sharp and often alarming smell of prairie fire, or catch the delicate scent of the wild roses in the coulees, or the rich odor of the prairie soil filled with the promise of spring. Often a herd of fleet but curious antelope would follow along at a safe distance to investigate this new intruder into their wild domain.

Crossing the prairie these riders felt the restless wind pulse against their faces and heard the calls of meadowlark and gopher, of coyote and buffalo wolf, and a dozen other prairie creatures. This was never a silent land, for even when the wild creatures were still, there was always the sound of the wind. Like the natives before them, these young peace officers came to know the wind in all its moods: they experienced its gentle caress in the easy days of summer and its terrible strangling fury during a smothering blizzard, or again its capricious moods when the warm Chinook swept over the rolling plain transforming the bleak, winter landscape into spring within hours. Many, though not all, of these Mounties came to love this land, and a few stayed after the railway came to become fine settlers and citizens.

Although the arrival of the Mounties and the signing of Treaty Number 4 with the Indians had opened the region for peaceful surveys, it was not until 1880 that the Canadian botanist, John Macoun, became the first of many surveyors and scientists to explore the district. These men, by their surveys, began the process that eventually changed the once wild buffalo ground into prosperous ranches and farms.

Today, surveyors and scientists have accumulated a storehouse of facts related to the soils, the native vegetation, the seasonal temperature variations, the precipitation, and the general suitability for agricultural purposes of this district. We now know that the land lying just south and southwest of Swift Current is characteristic of the dark brown soil subzone type. The balance of the district consists of the brown soil variety with occasional variations from lighter to darker brown soils. This topsoil was formed thousands of years ago from till, outwash, and lacustrine deposits left behind by the retreating Keewatin ice sheet. Here, on these fertile plains, medium-tall grasses are more abundant than in the short-grass prairie of the Cypress Hills region to the southwest. This region near Swift Current, then, is classified by scientists as being "mixed prairie."[7]

Nearly ninety years of local scientific observation confirms that, generally, the winters are long and rigorous, occasionally being interrupted by the warm, but short-lived, Chinook winds from the southwest. These welcome winds make the winters of this southwestern part of the province milder and more variable than elsewhere in Saskatchewan. Due to its dry atmosphere, the cold is less penetrating, and the extremely low temperatures are less discomforting than are moderately low temperatures in regions of higher humidity. The summers are comparatively short and warm, often with high day temperatures and many hours of intense sunshine, while the nights are occasionally cool. Extremes of temperature from forty degrees below zero in winter to one hundred degrees above zero in summer are frequent. However, dry, hot winds affect this region more than other areas of Saskatchewan. Sometimes they cause serious damage to grasses and crops, notwithstanding the fact that the soil may contain sufficient moisture to prevent wilting under ordinary conditions. Recorded data indicate that the last spring frosts occur commonly during the first week of June, with the first fall frost normally striking the district during the second week of September. Therefore, the average frost-free growing season is only about one hundred days. The mean annual precipitation is slightly less than fifteen inches. Nearly half of this amount usually falls during May, June and July. For this reason, together with the frequently high wind velocity and evaporation rate, the region is semi-arid.[8] Though ranching quickly succeeded where the buffalo had pastured so well in this Chinook belt, it took the combined determination and skills of generations of farmers and agricultural scientists to firmly establish grain growing in this often-hostile land.

In the years from 1880 to 1884, following John Macoun's trips across the district, numerous surveyors and geologists in the employ of the C.P.R. Syndicate and of the Dominion Lands Branch of the Canadian Government tramped throughout the region. They measured it off and marked it into squares; they analyzed its soils and mapped the features of its empty plains. This done, the stage was set for the expected tide of western settlement which, it was believed, would surely follow in the wake of the transcontinental railway.

Despite these preparations, almost a quarter-century was to pass before the long-awaited flood of homesteaders swept into the district to claim the unfenced land on which local ranchers grazed their herds. But these years of waiting were not without incident or value, either to the district or to Canada. It was in this period that the foundations were laid which made possible the orderly, sustained development of the district's farm lands and market centres at a record rate in the West. Early railroaders and trail freighters, steamboat and ferry men, half-breeds and Indians, militiamen and Mounties, buffalo hunters and bone dealers, aristocratic promoters and pioneer ranchers, missionaries and Mennonites, together with an incoming tide of homesteaders and townsmen from many lands, all played a part in Swift Current's frontier days.

Chapter II

RAIL AND TRAIL

Swift Current, like many neighboring prairie communities, owes its existence to the C.P.R. The final decision to cross this portion of the prairies with the transcontinental railway largely rested upon the advice of John Macoun. His report tipped the balance in favor of building by a southern route west of Moose Jaw rather than northwestward through Battleford. Even to this optimistic man, agriculture was the only potential industry in the region through which the Swift Current Creek flowed. Furthermore, whatever agricultural potential the area possessed could only be realized by the provision of dependable, relatively cheap, transportation facilities which would serve the needs of its settlers and carry such bulky products as grain and livestock to distant markets. Macoun correctly foresaw the area's ranching potential, but he was wrong in claiming that grain could then be successfully grown there, for this semi-arid district only became part of the grain belt when dry land farming methods were developed and widely used. Though the railway, therefore, created and justified the district, many years were to pass before the district was to justify a railway.

Since even ranching did not begin to develop in the district for some time after train service began, the hamlet had to rely for its existence upon the buffalo bone trade and trail freighting, plus the traffic and payroll of the C.P.R. itself. In this way, the hamlet was sustained until prosperous ranches and, later, farms developed around it. Its selection as a divisional point on the main line gave it further stature and stability — a selection due as much to the water that the Swift Current Creek could provide for the steam trains as to the fact that the creek is nearly equi-distant from the adjacent divisional centres of Moose Jaw and Medicine Hat. In addition, Swift Current was for several years the closest railway shipping point for the populous Battleford district. The traffic which passed over the trail between these two centres, especially while Battleford was under siege during the Riel rebellion, made Swift Current strategically important, for a time, to the whole of Canada. After peace was restored in the North-West, trail and rail traffic continued to support the tiny community. Throughout all the early years, bone merchants of the district benefited from the fact that they were in the heart of a huge, one-time buffalo pasture. Thousands upon thousands of tons of buffalo bones, destined to be used for fertilizer or in the refining of sugar, were gathered from the rolling plains as far away as Battleford to become the first, and, for years, the only cash crop to leave the district. By the time that a railway reached Saskatoon in 1890, thereby providing Battleford with a closer railway terminus, Red River cart freighting in the prairies was almost finished. With its passing, the métis, whose livelihood it had been, dropped out of the economic mainstream of life, their wooden carts unable to compete with the white man's steam locomotive. Fortunately for the economic life of Swift Current, when cart and wagon trail freighting ended, a new industry, ranching, had emerged to replace it.

As late as 1879 the route to be followed by the projected railway from Winnipeg across the North-West Territories to the Rockies was still the subject of debate. There was little scientific information available on the vast south-central plains region beyond the forbidding reports Palliser and Hind had furnished over twenty years earlier.

In order to determine the value of their assertions, the government, acting through the railway which it then owned, sent John Macoun into Rupert's Land and the North-West in 1879 to begin a study of the resources of the prairie region, including the area along the Swift Current Creek. Macoun and his fellow surveyors did not set foot on the lands along this creek in 1879, or even in what is now southwestern Saskatchewan and southeastern Alberta, the centre of Palliser's triangle. Still, based on their findings elsewhere in the West that year, early in 1880 Macoun published a sweeping report on the entire Canadian West. So far as his comments in this document on the heartland of Palliser's triangle are concerned, the report is both rash and over-generalized. Macoun claims in the report that both Palliser and Hind were largely mistaken regarding the arid nature of the plains. He did not appear to realize that while these two earlier surveys done by Hind and Palliser had taken place during a period of drought, his own and others' surveys of the West in 1879 were made when rainfall was abundant. As a result, he recklessly classified at least 150 million acres of the Canadian West as then being fit for dry land agricultural settlement. It took a revolution in dry land farming methods in this area beginning over a generation later to achieve the goal Macoun thought was attainable by farmers in 1880.

On hearing this encouraging report, the newly-formed C.P.R. Syndicate, successor to the publicly-owned C.P.R., decided to alter the route which the railway would follow, at least as far west as Moose Jaw Creek. A shorter line from Winnipeg to present-day Moose Jaw was surveyed and approved at the beginning of 1881. At this point, the private company was undecided whether to build to the northwest through Battleford, then the capital of the North-West Territories, and thus by the old Yellowhead Pass route through the Rockies, or to follow the shorter southern route through Calgary and the kicking Horse Pass to tidewater.

The syndicate's decision regarding the route involved more than economy in construction or a desire to head off future U.S. railroad competition in the southern Canadian prairies. As one historian, F. G.

Roe, rightly pointed out, higher construction and operating costs through the rugged mountains along the southern route probably made this route less economical than the original northern route. Moreover, the only U.S. railroad then building westward through the great plains near the Canada-U.S. border was the Northern Pacific, but it was being built sporadically on a route more than 200 miles south of the boundary line and, significantly, well over 300 miles south of Moose Jaw and the C.P.R. main line — too far distant to be an effective competitor with the C.P.R. for the carrying trade in the Canadian prairies. According to Roe, the railway financiers had a further economic reason for favoring the southern route. This was a greater opportunity for making windfall profits from real estate developments in and around any railway townsites that it created than would be possible in those communities, such as Battleford, where existing land holders and rival speculators would share in the profits from soaring land prices.[1]

Battleford's citizens, on the other hand, dismayed by the earlier change in route which had already left Prince Albert far from the all-important railway, saw themselves similarly threatened. The future of their land values, the arrival of settlers who would and could profitably develop both the hamlet and the agricultural potential of the district, even the continuance of Battleford as the capital of the North-West Territories, hinged upon the coming of the railway. Surely the railway would not forsake the existing settlements along the fertile, wooded valley of the North Saskatchewan for the dry and empty, windswept plains of Palliser's triangle! Surely no surveyor familiar with the country would suggest such a thing! Surely Macoun's faults were obvious!

Such wishful thinking proved futile, for the government in 1880 gave Macoun the task of evaluating the region west from Moose Jaw Creek. His report proved to be crucial to the future development of the south-central plains. He and his party first entered the Swift Current district in July, 1880, en route for Cypress Hills, and recrossed it while returning east the following month.[2] Carried away by his usual self-confidence and optimism, Macoun later reported to the hard-driving C.P.R. syndicate that almost all of the land lying between the north end of Old Wives' Lake and Cypress Hills was excellent soil with occasional wide, slightly undulating plains covered with tall, rich grass.[3] If the vast herds of buffalo had survived to graze upon these plains in 1880, as they had when Palliser and Hind explored them over twenty years earlier, perhaps the grass would not have been so lush, despite the abundance of rainfall in the latter period.

Macoun claims that his advice early in 1881 to J. J. Hill, George Stephen and R. B. Angus, C.P.R. directors, on the agricultural potential of the south-central plains was the deciding factor which tipped the balance in favor of the more direct southern route.[4] Had 1879 and 1880 been very dry instead of wet years, Macoun's report on the region must surely have been less favorable. A drought might well have resulted in the railway being built north-west from Moose Jaw to Battleford and on through Edmonton and the Yellowhead Pass to the Pacific. If Battleford's citizens had realized that abundant rainfall in these years meant heartbreak for them, undoubtedly the North-West would have witnessed the only prayers for drought in its history.

As a consequence, Swift Current, together with dozens of other southern prairie towns, came into being, and Battleford, its hopes frustrated, was replaced by Regina as Territorial capital on March 27, 1883. Thus, such centres as Regina, Medicine Hat and Calgary as well as Swift Current, gained by Battleford's loss. Had this decision not been made, the area now known as Saskatchewan and Alberta might have become one province in 1905 with its capital centrally located at Battleford, and Regina, if it existed at all, might today be merely another little prairie town known by its original name of Pile of Bones. The decision which the railway syndicate made following Macoun's report was extremely critical for the pattern of western development.

Once the decision on the route was made, the preparation for construction began immediately. By October, 1881, the surveyed line for the C.P.R. was staked out as far west as the Swift Current Creek.[5] Early the following spring, L. A. Hamilton, the C.P.R. lands officer, selected from the Mile Belt Reserve[6] along the main line the location for future stations and townsites. Swift Current, because of availability of water in the creek to supply the steam trains, was picked as one of those townsites and a divisional point as well.[7] Now actual construction through the region was begun.

Thrusting ahead at a rate of six miles per day, the C.P.R. roadbed grading gangs reached Swift Current Creek by September, 1882. Following them, but at half the speed, came the track layers.[8] While the graders pushed on towards Maple Creek, the track crew, laying their steel rails upon an unballasted roadbed, reached and passed through Swift Current in December, 1882. Consequently, this section of the line west of Moose Jaw was, at first, fit only to handle work-train traffic.[9] As the cold weather approached, the construction party that had preceded the track layers to Swift Current quickly staked out the locations for a depot, roundhouse and siding,[10] and built a loading platform. When severe winter weather finally came in January, 1883, the railway navvies were forced to halt. By that time the graders had heaped up the partly frozen sods to a point close to Seven Persons Coulee (Medicine Hat) and track had been laid almost to the site of the future town of Maple Creek. Swift Current then received its first of several minor set-backs. Plagued by the cold and a fuel shortage, the crew of one work train that had been hauling construction materials was forced to tear up and burn Swift Current's new loading platform in order to keep their engine's boilers working until they could reach their winter headquarters at Regina.[11] The C.P.R. left behind a caretaker, John Lindsay, to watch over its Swift Current property until spring arrived. With him was

William C. Tims, a brother and employee of Frank Fraser Tims who continued to run a small general store in Regina and owned the first hastily-erected tent store in Swift Current. Only the visits of Indian customers, recently camped nearby along the creek, or the Mounties on patrol broke their winter solitude.[12]

With spring came a large gang of workmen with carloads of materials. They first replaced the ill-fated plank platform. Then, they quickly built a freight shed, watering tank, section house, bunk house, small depot, and erected the indispensable C.P.R. dining hall complete with hotel rooms above. Later they replaced with a roundhouse and turntable the wye track used for turning engines. In the years to come, the dining hall, with its twenty-four bedrooms upstairs, not only provided welcome meals for travellers but also served as restaurant, hotel, public meeting house, makeshift church for various visiting missionaries, and a general gathering spot for the local citizens. Truly, the C.P.R. established Swift Current and dominated its life.

In April, the first freight trains, cautiously running over the still unballasted sod grades beyond Moose Jaw, crept into Swift Current. Then another brief set-back occurred, as almost immediately a blizzard piled snowdrifts into the cuts near Morse and brought traffic to a temporary standstill. This storm caused another problem to emerge which further delayed rail traffic. As the warm April winds melted the drifted snow, the Swift Current Creek flooded its banks, carrying off a portion of the temporary wooden bridge. Late in April, when repairs had been made to the bridge, the line was again opened. Falteringly, Swift Current's life as a railway centre had begun.

As the transcontinental neared completion and white settlement spread in the prairies, train service was gradually improved. Two mixed trains weekly began running east and west through Swift Current in 1884 and, to the delight of local residents, in April, 1889, a daily train service was begun. This daily service meant more railwaymen were needed at Swift Current to service and run the trains. The added payroll plus the passenger service trade was welcomed by the merchants, and all enjoyed the added excitement that went with it.

Early in this period the C.P.R. made extensive land selections in the district as part of its Dominion subsidy. Acting upon the report of a Professor Kenaston and certain Dominion Lands surveyors who had examined the district between 1881 and 1886, the C.P.R. land department selected most of those odd-numbered sections which it wished to receive in the townships around Swift Current.[13] This appears to have been a positive and much needed display of faith in the agricultural potential of the district and a confirmation of John Macoun's claims. Apparently, the railway considered this land fairly fit for settlement and gambled that future land buyers would likewise do so. This was one gamble that the syndicate came close to losing. It was 1888 before the C.P.R. could find its first buyer for

15

any of its land in the district. The syndicate's twenty year exemption from taxation on this land, calculated from the date it received patent to it, had expired on some of the land before the company succeeded in selling it. The railway's set-back, of course, was also Swift Current's.

Swift Current experienced yet another difficulty. The false-fronted offices and stores which had replaced the hamlet's first canvas-roofed structures by the summer of 1883, together with most of its seven houses built and occupied by the white residents, faced south towards the railway. The lots upon which these frame buildings stood should have lined up with the first sub-division survey done in 1883 by Hugh Kerr,[14] Dominion Lands surveyor. To the dismay of those concerned, they did not. Local half-breeds and Indians, squatting in tents, shanties or cone-shaped tepees south along the creek, of course, were unaffected. The Dominion Lands surveyor, R. C. Laurie of Battleford, attempted in 1886, without success, to locate the wooden survey stakes marking the town lots. Perhaps the Indians had used them for fire wood. It seemed ironic to some that even the newly-built office of the local Dominion Lands Agent bore no markings to indicate its exact location. Consequently, Laurie was unable to confirm any of the existing streets which had simply been laid out parallel and perpendicular to the four sets of tracks in the railway yard. Since the tracks themselves did not run due east and west, the result was, as Laurie reported, that the hamlet's buildings and streets were "skew-twisted".[15] However, the crookedness of the layout was soon remedied by moving the offending buildings to agree with Laurie's 1886 survey. During the moving process those walking about the hamlet at night who were unfamiliar with the situation risked falling into gaping cellars.

It is interesting to see that the physical pattern of community development in Swift Current contained two separate population centres, each oriented towards different avenues of transportation — the one technically advanced but joined to and dependent upon the world beyond, the other primitive but almost independent. The white citizens, either employed or indirectly supported by the C.P.R., built houses and stores clustered about the railway facilities — all facing, as if in dutiful homage, towards its tracks. The métis and Indians, in contrast, placed their log shanties and tepees along the local waterway — the creek — as their ancestors had always done. It supplied them with some fish and waterfowl, as well as game animals seeking drink. Moreover, it was a water supply linked to the Saskatchewan river system, and its verdant banks yielded firewood, slim poles for building shanties or lodges, roots and berries, and grazing for their animals. The separateness of these two communities signified and embodied the difference in their culture. The railway and its people belonged to the future of the district; the native people beside the waterway were of the past. It was only a matter of time before the natives with their *travois,* hide boats and wooden carts were thrust aside by the white man's technology of steam and steel. The death of the native com-

Swift Current's new general stores in 1883. Standing beside the two small boys is F. Fraser Tims wearing high-cut boots and his customary derby hat. Note that both Tim's and Curry's stores had living quarters above.

SWIFT CURRENT'S WHITE CITIZENS VISITING A NEARBY INDIAN CAMP south of the hamlet in 1884. Identified are (left to right): Alice Smillie (in white), Fraser Tims (wearing derby hat), Alex. Curry (immediately left of teepee in foreground), Frank Goodwin, N.W.M.P. (standing between Indians in front of teepee), Dave Woods of the C.P.R. dining hall (first man mounted), W. C. Tims (next man mounted), Wm. Rutherford (standing in front of W. C. Tims), Alex. Fenton, C.P.R. station agent (standing beside Rutherford).

munity along the creek was certain, but the dying was prolonged and painful, for the slowly growing white settlement took years to crowd the natives out of the district.

Although many people had eagerly bought townsite properties in Regina, Moose Jaw, or Medicine Hat, few had cared to buy lots at Swift Current. Even before the rails reached it in 1882, the Swift Current townsite, consisting of 640 acres of land,[16] less a few acres reserved for future railway expansion, had been transferred by the C.P.R. to the Canada Northwest Land Company, a British-Canadian syndicate. The railway company's need for immediate cash was its reason for selling this and many other main line prairie townsites to the land syndicate. The deal called for the C.P.R. to receive one-half of the net proceeds of land sales, with a body known as the Dominion Trustees of Town Sites, made up of two trustees from each of the syndicates, to administer the land. In the case of Swift Current, apparently no promotional campaign to sell building lots was carried on by the Trustees. In any event, by 1887 only a few lots in Swift Current had been sold. About that time, an official plan for the townsite, more in keeping with the hamlet's size and prospects, was prepared by L. A. Hamilton of the C.P.R., and was registered February 15, 1888. This blueprint detailed six avenues running north and south, and two streets running east and west, enclosing five blocks of nineteen lots each. The street facing the C.P.R., where almost all of the businesses and houses in the railway hamlet were built, was appropriately named Railway Street. Hamilton called the remaining street to the north Cheadle Street.[17]

No community, especially a railway divisional point, can exist without a reliable water supply. Recognizing this, the C.P.R. made a major addition to its and the hamlet's facilities. The flow of water in the creek had often fluctuated from the barest trickle to a flood. To offset this problem and to guarantee a certain supply of water to its steam trains, the C.P.R. in 1888 built a stone and plank dam almost 400 feet in length across the creek.[18] A pumphouse was constructed from which water was piped underground to the roundhouse and to the water tank near the station. For the convenience of the inhabitants, the C.P.R. installed a hand pump near the depot. As a result, the native who lived by hauling water from the creek for the whites was put out of business — a victim of progress. Still, the dam and pumping system meant that the railway hamlet, plagued by a water shortage when the creek dried up, would now have ample water.

Not only had the railway brought Swift Current into being, but it also fostered its early development. Its employees and their families comprised most of its residents; the company payroll helped to support the hamlet's businessmen; its dam and pump provided a convenient water supply; moreover, its transportation facilities promoted an extensive trail freighting business which brought excitement, color, and cash into its otherwise drab life.

The westward progress of the railway had also had a pronounced

19

THE FIRST OFFICIAL PLAN OF THE HAMLET OF SWIFT CURRENT, prepared by L. A. Hamilton, Dominion Lands Surveyor, in 1888.

effect upon the overland transportation routes in the West. The cart trails of the métis freighters had generally run east and west, but they now began to run north and south from the new railway. When, in the spring of 1883, Swift Current briefly became the most westerly C.P.R. terminus, it became, as a result, an important trans-shipping point. Cart brigades numbering in the hundreds came from as far away as Fort Edmonton to load freight bound for police posts, Indian agencies and settlements, and to haul goods to waiting steamboats that plied the South Saskatchewan River during high water.

The thriving business being done by Fraser Tims and other Swift Current merchants was reported on February 17, 1883, in the *Saskatchewan Herald:* "The new town at Swift Current has set out as a wholesale mart for the Saskatchewan Valley, as being more convenient than Winnipeg. . . ." Tims had brought in a large stock of goods by C.P.R. work trains during the previous winter, both to serve the profitable trade of the railway builders, freighters and Indians, and to sell wholesale to merchants elsewhere. In April, 1883, Tims began advertising his business in this newspaper thus: "Have no more tedious and expensive delays await-

20

AN INDIAN OR MÉTIS CAMP ON THE PRAIRIE. Note the canvas tent and the Red River carts.

ing stocks from Winnipeg, but purchase from the Pioneer Store of Swift Current Creek.'' So successful were he and his competitors, the Curry Brothers (Sam and Alex) of Regina, who had also opened a general store in Swift Current early in 1883, that a year later the same newspaper proclaimed: ''Swift Current is becoming an important supply point for this northern country, and many of our citizens buy largely there when they go down.''

Naturally, this business flurry attracted others. Besides these frame or canvas and rough board structures, two ''hotels'' (one of them a temporary structure, the other the C.P.R. dining hall), a billiard saloon, variety store and post office, mostly housed in tents, sprang up. Almost at once the merchants were reported by the Battleford newspaper to be ''doing well''. However, this flurry of business could not last, for the railway construction pressed rapidly westward. By mid-August, 1883, the main line was opened to Calgary, which became the new terminus for points west until 1884. This development caused the transient traders and floating population to strike their tents and board the train for this newest ''railway Mecca'', leaving only a handful of more permanent residents to mourn their departure. Fortunately, Swift Current continued to serve as freighting and supply centre for the almost 5,000 residents of Battleford district, then the second largest community in the North-West Territories.[19] Frame buildings were soon erected to replace the first tent stores, and the hamlet's commercial facilities, fairly well established thanks to the short-lived business boom, were prepared to handle the demands which accompanied this expanding northern trade.

Traffic between Battleford and Swift Current had begun as soon in 1883 as the spring winds had laid bare enough prairie to permit cart travel. Plans had been made by Battleford freighters that January to lay out an overland trail equipped with a ferry on which to cross the South Branch north of Swift Current.[20] Goodwin Marchand, a prominent métis freighter, had left Battleford on April 20, 1883, leading a party of men with some thirty-five horses, a large outfit of carts, and a wagon carrying a scow. This would-be ferry, bearing the optimistic name *City of Battleford,* had been built for A. Macdonald and Co., general merchants of Battleford.[21] It measured nine feet by eighteen feet — just large enough to carry two loaded carts at one time, each with its lone draft animal and driver.

This first freighting expedition went smoothly. A passable grade from the prairie land over the steep banks of the river was discovered about eleven miles due west of the mouth of the Swift Current Creek. Here, on the morning of May 2, the scow was launched and the river crossed. Two days later, Marchand's party reached Swift Current. When the freighting party laden with supplies returned to Battleford on May 22, they pronounced the new trail to be the best of the many that crossed the plains in every direction.[22]

Before the railway reached the prairies, Winnipeg had been the key distribution centre for the North-West. It had taken at least forty-nine days for loaded carts and their métis drivers to make the one-way trip from Winnipeg to Battleford, barring frequently adverse weather conditions or prairie fires en route. Now a round trip from Battleford to Swift Current, under favorable conditions, could be made with freight in sixteen to twenty days. A fast team of horses hitched to a light wagon or buggy could travel the 192 miles of trail from Battleford to Swift Current in only three days. Once there, passengers could board the train for the two day trip to Winnipeg.

This great saving in time was accompanied by a similar saving in transportation costs for Battleford's citizens. The "saving", however, was achieved at the expense of the cart freighters. In the beginning, the freight rate from Swift Current to Battleford was three cents per pound. Those owning freight wagons and teams of horses, usually white men, hauled loads of some 1500 pounds and earned a fair income. But each cart hauled only about 600 pounds, and the métis with a single cart grossed at most $18.00 on the one-way trip or about $2.00 for each day spent travelling, not counting the time required to load or unload. This was about the same pay as railway navvies then earned. If the carters could have secured a similar payload at Battleford for the trip south, they would have been fairly well off, despite the harshness of their life. This was rarely the case. Within four years, competition from newly-arrived freighters had reduced the rate to one-third of the former level. Mostly these late comers were other métis carters who, displaced from their traditional occupation by the white man's railway, steamboat and freight wagon, attempted to gain some portion of whatever cart freighting remained in the West. Necessity, together with their hardihood and resourcefulness, made it possible for both the métis and their animals to mainly "live off the land". Had it been otherwise, the local people would have been forced to pay higher freight rates. Even the low rate of one cent per pound failed to encourage freight exports, since Battleford produced nothing, beyond its newspaper and the mail, which could bear even these shipping charges to distant markets. Moreover, the small amount of express and mail from Battleford was shipped by a white man's passenger stage service that began using the trail late in 1883.[23] Thus the métis did not share in the profitable express rate of ten cents per pound. The future for the métis carters, like the Indian hunters, was bleak.

In bygone years the buffalo hunt had sustained these prairie people. Now all that remained of the great herds was a memory and a final legacy — their bones. The métis desperately needed a product to transport to the railway which cost nothing to produce and little to harvest. They found such a product in the sun-bleached bones which littered the prairie everywhere. They and the Indians picked up these bones along the trail to Swift Current where they either sold them to the merchants there or traded them for supplies. In this way the buffalo again supported the prairie people. Until 1889 the local price paid for bones was about $8.00 per ton. Thus a 600-pound cart load brought the métis $2.40 in merchandise at Swift Current. Bone gathering meant more than an income to the natives for it suited their nature and culture. Just as they had done in the days of the buffalo hunt, the natives and their families set out on the bone hunt, frequently in large brigades.

To illustrate the extent of this enterprise, in the fall of 1884 alone, one of the hamlet's businessmen, F. Fraser Tims, shipped 200,000 pounds of buffalo bones to market in Minneapolis. There some of the bones were ground into fertilizer, but the dry, old bones were eagerly sought for use in refining white sugar since the sun had bleached the oil out of them. This trade provided the only locally-produced commodity to be shipped to market from the district before 1890. Unlike the merchant middlemen, however, the Indians and métis who combed the prairie for the bones could only barely exist on this industry. And just as the great herds of buffalo had so quickly disappeared, so within a generation did the bones which they had left behind. The natives, most of whom could not adjust to white civilization, once more experienced great hardship when their final gift from the buffalo was gone. White civilization, bent on efficiency and "progress", pressed on.

When the freighters and stage operators became more familiar with the country lying between Battleford and Swift Current, they began to search for ways to shorten the trail and to improve its facilities. Beginning in the winter of 1883-84, they laid out a route which sleighs could continue to use. When spring came in 1884 they succeeded in having the territorial government build a good wooden bridge where the trail crossed Eagle Hills Creek. During that summer, Peter Ballendine, Battleford freighter and owner of the new express line, was hired by the territorial council to locate and mark out a still shorter trail. His route skirted the Bad Hills south of Sixty Mile Bush (south of later Rosetown) and thus saved freighters one full day's time on the trip. The retained sections of the trail soon displayed a dozen or more parallel ruts, for the freighters forsook a set of ruts wherever their wheels had cut too deeply into the prairie sod. There was speculation that the N.W.M.P. authorities would maintain a ferry on the South Branch at the mouth of Swift Current Creek, but as long as private interests would operate a convenient ferry service, the police chose not to take on the responsibility.

The first ferry, *City of Battleford,* was free for all to use, but no one was put in charge of it. Often when the ferry was needed, it was on the opposite bank of the river, thus necessitating a trip over by rowboat to retrieve it. Some enterprising Indians took charge of it late in the summer of 1883 and, for a moderate fee, they gave good, dependable ferry service. Seeing a possible profit in this service, the Saskatchewan Coal Company forced the Indians out of business in September, 1883, by placing there a larger scow running on a cable. They likewise opened the first small store at the ferry landing to cater to travellers. Despite this added service, until early in 1885, freighters complained in vain to a certain Mr. McGirr, the owner of the ferry franchise, about the wretched conditions, the bad management which caused expensive delays, and the high ferry charges at the landing. The good service given earlier by the Indians had not been equalled by the white men. The new ferry, moreover, had been built without sideboards. Waves blown up by the wind washed over its flat deck causing the freighters to fear that their carts would slide into the swift river. During one crossing, Goodwin Marchand, who had launched the first ferry, lost his tents, camping equipment, and the then considerable sum of $670 cash which was in his coat when the new ferry tipped and upset his buckboard into the rushing waters early in May, 1884.

It was unfortunate, both for the trail-users and Canada, that when the 1885 Rebellion broke out, the ferry facilities were so poor. However, the ferry business had just been purchased by F. Fraser Tims, an ambitious businessman, who had also bought one of the largest local wagon freighting outfits. He needed to improve the ferry service to increase his profits from merchandise sales and freighting in any event, but the military traffic made this doubly true. Shrewdly, he saw that the ferry and store business, at least until the Rebellion ended, would pay handsomely. Late that spring he installed a new scow, sixteen by forty feet in size, running on a quarter-mile long steel cable and capable of carrying four wagons and teams. In addition to providing service whenever necessary, Tims's ferryman served as clerk by running his well-stocked store at the landing.[24] When the Rebellion ended, the money that Tims had risked on this newest venture had earned a windfall profit. Still, risk capital was no more important to trail freighting than the freighter's readiness to accept physical risks.

Trail freighting was an occupation requiring courage and great endurance on the part of both man and beast. The first cart brigades usually set out in late March while snow patches still dotted the greyish-tan prairie and crocuses hid from the raw wind. Wheeled traffic continued until the snows of another winter forced those still travelling to use sleighs. Between fall and spring the freighters often withstood sudden snow storms and temperatures which fell to forty below. Not until 1885 could these carters expect to find warm shelter anywhere along the trail except at the log and frame depot at the river. Early that year way stations were opened for the convenience of stage passengers. Their location was determined by the presence of a good water supply and the need for rest stops at intervals of about thirty miles. The depots were mostly such crude structures as dugouts in hillsides or shacks built of rough lumber, but at Sixty Mile Bush, the second stopping place south of Battleford, a good log house served as waystation. One trail traveller described the stations thus:

Next stopping place north of the [Saskatchewan Landing] was Devil's Gulch, a dugout in a big ravine with a lumber roof, furnished with four bunks. It was warm but mice ran all over sleeping occupants. Next stopping place north was at Iron Spring (fine water with iron taste). Night stop was at Eagle Creek Station. It was a shack built of rough lumber on a hillside near a slough of good water. Here mail contractors kept spare horses. Next station is Sixty Mile Bush. Pretentious log house. Next stop was at the [Red Pheasant] Indian Reserve eighteen miles from Battleford.[25]

Apart from discomforts and hazards caused by weather, the trail from spring until late fall held other threats, such as that of prairie fire. One such incident was reported on September 29, 1883 in the Battleford newspaper.

When about forty miles from this place on their way in from Swift Current last week, Mr. Prince and party were caught in a fierce prairie fire, and in fighting it to protect his outfit he was seriously burned about the head and face. A yoke of oxen and a horse were so badly injured by the flames that fresh animals had to be sent for to bring in their loads.

Usually these fires were started by lightning, but bone gatherers were known to burn off the tall grass to reveal otherwise hidden bones. Another result of these prairie fires was that feed for cart animals and fuel had to be carried by the freighters, unless they skirted the huge wastelands of burned-over grass. Drought, which at times dried up the natural sloughs and water holes, brought similar hardships. The railway itself posed another hazard to the unwary driver of a skittish horse, as a pioneer merchant of Swift Current, Samuel Curry, recalled:

One of these freighting outfits arrived here one day just before a train had pulled in. The ponies and carts were lined up near the depot when the "steel horse" came in sight. The first blast of the whistle startled

PANORAMIC VIEW OF SWIFT CURRENT, *circa* SPRING, 1885. On the left, business and residential district; in foreground, C.P.R. dining hall with rooms above; (behind the tents), the C.P.R. roundhouse and shops.

the frightened cayuses, and they turned tail for the north country. They were easy to follow, for cart covers, cooking and camping outfits were strewn along the trail.[26]

As a final obstacle, there was the river itself. It was slow and often dangerous for a large cart and wagon brigade to cross over it while the ferry was running. When the river ice broke up in the spring or when ice was forming in the fall, the crossing was impassable. Only when firm, thick ice covered the swift waters was the river no longer a barrier to traffic.

Despite the hardships and hazards of trail freighting, the trail to Battleford, aided by the new ferry, was a well-established prairie highway by the spring of 1885. As for Swift Current, fostered and nourished by the railway, the bone trade and trail commerce, it had developed permanent businesses and efficient freight-handling services. With the outbreak of the 1885 Rebellion, rail and trail combined to bring the tiny hamlet of Swift Current to the attention of the Dominion.

Chapter III

SWIFT CURRENT — THE MILITARY BASE

Until the spring of 1885, Swift Current, and indeed the entire North-West Territories, did not attract much interest either as a promising region for settlement or even as a topic of casual conversation for people living elsewhere in Canada. It took an Indian-and-métis rebellion led by Louis Riel to make this region and its people the subject of a widely spread press — often a page one feature.

Early spring had long been the harshest season for most prairie creatures. Now that the buffalo was almost extinct, this was doubly true for the prairie Indians. What few game animals there were about were, like the Indians, the survivors of a long, harsh winter, and were lean and wary. Waterfowl had not yet migrated from the south, and fishing was difficult and poor during the spring break-up. Winter snows had halted bone gathering, thus cutting off a chief source of income to the natives. These once-proud buffalo hunters had lately been reduced to snaring gophers to get food for the empty bellies of their people, but at this season even these small rodents were still in hibernation beneath the frozen sod. The Indians were close to starvation. The white man's government in far off Ottawa had solemnly promised by treaties to care for them in exchange for relinquishment of many of their traditional rights to their vast prairie homeland. But the government had often broken its promise. The Indians on reserves in the North-West Territories in the early spring of 1885 were little better off than those who continued to roam the plains. In view of all this, it is little wonder that the rebellion broke out when it did.

The growing sense of frustration and desperation felt by the Indian and mixed-blood people of the North-West, and attributed by them to the neglect and injustice shown them by the Government of Canada, erupted into violent revolt at Duck Lake, some eighty miles east of Battleford. There, on March 26, 1885, a few aroused Indians, accompanied and led by a small party of métis who were determined to enforce the will of their new and rebellious Provisional Government, attacked and defeated a party of N.W.M.P. and volunteers. Three days before this violent clash, first-hand news of impending trouble had reached Swift Current when two N.W.M.P. officers, identified in the press simply as Kerr and Ross, were obliged to ride in from Battleford to send despatches by railway telegraph since the rebels had cut the telegraph line to Battleford. On March 29, fearing an attack by a large Indian war party, some 600 frightened Battleford citizens abandoned their homes and took refuge in Fort Battleford, which was besieged by the Indians on the following day. The Saskatchewan Rebellion was on, and its impact was soon felt in Swift Current and across the young Dominion.

Swift Current possessed several advantages which won favorable consideration from Canada's military commander at the time when bases for military operations were chosen. Its strategic location as the terminus of the Battleford trail made it an obvious centre from which the Canadian government forces could provision and direct an attack designed to defeat the rebels concentrated to the north in the District of Saskatchewan. Its well-developed trail-transport facilities, as well as the fact that it lay only thirty miles from Saskatchewan Landing on the South Saskatchewan River, were further advantages. Here supplies and men could be loaded aboard steamers and barges for fast and economical transportation to the north, at least during the high-water period resulting from the spring run-off. Finally, but most important, Swift Current was a railway centre with a rail yard, roundhouse, shops, rolling stock and stand-by locomotives. These factors caused Major-General Frederick Middleton, the British commander of the Canadian Militia forces, to select the hamlet as his main supply base.

On the morning of March 30, the same day that hostile Indians besieged Fort Battleford, a party of almost fifty police commanded by Superintendent W. H. Herchmer arrived by train at Swift Current with their equipment and horses. Major-General Middleton had ordered this small, lightly-armed force to proceed north by trail to protect the citizens of Battleford from the hundreds of belligerent Indians in and around it. The police, had a fight ensued, would have been greatly outnumbered. Perhaps it was fortunate for the Mounties that they found the river crossing impassable, as the ice was just beginning to break up. Upon notifying Middleton of this, Herchmer was ordered to have his force board the train on March 31 and proceed to Medicine Hat, there to protect the H.B.C. steamer, *Northcote,* berthed nearby on the river, from possible attack by a party of Northern Crees seen lurking near it.

If the Crees were planning to destroy the *Northcote,* as appeared likely, then they must have been aware of the potential threat to their cause that the river boat could be in transporting Canadian troops, supplies and equipment to strategic spots for use against the rebels during the coming high water season. The Indians obviously possessed a good grasp of war strategy. However, the prompt arrival of the police at the *Northcote's* berth forestalled any attack by the Crees upon the beached, unmanned vessel. The Indians, too wily to be taken by surprise, vanished without even being seen by the police party.[1]   Tension mounted among the citizens of Swift Current, as well as among those in many other prairie communities, as reports of the rebellion, often exaggerated in passing from lip to lip, caused many to fear an attack by the rebel forces. These fears were further increased when the farm instructor at Red Pheasant's Reserve south of Battleford, George Applegarth, reached Swift Current on April 2 with his wife and child. Applegarth told how they had escaped an Indian raid, thanks to the warning of a friendly brave, and had fled by buckboard south along the trail.[2] The family's account of their narrow escape heightened the general uneasiness of the residents of this tiny white community, for they had only a few guns to rely upon if a sudden Indian raid came. To make matters worse, the closest help was hours away at Maple Creek.

One can well imagine the great apprehension felt in Swift Current when, on the afternoon of April 3, there suddenly appeared a well-armed band of over thirty Cree warriors riding south towards the tiny hamlet. Wisely, the whites did not attempt to use force to prevent the Indians' entry. Had they done so, bloodshed would surely have followed, probably resulting in the death of many of the inhabitants. The Cree warriors, possibly the same party seen in the vicinity of the docked *Northcote* only four days earlier, while well prepared for a fight, apparently hoped to get what they needed without using violence.

The Indians wanted food most of all, but they also wanted tobacco, ammunition for hunting (they said), and news of the progress of the rebellion. They had almost no money and asked to be given most of the supplies as presents.[3] Under different circumstances, this would not have been an unusual request. The Hudson's Bay Company's traders had long advanced the Indians ammunition and supplies when they had no money to pay for them. In recent years, the federal government had distributed a diminishing quantity of rations that had kept at least some of the sick and weak from dying. On the individual level, the white man's feelings of humanitarianism had occasionally prompted him to extend a helping hand to his unfortunate red brother. But now a rebellion was afoot. The Indians knew that a show of force would be necessary to get what they needed. The white citizens, fearing this force, were prepared to make "presents".

With what little money the small band of Cree warriors had, they bought some provisions at Swift Current. The frightened merchants then gave them three barrels of flour, some sugar and tobacco but, prudently, hid all of the ammunition, claiming they had none to sell or give. None of the storekeepers intended that they should lose by their forced humanitarianism, for they later called upon the government to pay for the "presents". The Indians, probably realizing that the merchants were lying about the ammunition, became angry. Perhaps this development, or just the presence of so many armed Indians in their midst, caused the whites to put their women and children aboard the afternoon freight train for Moose Jaw where they remained until April 7.[4] The red men decided to spend the night with their generous "friends", and the whites had little choice but to act hospitably while hoping that their unwanted guests would soon depart. Their stomachs full and having got most of what they wanted, the Indians became peaceful. The news from the whites that many soldiers were coming to stamp out the rebellion also had had an effect. Discreetly, upon the arrival of the Indians, the railwaymen had wired Lieutenant-Governor Edgar Dewdney, asking him to send police protection, but this help was slow in coming. Happily, on the afternoon of April 4, before outside help reached Swift Current, the Indians quietly rode north out of town with their "presents", picking up a few "stray" cattle on the way to add to their meagre food supplies.[5]

For a brief time that must have seemed unending to Swift Current's citizens, they had faced greater danger than the hundreds of people, many well armed, who were sheltered behind the protective walls of Fort Battleford. George Applegarth, who had remained at Swift Current, must have felt especially uneasy, having narrowly escaped with his life only days before. The local people had acted calmly, strengthened their position by getting their women and children to safety, and stood their ground. Had they panicked and fled, the Indians would certainly have sacked the hamlet and possibly burned it. The Indian braves, for their part, had responded favorably to the calm, firm attitude of the whites. Had they not, Swift Current might well have been another bloody battle scene in the Rebellion.

Fearing that news of Swift Current's "charity" and vulnerability would attract more red men who might decide to attack and destroy the tiny but strategic railway centre, Dewdney had promptly requested of Middleton that Herchmer's police force be returned to Swift Current. After some delay, the British Commander gave the necessary order. Hastily, the police arranged for and boarded a special train at Medicine Hat at 8:30 P.M. on April 5 and reached the hamlet by 5:40 A.M. the following morning. The anxious white citizens greeted the dawn arrival of the Mounties with relief. Immediately, Herchmer sent a patrol north along the trail and placed a guard on Tims's ferry at the river crossing. But as before at Medicine Hat, they failed to detect the party of armed Indians.[6]

The townsmen had not, at the time, been aware of how violent the Indians to the north had become. They were soon to find out. On April 6, Constable Henry Storer and James Bird galloped into Swift Current from Battleford with despatches announcing the murder by hostile Assiniboines of a farm instructor and a rancher, James Payne and Bernard Frémont. Furthermore, the despatches stated that several Indian chiefs were gathering their bands on Poundmaker's reserve and that Battleford was without telegraph connections and was in a state of siege. Fortunately, the break-up of the river ice had prevented freighters from leaving Swift Current and travelling the now dangerous trail to Battleford, for only that portion of the trail between the railway and Saskatchewan Landing was then being patrolled by the police. On the 8th, Dewdney passed through Swift Current on a train bound for Blackfoot country. Once there, he secured Chief Crowfoot's promise that his powerful tribe would remain loyal. The following day the hamlet received its first soldiers, a detachment of forty-nine

Infantry School Cadets led by Lieutenant R. L. Wadmore. As the soldiers pitched their tents south of the depot, Herchmer moved the remainder of his Mounties out to the river crossing, there to protect the ferry and await the arrival downstream of the steamer *Northcote*.[7]

The improvements which had been made in the Swift Current-Battleford trail north from the South Saskatchewan made it a logical military and supply route, but Middleton was slow to grasp its strategic value. Another great advantage of this route, though not recognized by Middleton, lay in the freighting experience and ready cooperation, not only of resident white men, but also of the Battleford and local métis, nearly all of whom had refused to join the rebels. This was to prove an important factor in the success of the Canadian military campaign against the small insurgent force.

While several Westerners had immediately urged the prompt rescue of Battleford upon learning of the unhappy fate of its citizens, the cautious Middleton at first refused to consider sending soldiers up the trail to liberate the town. Instead, he would free Battleford by launching an attack up the much longer river route (down the South Saskatchewan past Prince Albert, then up the North Saskatchewan to Battleford), using water instead of land transport in an effort to reduce expenses. This required that Swift Current should become his major supply base for the main field force which was then marching towards Batoche, the rebel stronghold in the South Saskatchewan River. Men and materials were to be transported by trail only as far as Saskatchewan Landing, there to be loaded aboard steamers and barges. By using the river as his line of communication and attack, Middleton expected to be able to save money by dispensing with a large number of his high-priced transport teams.[8] However, shallows in the South Saskatchewan River prevented the early arrival at the Landing of the promised Galt steamers from Medicine Hat. Seeing the folly of this scheme, knowledgeable Westerners from Manitoba warned that the plan to relieve Battleford by following the river system was impractical. In part, their telegram to their Member of Parliament read:

> We know every foot of the country and that it is impossible to relieve Battleford either via Touchwood or Saskatchewan navigation. Only feasible way is via Swift Current.[9]

Despite this advice and the inability of any steamboats to reach the ferry landing when promised, as late as April 9 Middleton had altered his strategy only to the extent of ordering Lieutenant-Colonel W. D. Otter, commander of the second column of militia, to detrain at Swift Current and go by trail to the Landing, there to await the expected steamers. Upon the arrival of the steamers, Otter's column was to board them and proceed down the river to reinforce Middleton, who was plodding northward with his force towards Batoche. Only when it appeared certain that the Galt steamers could not for several days reach the river crossing, did Middleton alter his plans for the relief of Battleford.[10] At last, on April 11, he ordered

Otter to prepare his column for the one hundred and ninety mile march up the trail to rescue the town.

The following day, Lieutenant-Colonel Otter and a large part of his force stepped off the train at Swift Current. Their arrival, along with that of several more of Otter's inexperienced militiamen the day before, presented the citizens of Swift Current with a scene far more hectic and exciting than any produced by the incoming of the largest trail freighting brigades. Tons of supplies and equipment, almost five hundred horses, great mounds of fodder, over two hundred teamsters with as many wagons, heaps of rifles, cannons, cases of shells, together with almost five hundred untried soldiers wearing the distinctive uniforms of their various companies and battalions descended upon the tiny railway hamlet. The scene was one of noise, confusion and color. Military tents by the dozen mushroomed just south of the railway tracks across from the depot. The stores did a booming business, only pausing briefly on Sunday, the 12th, while the soldiers, teamsters and local citizens attended a Drumhead Service conducted by the Anglican Chaplain, Reverend G. E. Lloyd.[11] The troops, drawn up for the service to form three sides of a hollow square, were in good spirits. The sun shone down warmly through clear skies, and a feeling of excitement and comradeship buoyed up the spirits of the young volunteer militiamen.[12]

As soon as the church service and noon lunch were over, N.W.M.P. Superintendent L. R. Neale and his police party set out for the ferry with orders to camp there and patrol both sides of the river. When Otter's column reached the crossing, the police were to join it and act as an advance guard on the march to Battleford.[13] At 4 A.M. on the morning of the 13th, the 113 men of "B" Battery of the Royal Canadian Artillery and the fifty-one men who comprised "C" Company of the Governor-General's Foot Guards Sharpshooters[14] struck their tents, breakfasted on the poor fare of fat pork and tea, and started the march to the Landing, reaching it the following day. There the soldiers camped, mended their gear, bathed and admired the beautiful scenery of the river valley while awaiting the appearance upstream of the *Northcote,* and the arrival of the bulk of Otter's column from Swift Current.[15] A work force was detailed to ready Tims's ferry for service. No sooner was this task underway than the "amphibious" *Northcote,* damaged by winching itself over countless sandbars, floundered to the landing with two barges in tow, its whistle drowning the cheers of the young soldiers on the river bank. Captain Sheets and his steamboat crew at once began to repair and outfit the vessel for ferry duty.[16]

Now began the task of safely and quickly ferrying the column across the river. First, on the 15th, the police poled themselves across to the north bank of the river on Tims's patched up ferry in order to protect the landing.[17] The balance of Otter's 543 man force, including the 274 soldiers of the Queen's Own Rifles and the forty-nine man Detachment of "C" Company, Infantry School Cadets, plus some one hundred and eighty well paid teamsters with supply wagons, had reached the crossing on the 16th. Early the next morning, the day set for the crossing, a sudden snowstorm struck. Despite the swirling snow, the mended steamer, towing the two barges and Tims's ferry, began at dawn to shuttle back and forth across the wide Saskatchewan. By evening, every man, animal and piece of equipment needed was safely deposited on the north bank of the broad river.[18] The four-mile long column, composed of 745 officers, non-commissioned men and teamsters, together with 450 horses, set out at noon the next day to relieve beleaguered Battleford.[19]

Meanwhile, Swift Current had been a hive of activity after the arrival there of Otter's troops along with other units. With the militia came scores of railway cars filled with arms, horses, provisions and forage. Transporting this growing mountain of supplies proved to be a bonanza, not only to the C.P.R. and its employees, but also to the steamboat people and the trail freighters working north from the hamlet. To organize the stock-piling and shipping of the materials and to direct the men involved in this work required an experienced commander. Middleton, reluctantly, gave the task to a fellow British Major-General with more seniority — a Crimean veteran then living in Nova Scotia, Major-General John W. Laurie. Eager for action, Laurie willingly forfeited his seniority over Middleton and arrived April 16 to take command of this important supply base.[20]

The problems faced by Laurie were formidable. To begin with, the ferry at the river crossing had been poorly built and ran, when it did at all, upon a cable that was prone to break. When this happened, the ferry had to be laboriously poled across the river.[21] Even if the ferry had been well built and in good repair, it would often have been inadequate to carry the vast quantity of military supplies needed to sustain Otter's column, as well as to handle the backlog of demands placed upon it by the citizens of the Battleford district. With Otter's arrival the people of Battleford immediately returned to their plundered homes and stores and set about restocking them with goods that largely came by trail through Swift Current.

General Laurie realized that to make this supply route effective to serve both Otter's command and Middleton's main force he would have to have a large and efficient system of transport. This meant wagons and teams as well as cayuses and carts to haul supplies up the trail to Battleford, along with a much greater number of freighting outfits to move the mountains of materials from Swift Current to Saskatchewan Landing where it could be taken by steamboat and barge down river to Middleton. Laurie had unsuccessfully urged Middleton to delay Otter's force at the Landing just long enough for Otter's 230 teams to make one trip to Swift Current and back with stores. Some supplies were to be placed aboard the steamer *Northcote* and the two barges it towed for immediate transport to Middleton at Clarke's Crossing, north of Saskatoon, and the remainder were to provision Otter's force. Middleton had promptly dismissed this request,

MILITARY CONVOY FREIGHTING SUPPLIES TO MAJOR-GENERAL MIDDLETON'S FORCE, 1885.

stating that Battleford must be relieved without further delay.[22] As a result, Otter's column took almost all the supplies that had been stock-piled at Saskatchewan Landing for loading aboard the *Northcote*, since Otter's men, while waiting to cross the river, had used up much of the provisions that they had brought with them from Swift Current. Lacking a load for his *Northcote*, Captain Sheets decided to use the time while thus delayed in making repairs to his steamer and, at General Laurie's request, Tims's ferry as well. It remains a puzzle that Laurie did not have a new ferry built or at least order a new ferry cable to replace Tims's defective one.

Laurie's transport system was now totally inadequate. He had only thirty teams with which to provision the detachment at the Landing, provide loads for the steamers, and to supply Colonel Otter's column and the garrison at Battleford. The General at once sent out appeals in all directions for suitable wagon outfits. In addition to the use of the 230 teams and farm wagons that had accompanied Otter, as soon as they were available, he wanted 100 teams to load the *Northcote* and 150 more for the Battleford trail.[23] Through his appeal, and the excellent pay of $10 a day for drivers with a team of horses and a wagon (oxen drivers got $2 less),[24] he did attract a number of farmers from Regina, Moose Jaw and even from North Dakota. Still he was short of trail transport. In an effort to make up part of this deficiency, he contracted with Fraser Tims, who controlled some teams driven by half-breeds and Indians, to deliver 2,500 pounds of supplies daily on the north bank of the South Saskatchewan River for $25 per ton. Compared to the cost of hiring teamsters by the day, a practice Middleton insisted upon, this was a bargain rate for the army, for it was costing the government $32 per ton to land supplies just to the river's south bank.

A further and major problem arose out of the trail transport system itself. A team of horses needed eighty pounds of fodder a day, and Laurie estimated that another twenty pounds per team was either lost or wasted. To make matters worse, some of the hay that the Hudson's Bay Company arranged to have shipped to Swift Current was of such poor quality that Laurie had to condemn one carload of it.[25] And farm horses, unlike the native cayuses, could not survive, let alone work, on a small ration of oats along with whatever they could forage from the prairie at this time of year. Consequently, one supply wagon in ten was employed merely in hauling feed for the teamsters' own horses for each three days on the trail. If any delays took place, and they frequently did, such as rest breaks, lame horses, or prolonged waits at the Landing, then even a higher proportion of teams had to be used to haul fodder — all of which made the land transport system still more inefficient.

Nor were these the only difficulties Laurie encountered in this section of his command. To begin with, farm wagons, which were all he could hire, could not carry a large load of fodder. What Laurie wanted were wagons equipped with hay racks, or at least nets to secure a large load of hay on the farm wagons. He was unable to get either. While the wagon was technically advanced over the wooden Red River cart, it needed something that the carts did not — axle grease. Laurie had scarcely any on hand, and though he resorted to requisitioning all of the available tallow and coal oil from the local C.P.R. workshop, he constantly feared that it would not be enough to keep the wagon wheels turning. To add to his worries, some of the transport horses developed glanders disease, and only the prompt action of Laurie's Veterinary Surgeon checked its spread. But the greatest problem of all arose from the lack of blacksmiths to shoe the teamsters' horses. At one time there were sixty-eight teams idle and needing shoeing — all drawing daily pay — on the north side of the river. Some were so badly crippled that they died on the prairie. To make matters worse, when at last the army blacksmiths came, they arrived without their forges, and a further delay took place until these reached Swift Current. Finally, many of the teamsters refused to travel north from the river without an armed escort during the time when the Indians near Battleford were likely to attack. General Laurie, needing all the men in his command to handle the loading, unloading and stockpiling of supplies at Swift Current and Saskatchewan Landing, could rarely spare men for escort duty. He finally resorted to arming some of the teamsters with rifles and requiring convalescent soldiers returning to duty at Battleford to act as guards on the convoys going north.

The work was hard on animals and men alike. Each work day began at dawn for those soldiers assigned to transport duty under Laurie. He and his officers were determined that their men would not lose their fighting effectiveness or their military smartness, even though their duties kept them from combat. From 5:30 A.M. until 7:30 A.M. the soldiers were drilled in moving in extended order over broken ground and through underbrush, in practising their attack formations and in rifle shooting, outpost duty, and more drills.[26] At 8:30 A.M., after a monotonous breakfast of black tea, hardtack biscuit (which took powerful jaws to chew) and fat salt pork, they commenced their heavy work of handling supplies. More hardtack with tea and occasionally beans comprised their noon meal. Then more heavy labor until dusk when they were met with a final task of eating hardtack for supper.[27] The prospect of receiving their pay of fifty cents a day — if they lived to collect it — may have cheered some.

Some of the men developed dyspepsia from existing on the indigestible diet. Around the middle of May, Laurie and the medical officer decided to issue rations of oatmeal and molasses to the men in place of some of the hardtack, but they had only a small quantity of these foods on hand. Fortunately for the men, at this time General Laurie made a trip by train to Moose Jaw where he discovered some cattle which the beef contractor had delivered there by mistake, rather than to Swift Current. At once he ordered the beef sent to his men at the main supply base, where the soldiers enjoyed their first fresh meat in over a month. Still, these volunteers had a far from satisfactory diet. A few potatoes were eventually supplied, but other vegetables did not arrive, nor did bread. Even fuel for cooking fires was scarce,[28] but the more philosophical of the soldiers may have consoled themselves with the fact that there was little enough to cook anyway.

Work at the Landing was especially onerous. When the ferry cable broke, which it did more than once, the soldiers had to pole the ferry scow across the river. As the water level fell, the supplies had to be carried from the river banks across the muddy bed of the river on either side, as well as being unloaded and loaded in mid-stream when sandbars were encountered. The bulk of this back-breaking work was done by men from the Midland and Halifax Regiment — and to their credit, it was done well and cheerfully. On one particular day, the small work party at the river handled over 400 tons of supplies, as well as cutting piles of wood for the steamboats.[29]

While transportation was the main responsibility given to General Laurie, his other chief duty was to provide lines of communication for much of the field force. Action had been taken even before the General's arrival to provide instant communication between the railway's telegraph and Saskatchewan Landing. Following a suggestion passed on to A. P. Caron by Sir Alexander T. Galt, and after much confusion as to what was proposed,[30] a temporary telegraph line, built at government expense, had been completed by April 16 linking Swift Current to Tims's store at the ferry crossing.[31] Laurie had arrived at Swift Current on the day that the telegraph line was completed. He promptly arranged with the postal authorities at Winnipeg to have all mail destined for Swift Current and the troops carried by every freight train running west through the town, instead of by only the weekly passenger train. Quickly, he set up a Military Post Office to handle the mails, and organized a pony express system, with a line of relay stations along the Battleford trail to carry the mail and despatches, the heavier mail being sent by wagon. Laurie even extended this mail service to the citizens of Battleford.[32] Middleton suspected that the rebel leaders would attempt to flee to the United States while his main column proceeded towards Batoche. Therefore, on April 22, two days before the rebel forces checked Middleton's advance at Fish Creek, he ordered Laurie to set up a scout patrol between Old Wives' Lake and Cypress Hills to watch for fugitives. To form this patrol, Laurie at once withdrew part of the Intelligence Corps he had posted along the river and up the Battleford trail. A chain of posts was set up along the designated line and Laurie was kept informed daily of their findings. If they spotted a body of men, they were to report the most probable point that the fugitives would cross the railway line. Laurie arranged with the C.P.R. shops at Swift Current to keep the fires banked in a locomotive to be ready to take him and his soldiers along the rail line to intercept the fleeing rebels.[33] As it turned out, after the rebel capital of Batoche was captured on May 12, Gabriel Dumont, Riel's military commander, slipped through Laurie's patrols and made his way safely to the United States. Louis Riel probably could have done likewise, but he realized that in fleeing he would miss his chance for a public hearing.

Otter's column, meanwhile, had reached Battleford on April 24 and relieved it without a fight, since the Indians had fled before the soldiers' advance. Otter was determined to punish these Indians, who had gathered southwest on Poundmaker's reserve, and to prevent them from joining forces with Riel or the rebel Cree chief, Big Bear. His subsequent attack upon them came close to being a costly defeat for the Canadian militia, and he retreated ignominiously to Battleford from this battle at Cut Knife Hill on May 2.

During this time, Swift Current (the main supply base, trail freighting terminus and communications centre) and Saskatchewan Landing (the river port for the steamers and barges) were throbbing with activity. Before Otter's departure from Swift Current, two Gatling machine guns had arrived from the United States. Otter took one of these Gatling guns with him, the other was taken charge of by Captain Arthur L. Howard of the Connecticut National Guard, an experienced operator and champion of the new weapon. Only 20,000 rounds of ammunition had been sent with the Gatlings, half of which Otter had taken. Since the machine guns easily fired 100 bullets per minute, as Howard demonstrated to a much impressed audience at Swift Current, each gun had only sufficient shells for 100 minutes of firing. Laurie promptly telegraphed for more ammunition, but it did not arrive until a month later. At the Landing, the steamer *Northcote,* its ferry duty ended once Otter's troops were carried over the river, was preparing for the journey down river with reinforcements and supplies for General Middleton. On April 22, four companies of troops from the Midland Battalion with their commander Lieutenant-Colonel A. T. H. Williams, M.P., who later was to lead the impulsive charge that brought victory over the rebels at Batoche,[34] took passage for Clarke's Crossing. With them went a complete Field Hospital Corps, several tons of supplies, and "Gatling" Howard with his gun. All were loaded aboard the *Northcote* and the two barges that it towed, and, on April 23, this armed flotilla set off down the river to join Middleton.[35] Two days earlier, the first Canadian Red Cross Unit, newly formed in Toronto and consisting of ten trained men under the direction of a Dr. Nattrass, arrived by train at Swift Current. They were well outfitted, but Laurie could not provide transport to carry more than the most essential parts of their equipment and supplies. This they loaded into light wagons, and the untried, eager Red Cross Unit set out quickly to overtake Otter, now three days ahead on the trail.[36]

The first and smallest of Galt's steamers, the *Minnow,* reached Saskatchewan Landing on April 27. It had been slightly damaged as a result of having been grounded many times since leaving Medicine Hat, despite its shallow draft of barely sixteen inches.[37] Upon learning that the recently departed *Northcote* was aground near the Elbow, the supply base commander, Laurie, ordered the *Minnow* to proceed downstream immediately. There it removed the doctors, the guns and ammunition, along with Captain Howard, from the stranded steamer in order that they might more quickly reach Middleton at Clarke's Crossing.[38]

The *Minnow* had left Saskatchewan Landing towing two small barges, one of them loaded with oats that Middleton urgently needed. The barges had run aground near where the Swift Current Creek empties into the river and had been cast off by the *Minnow*. Upon hearing of this at the supply base, Lieutenant Weller and ten soldiers who were experienced raftsmen (and zealous for action), volunteered to leave that night, April 30, and to raft both barges down river to Middleton. Laurie consented to the idea at once, for he had a labor problem on his hands at the Landing. The civilians there whom he had been trying to persuade to rescue the stranded barges had gone on strike for higher wages. During that night the soldier raftsmen drove to the Landing, leaving there on foot at daybreak on May 1 for the barges down river before the striking crews knew that they had been replaced. They found one of the barges wrecked in the rapids at the mouth of the creek, so they transferred its salvageable cargo to the other barge and arrived safely at Clarke's Crossing fifteen days later. Lieutenant Weller then reported to Middleton that he strongly favored using the river as a transport route, provided proper equipment and trained men were available.[39] At this point only the Indians under Poundmaker and Big Bear remained to be subdued.

Traffic over the trail to Battleford shortly before this was heavy, despite the danger of possible attack by hostile Indians. Almost daily, small, unprotected supply convoys had left Swift Current for newly-liberated Battleford, though ferry breakdowns frequently caused troublesome delays at the river. The early success of these freighting trips to Battleford engendered a false sense of security among the authorities, including General Middleton. The events of mid-May promptly shattered it.

At noon of May 14, the Military Mail courier, Callach, galloped into Battleford with the news of an Indian attack upon the trail. That morning, five N.W.M.P. on patrol in a wooded area along the trail about seven miles south of Battleford were mistaken by Poundmaker's tribe, moving east finally to join Riel's forces, for outriders of an enemy force intent upon attacking them again without warning as Otter's force had done earlier at Cut Knife Hill. In the fight which followed, one Mountie was killed and another wounded.

Immediately following the flight to Battleford of the remnant of the police patrol, the hungry Indians had a windfall. South along the trail the Crees spotted a small supply convoy from Swift Current carrying eleven loads of provisions and twenty loads of oats. At once the warriors set out to capture the supply train. Ten teamsters frantically unhitched their horses, and though the Indians chased them for ten miles, firing at them, they escaped to Battleford. But the unfortunate oxen drivers had no chance to flee on their slow steeds. They and all the supplies were seized by the Indians. Within a few days, though, the Crees released these freighters unharmed upon learning that Riel had surrendered on May 15. As for the food and provisions, the Indians kept them, possibly choosing to consider them as past-due treaty payments.

Word of the attack on May 14 made General Laurie fear for two additional small convoys which were also on the trail. In the lead, but not many miles north of the Landing, was a convoy of fifteen wagons. It was escorted by an officer, Lieutenant Hume Blake (son of the Liberal Leader of the Opposition in Ottawa), and about a dozen armed men who were either newly-engaged scouts or recently convalescent soldiers returning to duty. Five of the fifteen wagons contained ammunition and rifles,[40] which, in the hands of the poorly-armed natives, could be disastrous for the whites. Had the ferry been running well, the number of wagons thus exposed to attack would have been greater. After having lamented for days that the ferry was out of service, the base commander, ironically, had reason to be thankful that the ferry cable had broken when it did. Laurie sent riders racing up the trail with orders to bring back the supplies and to abandon all the mail depots north of the Landing. This was carried out without incident.

It was not Laurie's fault that the supply convoys were unprotected, for General Middleton had insisted that the teamsters not be armed or provided with a military escort. Yet, aware of the danger, on his own initiative, Laurie had arranged for the make-shift escort to guard the important convoy carrying guns and ammunition to Colonel Otter. Furthermore, he had done so without reducing the strength of his forces at Swift Current or the Landing. Still, it was Laurie who was unjustly held responsible for the capture of the supply train on May 14.[41]

This show of Indian hostility caused only a brief pause in communications over the Swift Current-Battleford trail. Callach, the mail courier, like the Pony Express riders of earlier days in the United States, followed the motto: "The mail must go through." He set out from Battleford with mail for Swift Current on May 16th — the day after Riel surrendered. His pay was only $2.50 a day — much too little to cause a man less dedicated or, perhaps, less foolhardy than Callach to continue bringing the mail through alone. As soon as he had entered the wooded country south of Battleford, he was pursued by three mounted Indians. The mail courier, trusting in the stamina of his horse, sought to outrun his pursuers. Two of the Indians gave up the chase, but one brave riding a tough little Indian pony was still in pursuit as Callach neared Saskatchewan Landing. In desperation, Callach hid himself beside the trail and shot this man from ambush. Leaving the dead warrior where he fell, Callach rode on to the railway hamlet.[42]

Even before Callach brought news of his ordeal to Laurie at Swift Current, the base commander had decided to change the method of dispatching supplies north from the river. Instead of sending small groups of freighters up the trail without armed escorts, as General Middleton had ordered, Laurie decided to prepare a large armed convoy at the ferry.[43] This he had trouble in doing, for several teamsters stated that, if attacked by Indians, they would flee rather than fight, and furthermore, they would not take orders from the Assistant Transport Officer — a man who had earned their dislike while commanding them on a former occasion. When it was explained that an escort would be provided with scouts in advance, and that Otter's force must receive supplies, several teamsters volunteered to go. But before the freighting brigade could be organized, Otter telegraphed to Laurie that Poundmaker had released the captured teamsters unharmed and was ready to surrender. With the arrival of this welcome news, the trouble ended. A convoy of 158 teams, along with the freighting outfit of F. Fraser Tims, and, as a precaution, an escort of scouts and twenty-seven convalescent soldiers commanded by Lieutenant Blake, was sent to Battleford by Laurie on May 25, the day before Poundmaker surrendered to Middleton.[44] The convoy reached Battleford without event on June 4. The only larger freighting party ever to use the trail was the convoy of the previous month that transported Otter's column to Battleford. No further Indian attacks on trail traffic took place, and soon commercial freighting for Battleford merchants resumed.

During this time, river traffic to and from the Landing was at its peak. Major-General Laurie proudly reported that 800 tons of supplies had been hauled to the Landing during the first week of May. Melting snow in the mountains had begun to raise the water level early that month and kept it high until July. On May 3, the Boyd and Crowe contracting crew from Winnipeg, together with building materials, had arrived at Swift Current. At once, they set out for the landing, where they proceeded to build twelve barges to carry 220 tons of supplies to Middleton's force which, since being checked at the battle of Fish Creek days before, remained encamped down the river.[45] The barge builders encountered a problem at once. They had neither caulking tools nor caulkers to make the barges water-tight. Fortunately, the soldiers once more came to their aid. Experienced men of the Halifax and Portsmouth contingents made caulking irons and did the caulking, and by May 10, all the barges were finished and loaded with supplies. Galt's two large steamers, *Alberta* and *Baroness,* had both arrived at the Landing by May 7. Before the river convoy of barges and steamers could embark, a further problem, this time the result of a misunderstanding, had to be resolved. The Winnipeg contractors claimed that they had agreed with the Hudson's Bay Company to supply crews to man the barges only if twenty soldiers accompanied each barge to assist in working them and to provide protection. Laurie offered instead to arm the civilian crewmen, but the contractors insisted that the soldiers accompany them. At that point the impasse was resolved when an unexpected order came from Middleton directing the Midland Detachment and the 7th Fusiliers at Swift Current to join his force in preparation for the attack upon

A TRAIL FREIGHTING PARTY LEAVING SWIFT CURRENT FOR BATTLEFORD DURING THE REBELLION OF 1885.

Batoche. Laurie ascertained that there was no easier or faster way of getting the 400 soldiers to the front than by sending them along with the barges and steamers. This arrangement suited everyone. The soldiers got their longed for chance to see action, the contractors got their work crews and protection, and, although they had not been promised it, they received pay for transporting the additional troops down the river. Moreover, the contractors dismissed all but one of the civilian crewmen per barge and thus made a substantial saving in wages. The flotilla set out for the battle zone at 8 A.M. on May 11. Although the first three of the barges reached Clarke's Crossing only one week later, the soldiers, eager for combat, were disappointed, for this was six days after the fall of Batoche and three days following Louis Riel's surrender. That these barges had made better time than the other nine was due to the simple expedient the soldiers followed of throwing some of the supplies overboard to lighten their load.[46] As for the steamers *Alberta* and *Baroness,* they made a fast trip down river under orders to unload quickly and to bring back the sick and wounded from Middleton's camp to be treated at the make-shift base hospital which had been established at Swift Current.[47]

The word "hospital" conjures up an image of a clean, quiet, comfortable building with an antiseptic odor but the reality was far from this. Plans had been drawn by the military in 1885 to erect a suitable frame hospital in the hamlet, but the slow progress down river of the *Northcote* caused Middleton to abandon this original idea.[48] Instead, a make-shift military base hospital was set up by Deputy Surgeon General Roddick on April 16,[49] and Swift Current was to wait more than another quarter-century before a hospital was constructed in the town.

The second day after the military hospital was opened, the medical staff received their first patients — five militiamen belonging to Otter's column, suffering from sore feet, exposure, or ailments brought on by a steady diet of stale fat pork, hardtack and black tea.[50] The quarters chosen to house the hospital could hardly have been worse. As for the sick and wounded, if these unfortunate men were hardy enough to withstand the slow journey upstream to the Landing on the open deck of a steamer, and then the bone-jarring trip by wagon to Swift Current, they had a fair chance of surviving the appalling conditions that awaited them at the base hospital. This hospital was inspected less than a month after it had opened by the Honourable Doctor M. Sullivan, Purveyor-General. His report, part of which follows, is a scathing condemnation of the conditions he found — conditions in many respects reminiscent of the deplorable military hospitals of the Crimean War days.

> On my arrival at Swift Current I found the hospital car used as a dormitory by dressers, orderlies and surgeons, while the caboose was used as a dwelling by the Commandmant General Laurie and the Surgeon in Command of the Hospital Corps. On further examination I found that an old, dirty, dilapidated car, deeply embedded in the mud, was used as the hospital. It was close to the railway latrines, the odor

45

from which it could not escape; there were two or three sick soldiers in this and they were attended by 19 dressers and 4 surgeons. I immediately determined to make a change, and had two marquees or hospital tents and four small ones pitched on an elevated situation, and had the patients removed.[51]

It is little wonder, then, that following Sullivan's report to Middleton, the base hospital was moved on May 20 to Moose Jaw.[52] However, by this time, the need for this hospital was slight.

The fighting to the north of Swift Current had ended in May, and only the futile pursuit of Big Bear's band continued to occupy the militia. By the third week of June all of the supplies and reinforcements from Swift Current that had been required by Otter and Middleton had been despatched. There was now no reason to continue this military base. Indeed, since late in May, Middleton had been partly supplied by use of the trail north from Moose Jaw. Major-General Middleton, anxious to be rid of Major-General Laurie,[53] telegraphed A. P. Caron the following message:

> I directed Laurie by telegram on the 19th [June] to dismiss all his staff and to make up his accounts and proceed to Winnipeg where I should meet him in a few days. I also directed him to leave Captain White in charge of the stores at Saskatchewan Landing until brought away by steamer which would be sent up as soon as possible.[54]

The closing of the supply base and the passage through Swift Current from Battleford in July of two closely guarded groups of Indian prisoners from Big Bear's band destined for trial in Regina marked the end of the Rebellion.[55] By mid-October, the remaining militiamen stationed at Battleford boarded the train in Swift Current for home. Transporting these soldiers was the last employment of a military nature that the civilian trail freighters had, and, to the regret of the freighters, it was done at one-third of the earlier "rebellion rate".[56] The time of big profits in local freighting had ended months before. Likewise, the impractical vision that Louis Riel had had of creating a new nation for the métis and Canadian Indians had been shattered. Riel, for years a man obsessed with a single cause — founding his "new nation" — was a prisoner in Regina. His vision had been doomed from the start, and the fall of Batoche finally made this evident even to him. His surrender, conviction and subsequent execution on November 16, 1885, won more sympathy for his cause than anything else he had done in his lifetime. Most important, Louis Riel became to many a martyr which, it appears, had become his second ambition.

As for Canada, it had faced and suppressed a rebellion that threatened its new unity. In doing so its soldiers had won a measure of glory, some at the cost of their lives. Even the vanquished rebels had won a little, in that Parliament and the people in eastern Canada finally paid some heed to their troubles. But these prairie natives had lost heavily, and they had lost more than most of them knew, for this tragic rebellion marked the end for all time to their hopes for a return to the wild, free life of the nomadic hunter that they had loved. The civilization of the white man had proven itself supreme in the North-West Territories, never again to be challenged in such a manner by the native Indians or métis. The plough had defeated the prairie. In the Swift Current district, as in other areas, the last act in their tragedy was painfully and slowly played out over the next twenty years.

Chapter IV

THE AFTERMATH OF THE REBELLION AND THE END OF TRAIL FREIGHTING

The rebellion over, Swift Current returned to the usual trail freighting. Only five more years were to elapse before the advance of railway building in the North-West brought this colorful phase of Swift Current's history to an end. When this happened, the half-breeds of the district whose livelihood was freighting faced severe hardship. They and the local Indians had long suffered from the white man's bigotry, which sprang from his fear of the natives and his belief in his own superiority — an intolerance made worse by the racial nature of the rebellion. These children of the prairie were gradually forced to leave this, their homeland, by the insidious pressures of white civilization. But as the native people departed, a new group arrived whose influence upon the district was even greater than that of the earliest residents, for they came to test and develop the district's agricultural potential.

The "Indian scare" caused by the Rebellion persisted in Swift Current for at least two years after hostilities ended in 1885. In part this uneasiness, an aftermath of the rebellion, was kept alive by the refusal in 1886 of two bands of treaty Indians to leave the district and to return to the confinement of their reserve east of Regina. In order to force these wanderers from Piapot's band to return to Qu'Appelle, Superintendent Mc-Illree and a large party of N.W.M.P. had to arrest several of the leaders. Although the Indians threatened to take reprisals against the Mounties for forcibly curbing their roving nature, no violence developed.[1] Also during early winter in 1887, local citizens became alarmed over the presence of a number of half-breeds near Saskatchewan Landing. Were they preparing to attack the hamlet? The scout sent out to investigate the matter reported finding only the habitual gathering of métis engaged in winter festivities. This news only temporarily eased over-tense nerves in Swift Current. Reports early that spring of strange Indians lurking in the district caused its white citizens to demand a thorough police search which likewise proved fruitless.[2] Again in June, fearful railway men and merchants at Swift Current reported the presence of a large party of armed half-breeds near Gull Lake. Those most imaginative were convinced that another uprising was imminent. Superintendent Sam Steele and most of "D" Division of the N.W.M.P. were rushed to the scene and promptly combed the district

MÉTIS AT GULL LAKE HAULING BUFFALO BONES TO THE RAILWAY. *circa* 1887.

for potential rebels. They found only one forlorn group of natives near Gull Lake. The N.W.M.P. historian, J. P. Turner, describes these people:

> At the latter [camp] the destitute occupants of half a dozen lodges were gathering buffalo bones for sale; they explained it was their only means of procuring money to tide them over another winter. Two of the families in a starving condition were immediately given aid, and a thorough investigation revealed that there had not been the slightest cause for alarm.[3]

Sam Steele later wrote rather cynically that he suspected that the rumor of impending rebellion may have been started by Swift Current merchants hoping to bring about the stationing of a division of N.W.M.P. in their hamlet.[4] The white citizens' suspicion and distrust of the natives, at times approaching hysteria, apparently subsided and changed somewhat after this time, being replaced by an increased feeling of dislike and contempt. Underlying the local whiteman's attitude was his unshakeable belief in the superiority of his own race, language, religion and culture. In a word, he was a bigot.

The plight of the few Indians in the district and those half-breeds not employed in freighting remained serious, especially during freezing weather. During the winter of 1888, the police issued relief rations to a few half-breed families at Swift Current and Saskatchewan Landing whom they considered "deserving".[5] The culture of the Indians, including their attitude to employment, their language and religion, and their knowledge of the world, set them apart from the white men and even from the métis. By nature wanderers, many Indians left the district for better hunting grounds in Montana. The following year the district's Indian population had declined to only eight families. These non-treaty Indians, proud of their independence, eked out a living gathering buffalo bones and doing whatever few odd jobs the whites would give them. The police report for 1889 states:

> Polishing buffalo horns and selling them to passengers on the trains passing through is what they mainly depend upon for a living; some Indians have made as much as $7 or $8 some days by these means. . . . Buffalo horns are fast becoming as scarce as the buffalo themselves. It will only, therefore, be a matter of time before the Indian loses this, his principal source of maintenance.[6]

Local non-treaty Indians had not exchanged their self-reliance and freedom for the treaty payments and restriction of a reserve. Thus, except for rare occasions when government aid was provided for those who were actually starving, these Indians were left to fend for themselves in a changed and often hostile homeland. The government had no policy to aid the non-treaty Indian who wished only to help himself. He was not given land or livestock, nor taught to farm or trained for a job in the white man's world. This once proud buffalo hunter was forced to eat his horse, his dog, even carrion, to keep alive. His old people and children froze or starved to death in winter while huddled together in a tattered cloth tent. His women, in despair, sold themselves to the sex-starved gangs of railway workers or to the Mounties. The Indian men sought an escape in whisky. The only dignity left to the non-treaty Indian was his freedom to roam at will over his prairie homeland — and the settlement of white ranchers soon put a stop to that.

The Indian population in the district was only about one-tenth as large as that of the métis. Inspector Sanders stated of the mixed-blood residents:

> At Swift Current and neighborhood there is a shifting half-breed population which averages about eighty families. A few engage in freighting to Battleford and other points, others fish in the lake [Lac Pelletier] and remainder polish and sell buffalo horns.[7]

A few of these people had received what must have seemed a windfall in 1886 when the North-West Half-breed Commission held sittings at Swift Current and settled twelve claims for money scrip totalling $2,202.66[8]. As is the nature of people who long have had more wants than money to gratify them, the natives quickly spent their newly found wealth at the local stores. The merchants did a thriving business as a result, perhaps benefiting as much by this injection of new currency as did the natives. However, by issuing the scrip in settlement of the half-breeds' long-standing demands, the government was acknowledging the justice of their claims, as well as its own shortcomings which had helped to precipitate the Rebellion.

Probably no more than half of the twelve people who had received scrip in 1886 lived within the district. Therefore, it is safe to say that the great majority of the local mixed-blood population and all of the Indians (who were not covered by a treaty), received nothing from the government for remaining loyal during the rebellion. Indeed, several of them had helped the government to defeat their rebelling brethren in the north. Paradoxically, many of the treaty Indians and half-breeds elsewhere, who either had revolted or threatened to, received additional food, clothing or land scrip. The loyal natives of the district, meanwhile, were treated little better by the whites than the "bad" Indians and métis who had decided, in desperation, to fight for their rights!

The suspicion and contempt which most of the white citizens displayed towards the Indians was generally shown to the half-breeds also, although less openly. While the métis were more like the whites in culture, they differed from the white, English-speaking Protestants by being French-speaking Roman Catholics, albeit, ones who generally spoke English and an Indian language also. Such rapport as existed between the local métis and whites apparently was governed by the need of the white citizens for the labor or patronage of the métis. As long as fishing, hunting, gathering buffalo bones and trail freighting could be carried on in the district, they and the Indians could remain. When these occupations ended there was little else the original inhabitants could do but move on, for hardly any of them could farm. By December, 1892, most of the Indians and many of the half-breeds had moved out of the district. They had never given the police any trouble, despite the generally intolerant attitude of the whites and their frequent ordeals of starvation in a land seemingly unable to feed them. By this time, game animals were scarce locally, and the days of trail freighting to Battleford were just fond memories. Those who stayed to gather the remaining buffalo bones were forced to comb the distant prairie to keep a scant hold on life.

Although the rebellion had produced nothing of lasting economic value for the local natives, it had brought benefits to those engaged in trail freighting, especially to white businessmen such as F. Fraser Tims. Tims, a big, handsome man who wore a black derby hat, a dark, neatly-trimmed beard, a cutaway coat with trousers often tucked into knee-high boots, was an impressive figure, especially for a frontier hamlet. He had made a good deal of money from his ferry and store business at Saskatchewan Landing —so much so, in fact, that the authorities felt he could well afford to repair his own broken ferry cable, rather than expect the government to pay the cost.[9] In addition, Tims profited from his contract with General Laurie to deliver supplies from Swift Current to the north bank of the river at the rate of $1.00 for each 100 pounds.[10] Finally, he made further gains from the incidental business which had come to his store in Swift Current from the hundreds of troops and freighters stopping there. With these profits, Tims did replace the broken ferry cable and later installed a second one. He also substituted two new barges that measured twenty by one hundred feet and had a carrying capacity of 100,000 pounds each for his first ferry. Possibly these were "war surplus" barges, bought at bargain prices. The reconstruction of the temporary military telegraph line to the Landing in 1887[11] further aided him by providing him with the means of rapid communications between his two businesses. Thus, while his trail freighting facilities had aided the militia, their use by the militia had greatly aided Tims. Of general benefit to all using the trail, in addition to the telegraph connection to the river crossing, were the two bridges which Otter's column had built along it. The first was erected over Eagle Hills Creek and the other over the Battle River at Battleford. In addition, two mail stations, later used as depots, were built by Otter's force between Saskatchewan Landing and Battleford.

In fact, all the local white citizens and a few of the natives had gained from the rush of business brought on by the rebellion. Yet, except for the small group of transient bargemen who had struck, unsuccessfully, for higher wages, no evidence was found that the local people attempted to get more from the government for either their goods or services than was freely offered to them. This contrasts sharply with the generally damning report to the contrary which was applied to all the people of the North-West by three militia officers.[12]

The resumption of regular traffic over the trail, even before hostilities had ended in 1885, led the federal government in 1886 to take an interest in improving it still further. R. C. Laurie of Battleford, Dominion Lands Surveyor and the son of Battleford's newspaper editor, received instructions to locate and survey the trail. He began late in June, triangulated the

THE ROYAL MAIL ABOUT TO DEPART FOR BATTLEFORD, *circa* 1888. The Mountie in the pill-box hat seated next to the driver is William Milburn.

river at the crossing on October 27, and by early November of 1886 had completed his work. By altering the route from the Landing to Battleford, Laurie was able to shorten the trail somewhat.[13] Following this, the trail was declared a public road, and a considerable amount of traffic was maintained over it until Saskatoon replaced Swift Current as the closest railway point to Battleford early in the fall of 1890. Well before 1890, however, Fraser Tims had the foresight to sell his local businesses and to move to Fort Saskatchewan. There he continued to prosper as a merchant and rancher, becoming a member of the Territorial Assembly in 1894.

The requirements of Battleford did not account for all of the traffic which disembarked from Swift Current during the years before 1891, nor was the trail free of competition from other forms of transportation. Water transport was one of the trail's competitors, although the Swift Current Creek itself was found to be too shallow to float even the smallest freight boats. Almost as soon as railway service to Swift Current began in 1883, steamboats began to pick up freight brought by carts and wagons north to the river crossing — an arrangement which led in the following year to the abandonment of shipments via Lake Winnipeg and Grand Rapids.[14] That spring, also, a tug owned by S. R. Kerr of Winnipeg began hauling freight and passengers from the mouth of the Swift Current Creek to Saskatoon.[15] Two years later even some freight bound for Battleford was taken by tug or flatboat along this route to Saskatoon and thence by trail to its destination.[16] During this time, the C.P.R. station of Rush Lake (located seventeen miles northeast of Swift Current and only fifteen miles south of the South Branch), began to be used as a railway point by freighters hauling to flatboats and river steamers. So important did this route become that an application was reported to have been made in 1885 for a railway charter from Rush Lake to the river.[17] However, nothing came of it.

Shortly after this, the C.P.R. decided that a branch line railway would soon be needed in the Swift Current district. The Company made arrangements to survey such a line from Swift Current northwest to Red Deer Forks and then across the South Branch to Buffalo Lake. Beginning in May, 1890, a railway survey party led by an engineer named White mapped out this line.[18] Since the expected tide of settlement took another twenty years to come, the Company shelved the project. Still, this early survey was not entirely a wasted effort, for the Empress branch line, which was built during the years 1911 to 1913, follows a route from Swift Current that partly coincides with it.

It is impossible to say how many millions of pounds of freight were hauled from Swift Current by carts and wagons during the 1883-1890 period. From spring until fall in 1886 alone, over four million pounds of freight reached Battleford by the trail. The major consignees in Battleford, besides the stores, were the Indian Department, the N.W.M.P., and the Hudson's Bay Company. During this period, F. Fraser Tims and George Cowan, both of Swift Current, together with Goodwin Marchand and the partners Gibson and Ballendine of Battleford were the most prominent owners of local trail freighting outfits.[19] The freighters had an especially good year in 1889 due to the heavy demand and the increase of fifty cents per hundred pounds in the freight rate over the low rate of one dollar per hundredweight that prevailed in 1887. The Battleford newspaper on October 16, 1889 commented on this brief heyday, "Nearly every team in the country is engaged in freighting from Swift Current and the cry is still for more."

Cart freighting was responsible for the hamlet attracting its most distinguished visitor in the nineteenth century. Early in August, 1886, on his only trip through western Canada, the Prime Minister, Sir John A. Macdonald, alighted from his special train at Swift Current. He had heard much about the Red River carts but he had never seen one until he spied sixty or seventy of them at the depot awaiting freight for Battleford.[20] As he walked about viewing the carts and speaking to the native drivers, Swift Current's residents took the opportunity to greet the man who had done more than any other to build their nation.

While his merchandise and ferry businesses were thriving late in 1887, Fraser Tims had succeeded in selling his holdings at the river crossing to W. E. Russell of Battleford. The new owner built and operated an inn there called the Russell House and continued to manage the store and ferry venture. For a time business continued to be good, and a few métis began to settle at the Landing. The government recognized this development by granting the crossing a post office, the name of which brought forth the following *Saskatchewan Herald* editorial comment: "The post office at the Swift Current crossing of the Battleford Trail is now open. It has the absurdly long name of Saskatchewan Landing."

Russell, however, had the misfortune or lack of foresight to have purchased and developed the landing facilities less than three years before the railway reached Saskatoon. Traffic to Battleford over the trail virtually ended in September, 1890, and Russell was left with the equipment on his hands, although he tried in vain to sell it.[21] He was sustained until 1892 by his postmaster's pay and by a small police allowance for keeping the ferry open to accommodate the meagre amount of traffic that remained.[22] But the end came at last, and from 1893 to 1901 there was no public ferry at Saskatchewan Landing. During these years, however, James Smart ran a private ferry there for the convenience of himself and other local ranchers. When the steel ferry cable broke, he made a replacement from the abandoned wire of the old military telegraph line from the landing to Swift Current, resourcefully twisting the wires on a wagon wheel.[23] In 1902, as homesteaders at last began to arrive, regular ferry service was resumed. After 1905, this time with government assistance, ferry service continued until 1951, when a bridge was built at the old crossing.

A picturesque phase of Swift Current's history closed with the end of trail freighting to Battleford. The marriage of railway and cart had given birth to the hamlet. Railroaders and carters had kept it alive. During the eight years that trail freighting had lasted, the business derived from it had established Swift Current as a settlement equipped to survive. The impetus to development that resulted from the Rebellion had brought a brief period of hectic prosperity and, of a more enduring nature, it had secured a place for Swift Current in the pages of Canadian history. Sadly, the rebellion also heightened racial intolerance in the district, just as it did across Canada. As the trail freighters passed on like the buffaloes before them—a quickly vanishing breed — so did many of the native peoples of the district, unable to survive in the environment that the whites were developing. In their place had come a titled Englishman with a grand scheme for colonizing and farming the semi-arid plains. Three of his huge ranch-farms were to be established within the district, one just on the edge of Swift Current. This enterprise was to have an even greater impact upon the district's development than had either the trail or Riel.

Chapter V

THE NOBLE "76"

The rebellion had come and gone but still the plains around Swift Current remained vacant. Of the thousands of people who had passed through the district during the revolt, not one of them had settled. The region had the untested reputation of being too arid for farming, and even the claims of the government's botanist, John Macoun, that at least it was particularly well suited for ranching, were either ignored or scoffed at. Anyway, plenty of land said to be better was still readily available elsewhere.

The West's greatest landlords, the C.P.R. and the Dominion government, anxious to have their vast holdings in Palliser's Triangle settled, had each launched a program to attract land buyers. To test the region's suitability for agriculture, early in 1884 the C.P.R. established ten experimental farms along its main line west from Swift Current. The first of these was on the western fringe of the Swift Current district at Gull Lake. Sufficient rainfall during the growing season in 1884 and 1885 brought good yields, and, for a short time, it began to look as if Palliser's Triangle might be suitable for farming after all.[1] Also, in 1884, the federal government greatly relaxed its homestead requirements and opened the railway mile-belt reserve for unlimited homestead entry.[2] Of particular importance to the Swift Current district, the government chose Swift Current rather than the larger hamlet of Maple Creek as the location for a temporary Dominion Lands Agency to promote and facilitate settlement. The reason for the choice of Swift Current was that it was closer to the centre of the region that the agency was to serve. Despite the fact that the agent had all of present-day south-western Saskatchewan in his agency, he had little to do but mail out promotional literature and file reports. For the year ending October 31, 1885, there were only fifty-one land entries in all of this huge empty area of 32,290 square miles,[3] and most of these were made by people already living in the region.

In the Swift Current district, not one bona fide homesteader came from elsewhere expressly to engage in farming locally before the turn of the century. True, homestead entries were made in the district, but they were all like the first four entries which were recorded in 1885 when four men, already living and working in the district, were prompted to file on free Dominion lands. The average homesteader in the Canadian West generally had limited funds, crude farming implements and little, if any, knowledge of dry-land farming. Naturally he was unwilling to gamble all he had on the

57

slim chance that he could succeed in farming in a district where the land was said to be mostly of poor quality and drought-ridden as well.

Since the efforts made by the C.P.R. and the Dominion had failed to produce an influx of pioneers to the semi-arid region between Moose Jaw and Calgary, these great landlords were receptive to any reasonable scheme which promised to settle this area. They were especially attracted by any scheme that would cost them almost nothing, require no involvement or management on their part, and provide them with what was so vitally needed during this period of lagging settlement — land buyers with money to invest in the North-West. Just such a scheme had been developing in the imagination of a wealthy nobleman who envisaged a huge land development project for this very region. This gentleman-promoter was Sir John Pepys Lister-Kaye, a Yorkshire baronet described as ". . . a tall, blond, blue-eyed young Englishman with a deliberate, easy manner, a fine sandy moustache and a shapely head filled full of schemes."[4]

The full account of Sir John Lister-Kaye's activities and projects in the North-West and of the people in Canada and Britain who became involved in his schemes has never been told. Perhaps it never will be. As such, it is one more example of countless dramas from the frontier period of the Canadian prairies of which we know little or nothing — and, as a people, we are poorer for not knowing. This is a chapter of the story.

Sir John had arrived in the Canadian North-West in 1884, fresh from successfully promoting a land settlement project in California.[5] Convinced by what he saw at the vast farm of Major W. R. Bell, east of Regina, he concluded that the North-West held potential for agriculture and thus, for profit for a promoter such as he. That fall, in the grand fashion which typified the man, Lister-Kaye purchased from the C.P.R. and the Dominion a total of almost seven thousand acres at Balgonie, near the Bell farm. To house his workers and shelter the excellent livestock he had imported, he ordered extensive farm buildings erected. The following spring, despite the manpower demands made by the outbreak of the Riel Rebellion, he succeeded in having over two sections of land broken and planted to wheat, oats and barley which all yielded well.[6]

His first gamble in the North-West had met with success! This, plus the good crop reports for 1884 and 1885 released by the C.P.R. experimental farms, apparently caused him to turn his eye to the Swift Current district and to those waiting lands farther west. In all probability, Lister-Kaye also read and took hope from the government survey report published in January, 1886, which claimed that perhaps almost one-half of the area within the Swift Current Dominion Lands Agency was suitable for agricultural purposes. However, in the Swift Current district itself, the only land near the indispensable railway whose grain-growing potential was praised in the report was at Rush Lake.[7] This did not deter him, nor did the drought which plagued the south-central portion of the North-West in 1886. Travelling in style with his wife, Natica,[8] in a private railway car bearing her name, the thirty-three year old baronet made a reconnaissance of the region west to Calgary. He searched for blocks of good, well-watered land at intervals along the railway which were suitable for farming and stock raising. Favorably impressed by what he saw, he journeyed to Ottawa to acquire ten 10,000 acre blocks of land from the C.P.R. and the Dominion.[9] His syndicate (which he had yet to form) would establish ten ranch-farms modelled, he told a newspaper reporter ". . . upon the principle of an English estate."[10] Seven were to be at intervals west of the Swift Current district extending almost to Calgary, but, of vital importance to the district's future, three of these great estates would be located within it — one on the fertile plains of Rush Lake, another just south of Swift Current, and the third near the C.P.R. experimental farm at Gull Lake. All three were intersected by creeks. If his dream became a reality, then the total acreage of his eleven farms would dwarf Bell's farm in the Qu'Appelle Valley, then the largest in the North-West. This must have appealed to the titled Englishman's vanity, but the prospect for promoter's profit would doubtless have attracted him most.

Of first imporance to the Swift Current district and to the semi-arid region generally, the proposed scheme held out hope for the only large scale, diversified agricultural development project which might come along. Swift Current's hopes of becoming more than just a tiny railway hamlet depended on the local development of agriculture. This controversial nobleman must have appeared to some as the Messiah of the semi-arid prairies.

By late January, 1887, Lister-Kaye had concluded the land deal with the obliging representatives of the C.P.R. and the Dominion. He agreed to make six annual payments on the land and to fulfil certain cultivation conditions. In turn, the railway and the government would reduce the price of the land to less than $1.50 per acre by rebating about one-half of the purchase price when he or his assignees met all of the agreed conditions, and as well, the C.P.R. granted him freight rate concessions.[11]

Sir John immediately sailed for England and tried, unsuccessfully, to promote his scheme there among wealthy friends. He faced opposition from many quarters. The old opponents of the C.P.R. syndicate had painted a forbidding picture of the Canadian West in the minds of many British people. The collapse of the short-lived economic boom marked in the West by the bursting of the Winnipeg real estate bubble in April, 1882, made investors doubly cautious. The deep, long-lasting depression which followed this saw business slump to a low point in Britain by 1886. Furthermore, the North-West Rebellion in the spring of 1885, followed by the killing frost on August 23 which devastated all the late grain crops on the prairies that year, cast doubt on the political stability and farming potential of the North-West. Finally, the widespread drought on the southern prairies which caused an almost total crop failure there the next year made farming in this new and almost unknown region seem anything but promising. This kind of bad news travelled fast — and far. Certainly, the times were far from auspicious to promote the syndicate Lister-Kaye first called the Alberta and Assiniboia Land, Stock and Coal Company.[12]

The somewhat discouraged young baronet returned to Balgonie in the spring of 1887. He was almost prepared to abandon his grand scheme and, instead,|to promote a company to buy out the Bell Farm and acquire 100,000 acres north of it as well. The weather would decide the matter. Had he or western agriculture suffered another set-back that year, in all probability it would have caused him to abandon his first grand scheme entirely. But Dame Fortune smiled upon him in 1887, as good crops on the prairie were combined with a business recovery in Britain.

The successful harvest at his Balgonie farm over, Lister-Kaye, his confidence renewed, set out again for England. To aid him in convincing hesitant investors, he took along D. J. (Joe) Wylie, a charming Englishman who became M.L.A. for Maple Creek in 1905. The high-born promoter hoped that Wylie's four-year residence at Maple Creek would make him an acceptable authority on the general area. Wylie was promised a managerial position in the new company if his praise of the scheme helped turn the trick.[13] It did! A new syndicate, known as the Canadian Agricultural, Coal and Colonization Company (C.A.C.C. Co.), was formed January 26, 1888 to replace the first one. This company was to buy out Lister-Kaye's Balgonie holdings and, at a further substantial profit to him, take over his purchase agreement with the C.P.R. and the Dominion once the company's representatives had inspected the lands and given their approval. This they did in June, 1888.[14] Sir John immediately left for England where he quickly finalized the sale. Through foresight, luck, determination, charm and enthusiasm, coupled with some clever misrepresentation of land prices in the North-West, the thirty-five year old Lister-Kaye had earned a fortune from the deal.[15]

Some people in the North-West, already accustomed to disappointment, rather expected to see this too-good-to-be-true scheme dropped once this nobleman had made his promoter's profit.[16] To their surprise and joy, this was not to be the case. The C.A.C.C. Co. needed an experienced manager in Canada to launch the project. Lister-Kaye agreed to accept the well-paid position for five years, since he could not close the deal otherwise.[17] It remained to be seen whether he would be as capable in managing this largely experimental ranch-farm enterprise as he had been in promoting it.

One cannot write the early history of the Swift Current district without tracing the developments on Lister-Kaye's three ranch-farms within it. What happened on these three stations often mirrored or determined the fortunes of the entire scheme. Conversely, the progress of the scheme as a whole determined, to a varying extent, the company's operations within the district. Finally, and of utmost importance to this history, the progress of Lister-Kaye's estates in the district largely influenced the course of agricultural development around Swift Current. The one story is very much a part of the other. In the initial stages, however, before the ten new stations began to operate, the pattern of development for all was similar.

Sir John, always a man of action, at once set the project in motion. He had building sites selected, extensive fence lines surveyed, and two million board feet of lumber ordered for construction of excellent buildings for each ranch-farm.[18] To provide about 500 breeding cows at each station, he, in his usual grand fashion, purchased the entire herd, in all some 5800 American range cattle, from the Powder River Ranch Company — an English-owned firm with its headquarters in London.[19] Since these cattle bore the brand "76", the C.A.C.C. Co. decided to maintain the brand for all of its livestock — a practice which in later years caused the far-flung enterprise to be known in the North-West as the "76" Ranch. He sent his agents into the northwestern United States with orders to buy thousands of good Merino ewes, renowned for their wool, for delivery in equal sized bands to each of the eleven company properties during the following year. Sir John then selected and shipped from England nearly 300 pedigreed rams, mainly of the mutton type, such as Shropshire, to be distributed among the various farms to produce, by cross-breeding, a new variety of sheep with, hopefully, the best characteristics of both the dams and the sires.[20] In Ontario he bought hundreds of good mares in order to place a band of about sixty-five at each station for field work and breeding purposes. A choice Clydesdale stallion for each ranch-farm was imported from England, as, later, were Polled Angus and Galloway bulls, as well as sufficient Yorkshire boars and sows to establish eleven herds of about ninety pigs each.[21]

Those in the North-West were amazed and delighted by the scale of Lister-Kaye's enterprise. Commenting on the fine livestock then being imported, on August 31, 1888, the *Medicine Hat Times* proclaimed: "The number of pedigreed animals contained in the shipment is said to never have been equalled in the annals of the export trade." The editor of the Battleford newspaper a week earlier had boldly asserted: "This will be one of the most gigantic establishments on this continent." Be that as it may, as Henry S. King, Member of Parliament for Hull, England, and chairman of the board of directors for C.A.C.C. Co., rightly pointed out in his letter to Sir Charles Tupper, then the Canadian High Commissioner to London, the company's project was ". . . perhaps the largest scheme ever initiated for the working of Canadian land."[22]

A project of such size required the recruiting of a large work force. Lister-Kaye turned the task over to an aristocratic friend of his, Hubert Pelham Clinton, the younger son of an English lord. Through newspaper advertisements in England offering free passage to Canada, a one year contract including board, lodging and ten dollars a month wages to begin with the voyage, plus the chance to acquire "free" a 160 acre homestead adjacent to the company's land when their contract expired, some 110 young Englishmen were enlisted and sent to the North-West.[23] Two or three women, some married with children, were hired in the North-West for each ranch-farm to act as housekeepers and cooks. About the same number of additional farm laborers were likewise secured in eastern Canada and the prairies.[24]

The few residents of the Swift Current district were undoubtedly more pleased at the arrival of the C.A.C.C. Co. employees from England than were the employees themselves. Late in August of 1888 they arrived by train and were dropped off in groups of nine or ten at each of the company's properties. Some were obviously "greenhorns" who had neither farmed nor travelled before. They had been dismayed by their first glimpse from the train of the empty, treeless prairie, so unlike their English homeland. Their discouragement and sense of hopelessness increased when they reached their destinations. Rush Lake was only a railway siding in the wilderness. Gull Lake was little more, although it did have a station house and the C.P.R. farm. Swift Current, where Clinton himself was to be the company's manager, was just a tiny hamlet surrounded by the vacant, rolling prairie. At the future farm-sites, they discovered that neither the building material nor the construction crew had yet arrived. Clinton and his English foreman, James Smart, found a vacant shack to move into at Swift Current, but the balance of the men were obliged to sleep in tents until the large central farmhouse was completed late that fall.[25] They found them-

THE "76" RANCH HOUSE, identical to those built by the "76" at Gull Lake, Rush Lake and elsewhere in 1889. For a quarter of a century, these were the largest and finest dwellings in the Swift Current district.

selves in a strange, harsh land almost devoid of single women, where there was neither church nor pub to give them comfort at the end of their long day, and where nothing stronger than water could legally be had to drown their sorrows. And to make matters worse for those at Swift Current, the drinking water there was bad in taste and often dangerous to drink.

Falteringly, the lonely men set to work. The wagons, buckboards, mowing machines, hay rakes, and Scotch plows which Sir John had purchased soon arrived and somehow, had to be assembled and made ready for use. Native hay had to be cut and stacked to provide winter feed for the work horses then arriving. Some prairie sod had to be broken in readiness for seeding the following spring, and a start had to be made on erecting eighteen miles of unnecessarily elaborate and expensive wire fence, complete with wooden top rail, around much of the company's land at each location.[26]

Well before spring came in 1889, the contractors had completed the buildings on the company's farms. Each had a two-storey furnished house, by far the largest and best in their district, for the manager and some workers. At each farm they had built a stable to hold sixty work horses, with an attached machine shed, an overhead granary topped by a windmill for pumping water from a well and for cutting feed, a blacksmith's shop and a harness room. A cattle shed to shelter 500 cows, a sheep shed to accommodate 5000 animals, a piggery to house 300 hogs and frame bunk houses for the ranch hands made up the other main farm buildings. At Rush Lake and Gull Lake, the employees built dams of plank and earth across waterways on the farms to provide water for irrigation of small plots and for livestock.[27] Then, as soon as the frozen ground thawed in the spring, the men returned to the tasks of fencing and breaking the prairie sod.

Lister-Kaye's policy of diversified agricultural production extended from livestock to grain crops. But his farming experience at Balgonie, and in California and England, had not prepared him to farm successfully in the semi-arid region of the North-West. His managers and foremen, for the most part, knew even less than he did about crop raising locally. But to qualify for the $1.25 per acre rebate allowed by the C.P.R. for cultivation on lands it sold, and to fulfil his agreement with the C.P.R., Lister-Kaye had 2000-3000 acres of railway land broken on each farm early in 1889. His Scotch plows laid the sod furrows high in the air and, without bothering to backset the sod, as was usual, he ordered that the seed be scattered broadcast on the quickly-drying sods.[28] Only the lucky coincidence of abundant rainfall in the district during May of 1889 caused the uncovered seed to germinate. When the rains gave way to drought, the young shoots began to wither. Seeing this, Sir John immediately ordered from Winnipeg forty-four watering carts with which to irrigate his parched fields.[29] Fortunately, it rained and the cart-sprinklers were "retired",[30] which partly saved the baronet from the full criticism that his foolish irrigation scheme deserved. He next bought Massey binders and a horse-powered threshing machine to harvest the poor wheat crop. Late that fall Clinton, the manager at Swift Current, seeded 200 acres of oats on new breaking as an experiment,[31] which was fairly successful. Although the crop of 1889 was disappointing, Lister-Kaye's company did earn the much-needed rebate from the C.P.R., plus a further concession reducing the amount of cultivation required on C.P.R. lands from fifty to forty per cent. Best of all, on government land Sir John got the cultivation requirements dropped entirely.[32]

Both Lister-Kaye and his company were initially interested in the "colonization" of the North-West. Originally, they had planned to bring out 270 new settlers each year[33] but they soon found that this was impossible. However, a number of new men from the south of Scotland had been brought to the farms during the spring of 1889 by the company. Unlike the young Englishmen, said by James Smart to be a motley lot recruited from many walks of life,[34] the Scotsmen were looked upon as being a steady, industrious class, accustomed to farming, who would make excellent future settlers.[35] Lister-Kaye, always a planner and promoter, tried without success early that year to enlist financial help from both the Imperial and Canadian governments to launch a grand colonization project which would settle as many as 7,000 people from England and Scotland on land adjacent to the company's ranch-farms.[36] Since support for his newest elaborate plan was not forthcoming, developmental work on the proposed sites in the North-West was dispensed with. At the end of October, 1889, with the fencing, breaking and harvesting on the existing ranch-farms completed, the company dismissed most of those men it had first hired, along with several others.[37] However, some of these men settled in the North-West as ranchers, farmers or tradesmen. Never again was the company party to a deliberate colonization scheme in Canada, nor did it recruit employees for the purpose of making them future settlers. Still, a substantial number of people were employed on the ranch-farms in later years who did leave to establish small ranches or farms of their own. In this way the original idea of colonization was carried on, but indirectly and involuntarily.

During the fall of 1889 the excellent herds of livestock which the company had purchased arrived. That September, bands of 2000 ewes, part of the 19,500 head purchased in the northwestern United States and driven overland to Maple Creek, were placed on each estate.[38] To these were added the pedigreed rams from England. Earlier, each·station had received a herd of 90 imported pigs. The huge Powder River herd, bearing the brand "76", had been trailed to the company's estate at Langdon, near Calgary, that summer. Cows from this herd, plus bulls imported from England, were brought in lots of 500 by rail early that fall to each of the eleven locations of the company.[39]

During this time Sir John's fertile mind hatched a plan to vertically integrate the company's livestock operation. He ordered butcher shops and abattoirs opened at Dunmore and Medicine Hat and a large meat

Part of the flock of 19,500 sheep, belonging to the "76" ranch, being shipped from Maple Creek to the several ranch farms of the C.A.C.C. Co., Sept. 20, 1889.

packing plant built at Calgary to reap even more profits by selling the company's own beef, mutton and pork.[40] This venture met with success, but another idea he had did not. This was a scheme to process and sell butter and cheese. An Ontario "expert" advised Lister-Kaye that Swift Current, with its water supply and its trains from east and west arriving about noon daily, was the ideal spot for his company to build a creamery and cheese factory.[41] Built of concrete, it should be large enough to process the milk of 500 cows already on the company's farms. Once each day the milk would be shipped by train to the proposed plant for processing.[42] But one problem Sir John had overlooked stood in the way of this scheme. Half wild range cattle do not make good milk cows. The nobleman instructed his ranch managers to start the project, even offering a trophy to the one having the most cows milking by that fall. The hapless employees drove the cows into chutes, tied them with ropes and attempted to extract milk from the frenzied animals. Needless to say, it did not work.[43] Sir John's hope of making Swift Current the dairy capital of the North-West Territories was shattered as another of his schemes was stillborn.

Though this nobleman had experienced some disappointments in his attempts to promote his various schemes in the North-West, his failures thus far had not been too costly. He had quickly and efficiently established the far-flung project according to plan, but the plan itself was years ahead of the development of the Territories. Not realizing this, both he and the investors in the C.A.C.C. Co. were naively confident as the year 1890 approached that the company would prosper. Since they had known good fortune, they did not realize the great risk involved in raising livestock and especially grain in the North-West. But good luck was soon to desert the reckless Lister-Kaye and one setback after another was to befall the hapless company.

The worst winter weather in ten years struck much of the Canadian prairies, including the Swift Current district, during January and February of 1890.[44] Blizzards piled the snow into huge drifts making grazing on the range impossible for cattle. The Company's supply of stored winter feed diminished rapidly as the bitter weather persisted. When Sir John, then in eastern Canada en route for London, was informed of this, he immediately proposed one of his rash schemes. He knew that beef could easily be taken by refrigerated ships from Atlantic ports and marketed in Liverpool. He reasoned that since freezing weather then held sway across Canada, beef could be shipped east in regular railway cars. Accordingly, he instructed the managers on the C.A.C.C. Co. farms to slaughter 800 cattle and allow the dressed carcasses to freeze. Meanwhile, he arranged with the C.P.R. to supply about thirty freight cars to carry the frozen beef to eastern Canada.[45] His instructions were carried out, but before the huge beef shipment had reached Montreal a thaw set in, causing almost all of the 800 carcasses to spoil.[46] Lister-Kaye had gambled on the weather remaining cold, and had lost. This was a staggering blow to the already heavily-burdened finances of the company.

Meeting in London, the worried directors of the company decided that Sir John must be replaced. Under pressure, Lister-Kaye resigned and Thomas Stone, who had managed the Kincorth farm, succeeded him as general manager. To provide much-needed capital, the company was forced to offer its fine farm at Balgonie for sale.[47] Perhaps because of Sir John's position in British society and because he and his brother held shares in the company, his management was not publicly criticized by the company. Instead, in gentlemanly fashion, it was announced to the press that the Yorkshire baronet " . . . had given up the management, after putting the farms in good working order, to devote his time to immigration work."[48]

At first, no newspaper in the Canadian West spoke out against Lister-Kaye. But after the drought of July had devastated the grain crops in the North-West, western newspapers, perhaps partly in frustration, took up the attack on him. It was Sir John's bad management and not the agricultural suitability of the country that was at fault, they said. "The Kay [sic] system of management was radically wrong in its inception, and was carried out in a spirit of reckless extravagance and experimental ignorance such as no institution could long bear up under."[49]

What they said was true, but it was not the whole truth. It was foolish of Sir John to attempt to create eleven English estates based upon the ancient tradition of lord and servant in a region where social equality was engendered by a commonly-shared frontier experience. And due to his ignorance of conditions in the semi-arid region, as well as to his native rashness, Lister-Kaye had been guilty of some costly errors in judgment. But, in his defence, sound methods of dryland farming were not widely practiced in the North-West for decades after Sir John's first experiments. His farming methods were as good, or as bad, as most at the time. What is so regrettable in the criticism commonly expressed, both then and now, about Lister-Kaye's grand scheme is that the critics fail to give to him the credit that is his due. The Swift Current district, among others, had no livestock industry until the arrival of Lister-Kaye's excellent animals. In addition, at a time when the North-West was begging for immigrants, he brought in people who later settled in the area to establish pioneer ranches and farms. Finally, while economic depression plagued Europe and America and frustrated the hopes of the North-West, his scheme brought a large amount of investment capital into a region chiefly dependent on the buffalo bone trade and the C.P.R. payroll. It can fairly be said that, but for Sir John Lister-Kaye, the early history of the semi-arid region and the Swift Current district, in particular, would have been far different. Once launched, Sir John's great ranch-farm enterprise continued to dominate the agricultural industry at Swift Current and elsewhere for almost twenty years.

The troubles of the company did not end with Sir John's resignation. On April 16, 1890, a prairie fire started by sparks from a C.P.R. engine

HUBERT P. CLINTON (L.), MANAGER OF THE "76" RANCH AT SWIFT CURRENT, AND JAMES SMART, (R.) RANCH FOREMAN, *circa* 1890. Note the C.A.C.C. Co.'s barn topped by a windmill (background) and the wolf hounds.

trapped 2200 C.A.C.C. Co. sheep which were grazing near Gull Lake. Over half of them were killed or badly injured when their heavy fleeces caught fire. Since most were ewes soon to give birth and be sheared, the losses were doubly heavy.[50] The company's sheep, particularly the lambs, also fell prey to the numerous packs of coyotes which then roamed the prairie. Clinton, the farm manager at Swift Current, imported wolf hounds to deal with the coyote menace and, probably, also to enjoy the sport of "riding to the hounds" as he had in England. Apparently he devoted much of his time to the sport, for in the first three months of 1890 just one of his hounds killed ninety of these little prairie wolves.[51]

Despite the fact that the Territorial Government took such a dim view of the farming potential of the semi-arid region west of Moose Jaw that in the spring of 1890 it refused to distribute seed grain to settlers there,[52] the C.A.C.C. Co. that year seeded a large acreage of grain crops. They tilled or backset the previous year's breaking, and, at each of the estates, 500 acres of flax and almost as much wheat was sown broadcast on the soil.[53] Once more spring rains sprouted the seeds and gave promise of an excellent crop. Confidently, the merchants at Swift Current stocked up on binder twine to be ready for the immense harvest.[54] But the heat and drought of July wilted and shrivelled the once lush grain fields. Then, on July 15, a terrific hail storm struck the Swift Current region. Winds hurled hailstones with such force that most windows, including even the heavy glass in the C.P.R. passenger coaches, were smashed. The grain crops were hammered into the ground and covered by six inches of ice.[55] Not one bushel of grain was harvested in the Swift Current district that fall.[56]

Discouraged by their bad luck, the company decided late in 1890 that it must make changes. The cattle on the Swift Current farm would be moved to Rush Lake, and those at Gull Lake would go to the Crane Lake ranch, which would become cattle headquarters. The cattle division would be managed by D. H. Andrews, a shrewd little English bachelor who had worked for the Powder River company until the C.A.C.C. Co. had bought their herd and hired him as manager in 1888. A large summer camp for cattle was to be set up on the north-eastern slope of Cypress Hills.[57] The company's meat business, one of Lister-Kaye's best schemes, was doing well and was to be continued. In future, grain crops would be sown mainly at Balgonie and on the two farms near Calgary. Clydesdale horses and Galloway cattle were to be raised on the farms near Medicine Hat. Swift Current would become sheep headquarters, with the Scotsman, William Rutherford, an employee since 1888, as manager. Here a permanent shearing and dipping station to handle 20,000 sheep was to be established.[58] During the summer more than one-half of this huge flock of sheep was to be pastured down the creek north-east of Swift Current, and would be wintered at five camps at Lac Pelletier, where a great stock of hay could be put up. The Gull Lake ranch would handle the balance of 20,000 sheep.[59] The hay meadows which the company irrigated at Rush Lake promised to provide plenty of feed for its cattle there. As a result, the district became largely sheep country. Only a few small cattle ranches competed with the "76" for the available grazing along the creek's banks.

By reorganizing the operations of the company in this manner, the C.A.C.C. Co. allowed a large part of its investment on the various farms in elaborate fences, farm implements and large, specially-built barns, shops and granaries to either stand idle or to be only partially used. Lister-Kaye may have over-invested in these improvements, even in view of the diversity and scale of mixed farming that he intended to carry on. Yet when Thomas Stone and the company decided that in future they would concentrate on only one or two types of agricultural production at each estate, they made the company more vulnerable to the risks that are common to a one crop economy. True, overall, the company was still to produce several agricultural products, but by specializing at certain locations in raising one product only, they risked higher losses from such hardships as drought, disease, pests, hail, frost or prairie fire, which were often localized in scope. What they hoped to gain in efficiency by their reorganization had to more than make up for the lost advantage of mixed farming and the overhead expense of the now-unused improvements that had been made at great cost on each of the eleven farms. In view of the uncertainties of prairie agriculture and the company's seriously strained finances, the future was anything but bright for the "76".

It was ironic and unfortunate for both the company and the farming future of the Swift Current district that the C.A.C.C. Co. decided to give up large scale grain farming locally after their 1890 crop failure. Had they seeded a large acreage in 1891, it is probable that they would have harvested an excellent crop.[60] The following year, 1892, the crop conditions were also good. Probably two successful harvests in succession would not only have improved the company's finances, but would have helped to dispel the belief that the district was not suited for farming. However, not again until 1898 were local conditions so favorable as to be likely to produce fine grain crops with crude farming methods,[61] despite the fact that the C.A.C.C. Co. discarded their broadcast seeders and used seed drills from 1893 onward.[62]

Fortunately, the company's sheep ranching venture in the district, though, was a great success. In 1891, almost every ewe had a lamb, which increased the flock size by ninety per cent. By shearing time the fleeces were very heavy, averaging six pounds each. Both mutton and wool prices were high, and Manager William Rutherford cheerfully reported an excellent year.[63] James Woodsworth, Methodist Missionary Superintendent (and father of the first leader of the C.C.F. party), while travelling by train through the district in February, 1892, recorded that there were 30,000 sheep on the "76" ranches and about another 20,000 along the railway west to Maple Creek.[64] This sheep population was again sharply increased with the completion of an even more successful lambing season that spring.[65]

Since prices for mutton, wool, and sheep for breeding remained high, the sheep ranching division of the "76" continued to thrive throughout the four years following. This helped the company to partly offset the depressingly small returns that it realized from its farming and cattle and horse ranching divisions. By 1893, good range cattle brought only one cent a pound on the hoof, and the finest western wheat sold for as little as forty cents per bushel.[66] Pork prices, like mutton prices, were also relatively high, but the company had ceased raising hogs soon after Sir John resigned as general manager, and so missed this chance for good profits.[67] To be sure, Rutherford had had some worries with the sheep in his charge. The outset of the winter of 1892-93 had been severe, causing him to fear a feed shortage with a resulting heavy loss of animals, but Chinook winds in mid-winter cleared the snow from the grazing land just as they did again in 1894. The sheep of the "76" escaped the plague of scab or mange which struck the North-West in 1893-94,[68] thanks to the careful quarantine Rutherford imposed around his flocks. He added to his reputation and that of the flocks of the "76" by winning several prizes with his sheep at the 1894 Winnipeg Industrial Exhibition.[69] This caused the Winnipeg press the next year to take notice of the huge flock of 24,000 sheep that were sheared on the "76" ranch at Swift Current. The wool, much of it of the best quality, brought prices of up to twenty cents per pound[70] — an increase of seven cents since 1890.[71] This was the one bright spot on the company's gloomy financial statement.

The shearing over, the C.A.C.C. Co., claiming that it lacked enough money to carry on, decided to sell all of its holdings in the North-West. A new London-based company, The Canadian Land and Ranche Company, Limited (C.L. & R. Co.), was formed with A. F. Eden as chairman of the board of directors. With its new investment capital, the C.L. & R. Co. bought the assets of the "76". Oddly, almost all of the shareholders in the new company held stock in the old one,[72] which causes one to wonder why many of the shareholders had invested in the second company, unless it might have been to end Sir John Lister-Kaye's connections with the "76". D. H. Andrews, the cattle manager of the "76", was made general manager of the C.L. & R. Co.

Perhaps to provide additional working capital, or to raise funds to complete the purchase from the C.A.C.C. Co., or maybe to continue the trend towards greater specialization, the new company began at once to sell a great number of livestock from the "76" ranches. Almost 15,000 of the company's sheep on their ranches in the Swift Current district alone were sold in 1895.[73] Several employees were also dismissed. By April, 1897, the C.L. & R. Co. had reduced the number of breeding ewes it owned from 10,000 in 1895 to just 4,000.[74] It also cut the size of its herds of cattle and horses.

To consolidate the far flung enterprise, and also to cut expenses, the following year the company pleaded with the C.P.R. and the Dominion to allow it to exchange over 24,000 acres of arid, almost worthless prairie for better land. The lands which the company wished to give up included the entire ranch-farms at Kincorth (the next station west of Maple Creek), and at Bantry (about seventy-five miles west along the C.P.R. from Medicine Hat). As an even trade, they wanted as many more acres of good land at Gull Lake and especially at Crane Lake and Swift Current, in order to enlarge their prosperous ranches there. The company argued that if they were not permitted to make this land exchange then they would be forced out of business, and the North-West would suffer if this happened. In stating their case, the company's secretary wrote:

> As is well known to your Department and to the Canadian Pacific Railway authorities, the Company's agricultural and colonization projects have largely influenced the opening up of the Territories, and have been, and are, favorably referred to in pamphlets and official reports regarding that part of the Dominion. In addition to this, an off-shoot of the Company has established a cool store for dealing in chilled meats and pork packing on a large scale in Calgary, which has developed into an important industry in that town.[75]

At first the Minister of the Interior, Clifford Sifton, refused their petition. But the company continued to press for the exchange, saying it would irrigate some of the land that it desired and would greatly increase the size of its herds if the deal was made.[76] In July, 1897, the huge land trade was approved — perhaps the best stroke of business that the company ever concluded!

The company's ranches in the Swift Current district continued to do fairly well, despite the usual problems caused by prairie fires which burned thousands of acres of grazing land, coyotes and wolves which killed the sheep, and intense cold and blizzards that made the life of men and beasts miserable. Added to this, the price of wool by 1897 had fallen to less than half of what it had been two years earlier, with mutton prices also declining.[77] Fortunately, at this point, cattle prices began to increase, as did the demand and price for horses, which easily made up for the company's declining profits from sheep.[78] The trend towards higher livestock prices and accelerated demand continued in 1898 as more settlers came West. Ranchers in the North-West enjoyed a heyday. As the local N.W.M.P. Superintendent reported: ". . . this has been the best season the ranching industry has known in this part of the country."[79] The long term economic depression, international in scope, was ending. Despite the earlier depressed state of agriculture, the C.L. & R. Co. had continued the policy started by Lister-Kaye of importing purebred bulls, studs and rams from Britain to improve the quality of their herds. By 1900, the "76" had the largest herd of Galloway cattle in the world.[80] Exports from Swift Current in 1898 totalled 67,840 pounds of wool and 1,434 sheep, making Swift Current the sheep capital of Canada! The next year almost the same amount of wool was clipped on the "76" sheep ranch and nearly double the number of sheep were exported.[81] The sheep division, under the management of William Alexander since 1895 when he replaced William Rutherford soon after the "76" was reorganized, continued to do quite well into the year 1900. Perhaps because wool prices remained below the 1895 level, the company had decided not to increase the size of the breeding flock, although there was a strong demand and a profitable price for mutton. For ten years now sheep ranching had been good and had often been excellent for the "76". Not since 1890, when they suffered the heavy loss of sheep by prairie fire, had this division had a major setback.

Those made pessimistic by suffering repeated disappointments in the North-West would have said that it was too good to last. It was. To shear its huge flock of sheep in 1901, the company, as usual, hired several expert shearers. Among them were two men from Australia who, unknown to the "76" sheep manager, had recently clipped sheep infected with the dread disease anthrax.[82] The wool crop was heavy;[83] the shearing went quickly. But since wool dealers offered the company such low prices, the company decided to bale and store the thousands of fleeces, intending to sell the wool crop directly to eastern manufacturers. Soon after the shearers departed in July, some of the sheep began to sicken.[84] Manager Alexander summoned Dr. J. C. Hargrave, the veterinary at Medicine Hat, who correctly diagnosed the trouble. It was anthrax, and it was spreading quickly.[85] Since anthrax, or blackleg, also attacked horses and cows with the same fatal results, the veterinary knew that he must promptly take steps to protect all the livestock that might have been exposed. Once contracted, there was no known cure for the disease.

The only hope of saving the remaining 16,000 sheep,[86] plus the horses and cattle in the Swift Current area, was to immediately launch a colossal vaccination program that would treat every animal likely to be infected. A team of fourteen men assisted Dr. Hargrave and Dr. C. H. Higgins with the huge task. By working long hours every day of the week, and despite an early fall blizzard lasting four days that dumped two feet of snow on the district, the dedicated crew completed the operation in less than two months.[87] Meanwhile, seventeen townships surrounding Swift Current were quarantined, the dead animals were buried, and orders were given to burn off all the range where infected animals had grazed.[88] Through their prompt action, the veterinaries confined the disease and stamped it out entirely by early in November.[89] Ranchers for miles around heaved a sigh of relief when they heard this good news.

The "76" lost 650 sheep,[90] a few horses and only one or two cows to the scourge.[91] Unlike the terrible fire loss in 1890 that killed over 1100 pregnant ewes before shearing time, the company's loss in 1901 was just one more hardship, for by this time the company was financially sound. Moreover, in this case they still had all of the fleeces from the dead sheep to sell and, while the losses were mainly among breeding ewes, almost ninety per cent of their breeding stock remained. Just after the anthrax outbreak but before the quarantine was imposed, the "76", perhaps as a precaution, shipped almost all its cattle — two entire train loads — from its Rush Lake ranch to English markets.[92] The losses from the anthrax had so little effect on the overall profits of the company that at their seventh annual meeting held in Winchester House, London, on January 25, 1902, the directors were able to declare both a ten per cent dividend for the year ended October 31, 1901, plus a further ten per cent bonus on subscribed capital. In addition, the sum of two thousand pounds sterling from the year's substantial profits was added to the growing cash reserves of the company.[93] General Manager D. H. Andrews, upon returning to the North-West from this meeting, was generally optimistic about the company's prospects. In particular, he declared that the outlook for the cattle trade was exceptionally bright, with higher prices and an increased demand in Britain expected.[94] However, he made no comment about the prospect for the company's sheep industry centred on Swift Current, as it was the one depressed sector of the C.L. & R. Co. operations.

The days of the large scale sheep ranch, when the "76" could pasture its flocks along fifty miles of vacant, unfenced prairie beside the Swift Current Creek, were numbered even before the anthrax outbreak in 1901. More and more small cattle and horse ranches were being established in the area, and the cattlemen began to protest vigorously that the sheep were depleting the range grass.[95] Long before this, in 1894, the huge lease comprising 34,302 acres[96] which the "76" held on grazing land in the district, had been cancelled. Over the years, dry-land farming methods and grain varieties had steadily improved, and, since 1894, the district had been blessed with a series of good growing seasons.[97] Farmers bent upon plowing and fencing the rolling prairie of this "last best West" were soon to arrive and to begin to crowd even the small ranches off of the open range. When this happened, the almost forty thousand acres of land which the C.L. & R. Co. owned locally increased so dramatically in price as to be too valuable to keep for sheep pasturage or even to convert to the somewhat more profitable business of cattle or horse ranching.

To hasten the end of the "76" sheep ranch in the district, the vicissitudes of nature dealt the company and the district some damaging blows. The lambing and shearing seasons of 1902 went smoothly enough, but still mutton and especially wool prices continued at their low level. World supply exceeded the demand. Then from June to October the sheep of the "76" were again quarantined due to another anthrax scare. As a result, the sheep were short of grazing land. On May 16, 1903, just after lambing season, a severe snowstorm set in which hung on for nearly a week. The company's lambs, like the rancher's calves and colts, being especially vulnerable, perished in large numbers. Other weak livestock, plus hundreds of newly-arrived stocker cattle from the east, died of exposure, even though many were sheltered in stock yards or in the railway cars in which they had been shipped.[98] To make matters worse for the producers, livestock prices began to fall.[99] The only way for the company to combat falling prices was to reorganize production.

THE CRANE LAKE RANCH, CATTLE HEADQUARTERS FOR THE "76".

FIRE DESTROYING THE "76" RANCH BARN AT GULL LAKE.

In the summer of 1903 the C. L. & R. Co. decided to sell all of its sheep and to cease ranching at Rush Lake and Swift Current. Since 1901, the "76" cattle ranch at Rush Lake had been rented on a share basis to Robert Cruickshank, a rancher and early employee of the C.A.C.C. Co., who then bought most of this ranch.[100] At the Swift Current ranch the thousands of excellent sheep were advertised and sold during that fall and winter.[101] Sadly, the remaining shepherds and their faithful dogs bid farewell to the old ranch the following spring.[102] After that, a caretaker watched over the deserted ranch buildings until October of 1905 when the Denny Land Company of Swift Current, together with the Rose Realty Company of Yellowgrass, Saskatchewan, purchased the land and buildings which comprised Lister-Kaye's original ranch-farm.[103] They quickly divided it up and sold it profitably to the land hungry settlers then crowding into the district. Swift Current had reached the end of an era. In the beginning, the natives had been gradually forced out by the sheepmen, then the shepherds had slowly, peaceably given way to the cattlemen, who, in their turn, would be forced to yield to the incoming tide of farmers.

At Gull Lake, the company converted the original farm into an exclusive cattle ranch.[104] It was fairly close to the cattle headquarters at Crane Lake, and the company did own some additional land some fifteen miles south of Gull Lake along the Swift Current Creek. Here it improved the buildings and fences[105] to handle its Galloway cattle. But the westward tide of settlement was rising and the pressure was on the company to sell its vast landholdings. In 1905 it sold the 10,000 acre farm by the railway at Gull Lake to the real estate firm of Conrad and Price.[106] At this time, also, the larger farm at Stair was sold and the horse herd from there was driven to the Dunmore farm, which became the "76" horse ranch. The Stair cattle joined the thousands of head that the "76" had at Crane Lake and Gull Lake.[107]

In spite of frequently low livestock prices, of the death of many horses and cattle by blizzard, fire or drowning, and the loss of stacked feed and range grass to prairie fire, plus numerous other large and small tragedies which the weather or human error caused, the C.L. & R. Co. still managed to earn sufficient profits to pay both dividends and bonuses on its capital stock.[108] It also could afford to pay a handsome salary to its general manager, D. H. Andrews.[109] The company's directors relied heavily upon the management ability of Andrews and he, in turn, upon that of his competent ranch managers and foremen. The English shareholders knew that the profits they earned from the company were largely dependent upon the good management of Andrews. He had always done his job well, and the company had reason to be pleased with him.[110] Naturally, the shareholders were shocked when in May, 1905, at the age of fifty-two, Andrews was stricken with a fatal illness. Suddenly "the little Duke", as he was referred to locally, was dead! The company then appointed A. R. Springett to be general manager. While he directed the ranching enterprise, he was mainly engaged in disposing of the company's holdings.[111] The enormous "76" cattle operation was struck a mortal blow by the terrible winter of 1906-07, when almost two-thirds of their huge cattle herd perished on the open range.[112] Assisted by the large profits earned from the sale of their lands, the company was able to carry on until, in 1909, it decided to give up ranching entirely. In that year the firm of Gordon, Ironsides and Fares of Winnipeg acquired all that remained of the ranch holdings of the company. Thus ended the noble "76" which had first been conceived by the fertile mind of Sir John Lister-Kaye.

The end of the English company did not mean the end of its influence upon the Swift Current district. Indirectly, through former employees who settled locally, the agricultural industry, which the company had fostered and dominated, developed into the major industry of the region. Many young men and women who had come to the district to work for the "76" earned enough money and experience there to enable them to begin small ranches or businesses of their own. And most important to the future of the Swift Current district, many came to love its wild prairie landscape enough to call it home for the rest of their lives. These were the pioneers.

Chapter VI

SETTLING A BUFFALO PASTURE

The "76" ranches, in their time, had done more to establish, stabilize and promote the agricultural industry of the Swift Current district than any other individual or agency. Together with the railway, the "76" had ruled the daily life of the majority of the district's white residents for close to twenty years. Even most of those settlers who by 1907 worked neither for the C.P.R. nor the "76", had first come to the district as employees of one of the two enterprises, mostly of the agricultural company. Initially, Lister-Kaye's syndicate had intended to bring out from Britain to its ranch-farms a great many "colonists" annually. They would be given only a one year employment contract and, when it expired, they would be encouraged to settle near the company's land. Though this policy had been abandoned after the second year, a steady, though much reduced, number of employees had continued to be recruited and brought to the "76" for fifteen years thereafter as replacements for those who eventually left the company. This trickle of new settlers, possessed of those qualities so essential to success — experience with local agriculture, good health, some money, and a liking for the country — had made excellent pioneers.

Until the thousands of land hungry "sod-busters" crowded into the sparsely-settled district after 1903, these people, plus a few other ranchers, big and small, prospered by grazing their livestock where buffalo so recently had pastured. The life they knew and shared was different in many ways from the life of the farmers who came to plow the grasslands and trails and cut down the few trees for fence posts. The ranchers had scarcely altered the natural wild beauty of the treed coulees and ravines or done more than cut the native grass for hay. Neighbors were few and far apart in the ranching era. Perhaps partly for this reason, they valued one another more. The fact that they were stockmen and not grain growers certainly gave them a different community of interests. Competition between the long-established ranchers and the newly-arrived farmers for the available well-watered land sharpened this contrast in outlook between the two groups. Finally, since their way of life differed, they tended to develop a somewhat different point of view — not unusual for men who rode horses rather than following them.

Still, the future of the district was with the farmers. The Dominion government, through its land lease and settlement policies, made certain of this, as did the C.P.R., the territorial government, and later, the provincial government. Largely because of shortcomings in these policies, thousands of acres unfit for farming were taken away from successful livestock producers and granted or sold to people who would try to raise grain. These unfortunate folk broke their hearts on their sub-marginal quarter section farms soon after they broke the sandy prairie sod. Through bitter experience, the farmers learned what land would produce grain crops and what was fit only for pasture. But this process took many years to work itself out and resulted in a tragic waste of time, work and money for those concerned. Aided by the development of new farming techniques, and new crop varieties and machines, the farmers succeeded in adapting to the district and, to a lesser extent, in modifying their environment sufficiently to permit them to carry on grain farming successfully on most of its lands. They peopled the district and made it prosperous. Their coming sparked a period of hectic prosperity such as the region had never known. They caused its railway hamlets to grow at an amazing rate, and transformed tiny, placid Swift Current into a boom town. This, of course, was progress. But "progress" had a price which the ranchers, like the natives before them, largely had to pay.

To say that over thirty former employees of the local "76" ranches had settled within the Swift Current district by 1907 does not seem impressive. And to add that many more settled in other parts of the North-West scarcely increases the significance. As an increase to the present population of the district, this small group of people would go unnoticed. But as late as 1901, when most of these people were already pioneer homesteaders, albeit ranchers, the population of Swift Current was only 121 — men, women and children.[1] Moreover, all but three of the former "76" employees who settled were men, and most of these soon married and raised families locally. They bulked large in the population of the time. In relation to those privately engaged in agriculture, they easily made up two-thirds of the total.

Only ten of these pioneers had worked for the "76" while Sir John Lister-Kaye was still in charge. Five of these ten were James Smart, George E. Smith, James McNee and his brother William, and Robert Cruikshank, all of whom established ranches along the south bank of the Saskatchewan River in the northern part of the district. William Rutherford, William Alexander and Edward Hogg built ranches closer to Swift Current, and George E. Williams was perhaps the first farmer in the Beverly district.[2] Finally, E. E. Williams retired at Gull Lake after many years as foreman of the "76" ranch there.[3] They and all the others were good citizens as well as good settlers who, by the example of their own success, encouraged and fostered the development of the district.

Lister-Kaye was not the first to experiment in grain growing near Swift Current. Just before the railway's arrival, Robert Julian had squatted on the adjoining quarter section of Dominion land east of the townsite. He built a shack and eventually broke several long strips of land. Plagued by drought, he attempted to irrigate a few acres from the creek, but with little

This is the ranch originally established about 1896 by James and William McNee, former "76" employees. It was located along the Swift Current Creek, almost twenty miles north-east of Swift Current. This photo was taken late in the 1920's when the ranch was owned by Col. W. M. Yates.

success. Meanwhile, he took a job as wiper in the C.P.R. roundhouse to earn a living.[4] After the rebellion in 1885 he made an official homestead entry for the land. But the widespread drought of 1886, followed by a severe winter, so discouraged Julian that he gave up his homestead and took a job transfer to Banff.[5] Also in 1885, three other men then living and working in Swift Current decided that they had little to lose and perhaps something to gain by likewise filing on homesteads close to the hamlet. Like Robert Julian, all picked land intersected by the creek. They were Walter G. Knight, the local Dominion meteorologist and Notary Public, Charles H. Powell, the C.P.R. telegraph repairer, and Alfred Fenton, the hamlet's railway agent.[6]

The government saw fit to make special homestead arrangements with Knight, Powell, Fenton and Julian. This decision was prompted by the Dominion's desire to have its local lands settled in spite of the commonly-held belief that the district was not suitable for grain farming. Probably this opinion was strengthened by Julian's discouraging attempts to raise crops. Rather than having to break and seed thirty acres on each homestead, or, in lieu of that, to place a specified number of cattle on the land, as was customary, the Minister of the Interior merely required the four homesteaders to plant some trees![7] Seemingly, even the Minister had little confidence in the agricultural potential of the district, and he probably felt that the trees would make a welcome change from the otherwise bald prairie — if they would grow. Still, Powell and Fenton did break a few acres of land in 1886, but their crops, like Julian's, were a total failure. The following year, the ambitious Fenton hired James McNee to help him plant more trees and to care for the livestock he then began to acquire.[8] Since he had a steady income from employment, Fenton was able to increase his herd to 100 cattle and a few horses by 1890.[9] By the time that he died of tuberculosis in 1893,[10] he also had a fine grove of trees, including Manitoba maples, established by the creek. Fenton's grove became the favorite picnic grounds for the community, but was destroyed when the town constructed a dam on the site in 1913.

Grain farming, the early homesteaders concluded, was a waste of money and time in this region. Apparently others thought likewise, for in 1886 the Dominion Lands Agency at Swift Current, with all of the area of present southwestern Saskatchewan to look after, was the least active office of any in the North-West Territories. In fact, settlement in this huge region, already sparse, went backwards, as 102 more acres of homestead and pre-emption land were cancelled through the office than were applied for.[11] Apart from the attempts made to raise grain and fibre flax on the C.A.C.C. Co. farms, plus the experiments carried out by the C.P.R. at Gull Lake during the latter part of the 1880's, no one tried grain farming again in the region until early in the twentieth century.

At first it was believed that the district was not only too far west for grain growing but was also too far east for stock raising.[12] That belief was slowly changed by the few homesteaders who filed locally from 1885 to 1902 and who were successful in raising livestock. These typically small ranchers often did seed a few acres to meet the homestead requirements and to provide fodder, but not to grow grain for sale.[13] Their oat crops, which were frequently good, were cut, stooked and stacked rather than threshed. Possibly in order to guard their valuable open range from farm settlement, they did not advertise their successful crops. Ranching was a good thing, so why jeopardize it? Moreover, it was the only avenue open locally to ambitious individuals with limited funds to invest. Even those who had businesses or jobs in the district often engaged in ranching as a sideline.

As it was for most of the North-West Territories during the 1890's, ranching was the mainstay of the district. Many, at the time, thought that even mixed farming was impractical locally,[14] despite the glowing recommendations of it written by the local Member of Parliament, Nicholas Flood Davin.[15] In 1894, when Swift Current received less than ten inches of precipitation [16] and suffered terribly from drought, an accurate, if locally unwelcome, prophecy was made: ". . . the time will come when the agriculturalists will slowly but surely crowd the ranchers off the lands."[17] At the time, the local ranchers might have scoffed at this prediction, but within a dozen years it had proven to be true.[18]

The growth of the local ranching industry, apart from the "76" ranches, was slow until the mid 1890's, when it suddenly accelerated, then subsided, only to boom again between 1900 and 1905 when it reached its climax and quickly began to decline. While the C.P.R. agent, Alfred Fenton, was one of the earliest to establish a prosperous small ranch locally, he was not the first to do so. The Curry brothers, Alex and Sam, pioneer storekeepers, secured by lease for ranching purposes 11,000 acres of Dominion land and 5,120 acres of C.P.R. land bordering the river at Saskatchewan Landing in 1886.[19] It is probable that they began raising livestock near Swift Current as early as 1885. Charles Reid, who became a pioneer merchant at Swift Current, developed a ranch in 1886 where the north fork of the Swift Current Creek flows out of the Cypress Hills.[20] The outset of the 1890's saw two more ranches started. The first of these was begun by two young Englishmen, the partners H. Y. Jones and James Smart. The owner of the other was the purchaser of the old Tims store, the ex-Mountie, William Milburn. Since the last two ranches merely replaced those owned by the Currys and Fenton, who had sold out, the industry had scarcely grown. But the cancellation of the huge lease of the "76" in 1894, the availability of small leases, the reorganization of the "76" ranches in 1895 (which left several former employees to find other occupations), the end of the drought in 1895, coupled with the prosperity enjoyed by the few independent ranchers locally, prompted no less than fifteen men during 1895 and 1896 to begin ranching in the district.[21] Ten of the new ranches were located along the south bank of the Saskatchewan River, where the wooded coulees and ravines provided shelter for livestock, the river flats could be irrigated to grow hay,[22] the fine table land above the ancient river's banks offered good grass, and water was plentiful regardless of drought conditions. The range by the Swift Current Creek, for some of the same reasons, attracted the remaining five men to secure leases there.

This five-fold increase in the number of local ranches corresponded to the sharp increase in the number of homestead entries made through the Swift Current Dominion Lands Agency during 1895 and 1896.[23] That is remarkable for two reasons. First, this agency in both 1891 and 1894 had been the least active and had the lowest receipts of all agencies in the North-West Territories![24] Secondly, 1896, which marked the election of the Laurier government, saw fewer homestead entries recorded in Canada than in any previous year as far back as 1879. Whereas the number of new homesteaders did slowly increase in the rest of Canada from 1896 to 1902,[25] in present-day southwestern Saskatchewan they abruptly declined in 1897 to one-half of their 1896 level,[26] and remained fairly low to the end of the century. Locally, only two more men decided to start ranching during this period,[27] but not one person tried farming.[28] Since almost nobody wished to settle in the Swift Current district from 1896 to 1901, the government closed its inactive agency there in 1898.[29] Clifford Sifton's immigration policies, it seems, failed to attract any immigrants to the district during these years.

As is always the case with an industry dependent upon an export market, happenings in far off places often had an effect upon the local ranchers. The discovery of gold on Klondike Creek in 1896, which sparked the great Yukon gold rush, opened up a welcome market for western cattle, sheep and horses. News from the goldfields was a daily topic for conversation locally. To the ranch partners Jones and Smart, it became much more than that. Henry Yates Jones had started ranching at Saskatchewan Landing with James Smart in 1891 after accumulating both ranching experience and a little money in Texas, Wyoming and the Cypress Hills.[30] Both men heard the tales of the fantastically high prices being paid in the gold camps for fresh beef, and decided to try for a share of the newly-found wealth. The daring Jones was eager for adventure, so it was decided that Smart would take care of their ranch while he drove 100 steers by a new overland route through Edmonton to Dawson City.[31] They would need pack animals, and what could be better than big, strong oxen which would also make beef at the end of the trip. Twenty such placid animals were brought in from Manitoba.[32] In April, 1898, Jones, together with his métis guide, Jean Louis Fayant, his drover, "Peck" McDonald, his oxen and his herd of 100 mature steers, crossed the South Branch and began the long, dangerous trek to the Yukon.

For a long while everything went well. The trail drive reached Edmonton safely within only twenty-nine days. Here Fayant left the drive and returned to his home at the Landing. He reported that the trip had been pleasant and that Jones planned to winter the herd in the Peace River area before driving on to Dawson City the next spring.[33] But plans change.

Jones chose a good trail from Edmonton west and north, the route now followed by the Alaska Highway. At the old Hudson's Bay posts of Fort St. John and at Fort Grahame on the Finlay River in British Columbia, he found a ready market for one-quarter of his trail-weary steers. Whereas at Swift Current he would have received less than five cents per pound, live weight, for these animals, the beef-hungry people at these posts gladly paid him between thirty and forty cents a pound.[34] To Jones, this was just a sample of what lay ahead, for fresh beef that winter brought two dollars a pound in the gold camps. Jones had more than the lure of high prices to urge him to press on through the Cassier Mountains to Dawson City. Winter fodder for his herd was scarce and expensive. Furthermore, since the river valley largely determined his route north-west through the mountains, and since he calculated that the river would soon freeze over to become an ice highway for his herd, he decided not to wait until spring but to press on despite the dangers.

Scarcely any cattle herds during these years did complete the overland drive to the Yukon, and it is not certain whether Jones got his cattle to the gold camps or not. One report claims that all of his oxen and steers were swept over a waterfall while crossing a river.[35] In any event, Jones, himself, did reach Dawson City for a share of the excitement and adventure before he returned to the ranch at the Landing in 1899. How much money he made or lost by his daring gamble is not known. Apparently, the only money he brought back came from the sale the previous fall of the twenty-five steers along the trail, so the experience that he had gained was, perhaps, his only enrichment.[36]

The prosperity which the local ranchers enjoyed during the last years of the nineteenth century and the first years of the twentieth can be attributed to several factors. Among them were the lack of competition with farmers for grazing land, the increased rainfall after 1894, the rising prices and demand for cattle and agricultural produce, generally, beginning early in 1897,[37] and the readiness with which the small ranchers adjusted their output to match the market trends. As there was little demand for western horses during the 1890's, the local ranchers reduced their horse herds and increased their herds of cattle to profit from that favorable market.[38] To augment local production, they shipped in young eastern cattle to their ranges. These stockers or "dogies" soon fattened on the highly nutritious prairie grass, and, when mature, they brought good prices in distant markets.[39] It is impossible to say exactly how many livestock entered or left the district by trail, but by comparing the import and export of district cattle by rail, as given in the police reports, it is possible to gain some understanding of the growth and extent of the stocker trade locally. In 1897, when the trade was being established, 305 cattle were shipped in and 199 were exported.[40] By 1899, cattle imports by rail stood at 203 while exports had risen to 1,089.[41] In 1901, imports numbered 482, and export totals reached 2,105 head[42] — double the number of two years previous. Apparently several times more cattle and horses were herded into and out of the district during all of these years. Certainly a growing number of cattle were also slaughtered and sold in the district to supply the local population and the rapidly increasing number of travellers stopping at the railway dining hall.

Not only the Swift Current district, but all of present south-western Saskatchewan and southern Alberta shared in the prosperity from ranching. The N.W.M.P. report for 1899 on the Swift Current-Maple Creek regions reflects the joy felt by the pioneer settlers:

> The district is in a most prosperous condition, and the livestock industry, in which almost the entire population may be said to be engaged, to a greater or a lesser extent, is bringing large sums of money into the country. I doubt very much whether there is in the whole of Canada a district where all the residents are in such easy circumstances as they are here.[43]

That the Swift Current, Maple Creek and Medicine Hat districts were finally becoming important cattle producing areas by 1899 is clear. Over one-third of the total Canadian cattle shipments for that year came from these districts.[44]

After a lengthy slump, the demand for horses suddenly quickened in 1900, as army mounts were needed for the Boer War and dray and driving horses in larger numbers were sought by Canada's expanding population of townsmen.[45] While no data exist, it appears that horses were trail driven into the district in proportionally greater numbers than were stocker cattle. Official records for C.P.R. shipments in 1900 show that local ranchers imported 454 horses,[46] nearly all young eastern animals, to grow, mature and train on their ranges. While in 1899 not one horse was reported to have been shipped from the district,[47] in 1901 there were 164 exported.[48] It is little wonder that this kind of market adaptability by the ranchers brought them good profits.

The result of these prosperous times was that the rolling prairie and river hills around Swift Current gained the widespread reputation of being well-suited for ranching. The good money and the available leases attracted prospective ranchers like a magnet. Fully twenty-five new ranches were begun in the district by individuals, partnerships or companies between 1900 and 1905. Former "76" employees and other local people still bulked large in the total of new ranchers, but, for the first time, American cattlemen and ranch companies also arrived. These Americans, many of whom became Canadians, started almost one-half of the total of new ranches. One of these — the Turkey Track — ranked with the three local "76" ranches in size.[49]

A. J. "Tony" Day of Pueblo, California,[50] the manager of the Turkey Track Ranch, and his foremen, John Day and Joe Driscoll, drove their huge herd of some 25,000 cattle and 600 horses from South Dakota, where they had been crowded off the range by settlers, to newly-leased land in present south-western Saskatchewan in 1902.[51] One of Day's leases comprised 65,760 acres.[52] They established several ranches along the prairie waterways; the closest one to Swift Current was located near today's Hallonquist. At this ranch they also raised some donkeys for sale in the West,[53] but cattle ranching was their main concern within the district as elsewhere. Late in August, 1906, one shipment of their cattle from Rush Lake to the British overseas market alone totalled 600 head.[54] Like the "76", the Turkey Track was squeezed out by farmers and frozen out during the winter of 1906-07, when almost two-thirds of their stock perished on the open range. Again, like the "76", the owners sold the remnants of their ranches in 1908 to Gordon, Ironsides and Fares Company, Limited, of Winnipeg.[55]

Murdo MacKenzie, manager of the huge Scottish-owned, Colorado-based ranching empire known as the Matador, secured a twenty-one year lease for his company on over 130,000 acres along the South Saskatchewan River north of Rush Lake on November 1, 1904. The range was to become perhaps the largest feed lot in the world. The Matador, unlike nearly all of the other local ranches, concentrated their operations on their Canadian ranch just on range feeding and finishing young Hereford cattle from their U.S. ranches for the American market. They raised no cattle in Canada. Instead, they shipped in train loads of two year old cattle "in bond", to avoid paying duty, fattened them for two more years, and then sold them at Chicago.[56] In June, 1905, their first herd of 6,000 stockers was unloaded at Waldeck. After two weeks they succeeded in driving their young cattle across the river to their new ranch under the management of David Sommerville.[57] Though their ranch hands always cut and stooked a large supply of native hay or "prairie wool", this did not prevent the Matador from sharing in the heavy stock losses during the bitter winter of 1906-07. While they lost nearly one-half of their local herd, this was not a crippling blow to a company whose American herds numbered 65,000 cattle, and they continued their huge "feed lot" operation until their ranch lease expired in the mid 1920's.[58]

Still another ranch operation which, like the Matador, imported stockers for range feeding, was the fairly large Gull Lake Ranching Company of James G. Millar. This company secured a large lease north of Gull Lake about 1903. A year later Millar acquired the ranch of H. Y. Jones on Miry Creek to further expand his lease. To increase his herd, he purchased 300 Mexican yearlings as stockers out of a shipment of 900 that were brought to Rush Lake in 1904.[59] The following year he travelled to Manitoba where he bought several hundred more young stockers for range finishing.[60] This operation proved to be so profitable that in June, 1906, his company arranged for another 500 head of yearling stockers from Winnipeg for delivery to his range. A large number of these "dogies" perished during the following winter,[61] and Millar was soon forced out of business and off the range as settlers moved onto his lease.

The rancher's life was always a struggle to overcome adversity. Even favorable changes from drought to downpour brought some misfortune, for the rain created sloughs where mosquitoes and flies bred by the millions to attack both the rancher and his livestock. Despite this, the rain was almost always welcome, for it improved the grazing and, at the same time, it reduced the threat of prairie fire. Still, dry periods were frequent, and hardly a year went by when huge tracts of parched grazing land were not burned over in the district.[62] While some of the fires were caused by carelessness, most were started by lightning or C.P.R. locomotives. The fear of being "burned out" was a constant threat to the homesteaders until snow covered the ground. Then, in turn, they could start worrying about providing winter feed for their livestock. Coyotes and buffalo wolves, which particularly menaced the rancher's livestock from 1896 to 1900, brought them additional trouble.[63] Each rancher did what he could to deal with these killers, but wolf hunting was both time-consuming and difficult. The government and the Western Stock Growers Association increased the bounty paid for killing wolves and coyotes, which helped the ranchers. This prompted several métis to become professional wolf hunters.[64] Gradually the buffalo wolves were all either trapped, poisoned or shot, and most of the coyotes or "prairie wolves" met a similar fate, though big, fast hounds were also used effectively against these smaller predators.

The main natural adversity which challenged the local ranchers, however, came from wintry weather. The unseasonable six-day snowstorm, starting May 16, 1903, caused a heavy death toll among the calves, colts and lambs, but struck hardest at the large numbers of newly-arrived eastern stockers which were unaccustomed to the rigors of the western climate. They died by the hundreds, along with the weaker livestock throughout the district.[65] The loss fell mainly upon the importers of livestock,[66] and, since that included many district ranchers, the local livestock industry suffered a major setback. The next winter brought more severe storms and cold during February, 1904, and was followed by yet another May snowstorm,[67] although this did not trouble the ranchers nearly as much as had the May blizzard of 1903.

In the spring of 1904 a plague of mange parasite, which struck cattle throughout the southern ranching country, resulted in both financial loss and much extra work for the cattlemen. The task of rounding up the half-wild cattle was even more difficult than constructing the huge dipping vats and prodding the rebellious animals into leaping into the dug-outs filled with chloro-naphtholeum.[68] By dipping the cattle on two separate occasions, the mange mites were soon nearly eliminated from the range.[69] At this point the local ranching industry entered its final and most favorable phase.

Over the years the local ranchers had been tested by drought, prairie fire, mosquitoes, wolves, coyotes, livestock diseases, increasing lease rentals and restrictions, storms and intense cold. They had not only survived these challenges but had prospered. Like the tough, thorny cactus that clings to the parched prairie sod, determined to put forth its showy but short-lived bloom, the ranchers had persisted, and their industry "bloomed" in 1905 and 1906. The winters of 1904-05 and 1905-06 were fairly mild, and the grazing from spring until fall was good. The expanding and increasingly affluent population of Europe and America provided a growing market with rising prices for cattle and sheep. The influx of farmers needing work animals brought profits to the horse ranchers. These factors helped make Swift Current king of the ranching industry in Saskatchewan in 1905. In that year more livestock were exported from this point than anywhere else in the newly-created province.[70]

Sheep had long dominated the ranching industry around Swift Current and Maple Creek. In value terms, beef exports had exceeded mutton and wool by 1901, and by 1906 the cattle population of this region even surpassed that of sheep (117,206 to 105,440), with horses ranking a good third (63,096). This sparsely-settled south-western corner of the province, then the kingdom of the ranchers, accounted for nearly one-third of the total of Saskatchewan's range cattle that year.[71] Maple Creek, having Cypress Hills as a ranchers' sanctuary, edged out Swift Current in 1906 as the most important livestock producing centre. Meanwhile, at Swift Current, cattle exports, all to the east, declined from the high of 6,451 in 1905 to 5,237 in 1906, while horse exports were halved from 109 to 52.[72] In 1907, after the terrible winter, exports of cattle from the district plummeted to 2,915 head, with only 58 of these coming from Swift Current. The remainder came from Waldeck or Rush Lake[73] — the shipping points of the Matador, the Turkey Track and the fairly large Cruickshank ranch. The lands around Swift Current were being quickly settled by farmers at this time, and the ranching industry was in full retreat before the incoming army of "sod busters".

Several factors had combined to prompt those wishing to grow grain to turn their attention to the Swift Current district. From 1896 onward the district had received more rainfall than it had during the drought years of 1893 to 1895.[74] This helped dispel the belief that the district was too arid for farming (see Table 1, p. 90, for local precipitation rates from 1886 to 1906). Next, some dry-land farming techniques had been developed in Manitoba, largely by the Mennonites, in the mid-western United States by settlers there, and in the regions around Regina, Indian Head and Saskatoon. It would be a mistake to conclude that these farmers had mastered the problems of dry-land farming. Indeed, if any of them had, they certainly managed to keep their secrets from the provincial Department of Agriculture, for the Minister, the Honourable W. R. Motherwell, as late as May, 1909, was advising the farmers at Swift Current to plow early and deep, and to burn their stubble before fall plowing[75] — two bad practices that resulted in the loss of precious soil moisture, nitrogen-producing fibre and also in much greater soil erosion by water and wind.

TABLE 1

Precipitation During Growing Season at Swift Current, 1886-1906[a]

Year	May	June	July	Aug.	Total	Annual
1886	1.86	0.85	1.35	0.60	4.66	10.62
1887	1.56	3.85	3.70	1.62	10.73	18.01
1888	0.63	4.92	0.67	2.34	8.56	14.09
1889	2.42	1.44	2.77	b	6.63	10.46
1890	1.30	3.44	0.88	2.70	8.32	17.50
1891	1.16	6.80	3.36	3.20	14.52	24.55
1892	3.16	3.96	1.00	1.76	9.68	20.25
1893	0.37	0.37	3.22	2.28	6.24	13.87
1894	2.64	1.35	0.62	0.56	5.17	9.66
1895	1.77	3.02	3.32	0.34	8.45	12.29
1896	2.90	1.40	0.26	2.68	7.24	14.11
1897	0.26	0.83	6.27	1.28	8.64	16.24
1898	1.31	2.56	2.81	1.79	8.47	15.25
1899	2.40	3.17	3.95	4.75	14.27	19.38
1900	2.49	1.38	2.42	2.75	9.04	14.60
1901	1.99	4.18	4.29	0.56	11.02	18.58
1902	5.07	4.47	2.28	1.44	13.26	17.64
1903	3.23	3.26	4.11	3.04	13.64	17.96
1904	1.16	2.37	2.34	1.06	6.93	12.84
1905	3.75	3.62	0.91	0.14	8.42	11.47
1906	3.08	7.24	0.30	1.56	12.18	18.40
Mean*	2.120	3.070	2.420	1.823	9.433	15.608

[a] Canada, *Sessional Papers,* 1903, No. 25a, p. 22 and Saskatchewan, *Eighth Annual Report of the Department of Agriculture of the Province of Saskatchewan, 1912* (Regina: Government Printer, 1913), pp. 296-303.
[b] No figures given.
*Precipitation figures given in inches.

But the main factors which brought farmers to this cattle kingdom during these years were not, in the first place, the changes in the climate, Clifford Sifton's emigration propaganda or new farming techniques. The factors were almost purely economic. The population of Europe and the U.S.A. was growing rapidly in numbers and in affluence, which created both an expanding and profitable market for agricultural produce and a surplus population ready and able to emigrate. To meet the demand for wheat, the area of wheatlands had to be enlarged. Then, because the last of the best "free" land in the U.S.A. was taken up by about 1896, land prices in the dry-land farming regions there quickly increased. Next, even the poorer quality land in the U.S. was settled. Many sons of U.S. farmers could not afford to buy land and begin farming in their home districts, and they began to look to the Canadian West as a place to secure a good free or cheap homestead. Other American farmers simply decided to sell their land for the high prices that they were offered and move to Canada to begin the homestead process over again. Naturally, they preferred farm land where taxes were low, a railway and a trading centre were handy, and which was located in a district known to be suited for raising wheat. Since the price of wheat on world markets began to go up in 1897, averaging seventy-five cents per bushel for number one Northern at Winnipeg in 1901, and rising to ninety-two cents per bushel three years later,[76] an increasing number of people felt that grain growing was profitable, and they decided to become Canadian prairie farmers. The fact that transportation costs reduced, meanwhile, by almost the same proportion as wheat prices rose, further persuaded these people to seek farm land on the prairies. Grain growing seemed to be the road to riches to many poor folk in Europe, the U.S., and eastern Canada. Once they had settled all the free or cheap land in those districts reputed to be best for raising wheat, they began to settle around Swift Current and in other districts whose farming potential was, at best, considered dubious. Those locally with land to sell enjoyed a thriving, profitable seller's market. Under these circumstances, it is not surprising that the federal government was able to give some of its land away.

In addition to the powerful, almost irresistible forces which brought about farm settlement on good district land located well away from the water needed by the ranchers' stock, the government, through its modified lease and land settlement policies, facilitated the incursion of farmers into land that should have been left to the ranchers. In 1903, the ranch lands under lease in Assiniboia West were opened to homesteaders.[77] Ranching was made more difficult and insecure by the passage of the regulation which stated that all leases were subject to a two year cancellation clause,[78] unless the Minister of the Interior (then Clifford Sifton) declared the land under lease to be unfit for farming.[79] Since he and his successor, Frank Oliver, failed to do so to anything like the degree that was justified, many thousands of acres of land entirely suitable for ranching, but unfit for grain growing, were later settled by farmers. In the process, both the established ranchers and the ill-fated farmers lost heavily, as, in turn, did Canada. At the urging of the railway companies, the Saskatchewan Government also passed an act in 1906 stating that any animal that strayed within fifteen yards of a railway crossing would be considered to be trespassing. This meant that ranchers would no longer be able to hold the railway companies

91

liable when the trains killed their livestock at rail crossings.[80] Apparently the ranchers, being a small voting group, could safely be ignored by politicians dependent for support upon the rapidly increasing farm vote. Of 1905, the peak year for ranching in the Swift Current district, the report of the Saskatchewan Department of Agriculture states:

> The ranching districts in general are gradually being given over to the cultivation of grain crops; particularly is this the case in the lands around Swift Current and Herbert.[81]

And the report of the Dominion immigration agent at Swift Current for the year ended April 1, 1907, commented on the acceleration of this trend when he wrote:

> . . . Possibly 300 cars of settlers' effects came into this district, and the number of arrivals at all points on the main line which are tributary to the sub-land agency exceeded 3,000 adult settlers during the period covered by this report. . . . The large cattlemen are practically out of business as a consequence of the inflow of homesteaders.[82]

The ranchers were strongly resentful over the way they saw their interests being sacrificed by all levels of government, as the report of the provincial department of agriculture one year later clearly reveals:

> The ranchers complained bitterly of the encroachments of the homesteaders, the resulting introduction of herd law, and the curtailment of range and water privileges. Many of them assert that a well-established and long-tried industry is being destroyed for the sake of a precarious one — as they consider farming in the semi-arid southwestern portion of the province to be. They appear to consider their industry doomed, and statistics justify their contention.[83]

Following local agitation to reopen the Dominion Lands office at Swift Current,[84] on April 2, 1903, a sub-office was established, and William Milburn was appointed local agent. By June 30, 1903, Milburn had received sixty-three applications for homesteads.[85] Another 132 homestead entries were handled by him later, during the following twelve months, [86] and a year later, a total of 233 entries were recorded locally. Due to the increased work, Milburn demanded and got his salary raised from $307 to $420 a year.[87] The next fiscal year, from July 1, 1905 to June 30, 1906, saw an increase of almost 350 per cent in homestead entries received in the local sub-office, as the total reached 793,[88] averaging over 66 entries each month. This rapid pace set by those filing on homesteads locally in 1905-1906 was almost maintained through the next fiscal year ended March 31, 1907.[89]

These figures only illustrate the rapid pace of farm settlement in the district from 1905 to 1907. They do not include the number of homesteads in the district that were filed on at the Dominion Lands agencies in Maple Creek, Moose Jaw or Regina, nor do they include land sales by companies or individuals locally. They do, however, show the trend to farm settlement (see Map 3, p. 93, and Map 4, p. 94). It is little wonder that those engaged in ranching near Swift Current saw their industry doomed by the arrival of such a great number of farmers.

The American ranchers who moved into the district between 1900 and 1905 were the forerunners of a rising tide from the north-central U.S. who, from 1903 onward, came to buy, as well as to homestead, farm land.[90] A Medicine Hat newspaper reported:

> Americans have moved to Swift Current where they've bought from ¼ section to 40 thousand acres of land. They are very pleased with the district.[91]

These U.S. farmers possessed several qualities which made them desirable settlers, except, of course, to those local ranchers whose leases they began to occupy. In language and culture most of them were nearly identical to the older residents of the district. Not a few of them were returning to their native Canada after having spent a few years in the U.S. Many had

MAP 3
Rural Population Growth and Settlement Pattern in Swift Current District, 1901 and 1906[a]

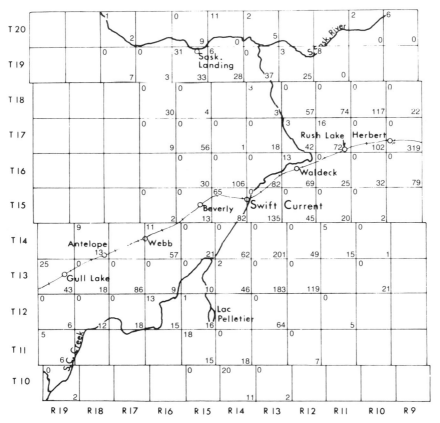

[a]Canada, *Sessional Papers,* 1906-7, No. 17a, Part I, pp. 28-31.

The top figure in each township represents the population in 1901, the lower figure that of 1906.

previous experience of dry-land farming and brought with them an outfit of farm implements. Nearly all of them had money to spend and invest locally — a welcome thing to the newly-formed Swift Current Land Company,[92] which had bought up for resale a large amount of local land. Of course, the government had a great many quarter-sections available for homesteading upon the payment of a ten dollar filing fee, but it had withdrawn the right of pre-emption in the North-West Territories in 1890 and did not reinstate it until 1908. If a settler wished to acquire the quarter-section adjoining his "free" homestead during this interval, then he had to buy it. Usually the owner was the C.P.R. or the Dominion, a local land company or the Hudson's Bay Company. Prices for land considered suitable for farming in the district ranged from $5.50 per acre in 1903 to $10.00 per acre in 1906, and continued upward in later years.[93]

MAP 4

Number of Occupied Farms and Ranches in Swift Current District, 1906[a]

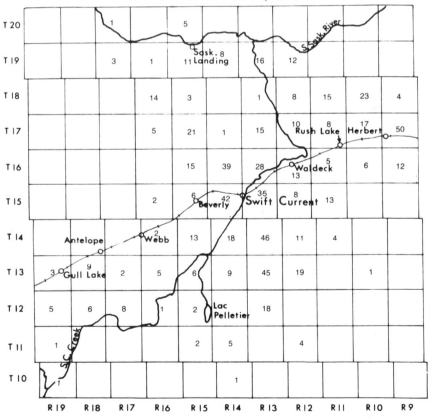

[a]Canada, *Sessional Papers,* 1906-7, No. 17a, Part II, pp. 137-138.

TURKEY TRACK COWBOYS RELAXING OVER A DRINK AND A CARD GAME.

The steady flow of U.S. farmers to the district between 1903 and 1907 was matched by the number of local C.P.R. and "76" employees and by former "cowpunchers" and small ranchers who also homesteaded or bought the better lands to begin farming.[94] These people saw that the farmers who were arriving would soon force almost every rancher to give up much of his lease land whether fit for farming or not. Some of them were themselves victims of this transformation. And clearly, it did make better sense to raise grain on the good land that was located too far from the waterways for grazing but was close enough to the railway to make grain hauling practical, rather than to pasture livestock on it. It was reasonable to think that, acre for acre on this land, grain growing would prove to be more profitable than ranching. Indeed, the government and virtually every segment of business in central Canada and in the West stood to gain from prairie farm settlement. More western people meant more profits and prestige — except for the established ranchers, naturally. It is not surprising that prairie settlement was pushed with such vigor and recklessness by both businessmen and elected politicians!

The government's decision in 1903 to open for settlement its lease land along the railway east from Swift Current to Herbert immediately sparked activity there. The Moose Jaw Saskatchewan Land Company acquired a large tract of this land at once and blatantly advertised it for sale as "The

World's Choicest Wheat Lands". It quoted prices ranging from $5.50 to $7.50 per acre, and made the exaggerated claim that there was plenty of timber to be had along the creek and the river for shed, stable and fence building.[95]

Large trees along the creek and river were never plentiful, but the settlers soon chopped them down, almost denuding the waterways. The trees had provided shelter for the ranchers' livestock — both from the hot summer sun and the winter wind. Naturally, the ranchers were resentful when they saw them all being felled for building material, fuel, or worst of all, fence posts to cut up the open range. Recklessly, the federal government, through its Dominion Lands agencies, continued to issue an increasing number of timber permits locally from 1903 to 1907,[96] which soon resulted in the destruction of nearly all the shade trees along the waterways. This also threatened or destroyed the habitat of many species of wild game. The trees, once cut down by the wood-hungry settlers, were never permitted to re-establish themselves again.

The land company's misleading advertisements succeeded in catching the attention of the Mennonites settled in southern Manitoba. This evangelical Protestant sect had come to the Canadian prairies from Russia during the years 1874-1876 to preserve their culture and religion from governmental influences. They opposed military service, the taking of oaths, and the holding of public office, and wanted as little as possible to do with governments. They were peace-loving, dry-land farmers who believed in plain dress and plain living. Since coming to Canada, they had increased in numbers until they faced the same problems as did many farmers in the earlier settled parts of Canada and the United States — there was no more free or cheap land of good quality for expansion near their home districts. For their young people, they wanted blocks of farm land where they could build their communities, with their unpainted frame houses in a row flanking a road. Behind and attached to each tall house, they usually erected a hall-like porch, then a stable; and finally a chicken pen. Apparently, the Mennonites felt that the economy and conveniences of this style of construction more than offset the obviously disagreeable features of nearly living with their livestock. As for residing in hamlets, this did offer social advantages, convenience for church attendance, and economy in water supply.

The Manitoba Mennonites, having a considerable communal fund of money, decided to send a delegation of over 100 of their brethren to inspect both the company-owned and the Dominion lands in the eastern half of the district in October, 1903. They found the clay-loam plains covered by a heavy growth of grass that year, and the Mennonites were convinced that they could raise grain there. They promptly bought some land north of Herbert and Rush Lake and filed on more to form one settlement block. However, they wanted additional land in blocks and, like everyone else, they preferred to receive most of it "free" under the homestead land grant system. They asked Clifford Sifton, the Minister of the Interior, to set aside reserves for them where they could homestead under the hamlet system, rather than each homesteader residing on his own quarter-section. Furthermore, when they had received land patents, they wanted the right to purchase the section adjoining their homesteaded land within three years for $3.00 per acre, payable in ten annual instalments with five per cent interest on the unpaid balance.[97]

The land south-east of Swift Current appeared to Sifton to be ideally suited to the requirements of the Mennonites. In a block comprising six townships there was but one settler, David Ellems, who had built a log house and stable and fenced a quarter-section about ten miles south of Waldeck. The C.P.R. owned only a few odd-numbered sections in the block, and the four sections of Hudson's Bay Company and School Lands in each township made up the remainder of the land holdings not available for free grant for sale by the government. Since the level tract was well away from the Swift Current Creek, so essential for livestock watering and grazing, the ranchers apparently did not object to the establishment of the proposed Mennonite settlement. Whether or not the Turkey Track Ranch owners, who occasionally grazed cattle on the eastern edge of this block, were advised of Sifton's plan to establish a colony there is not recorded. Sifton urged the government to grant the Mennonites' request, implying that the land was of little value by stating that it was considered arid.[98] The Laurier government, by Order-in-Council dated August 13, 1904, granted the land as requested by the Reinland Mennonite Association, except that it withheld the right for them to homestead under the hamlet system.[99] Perhaps the government felt that the Mennonites would be assimilated more easily if denied their hamlets.

The Mennonites who had purchased or filed for homesteads upon land north of Rush Lake and Herbert were the first to arrive in the district. A small group of fifteen, led by Benjamin Janz, arrived at what is now Main Centre, north of Herbert, on April 9, 1904. They were not strangers to either prairie life or farm work. At once they began to break the sod and erect buildings. To them, their church was the very heart of their settlement. They gave priority to its building, and by June 18, 1904, they had completed and dedicated to God their first Mennonite Brethren Church.[100] In addition, they had seeded a few acres of grain which yielded well.[101] Since seed was scarce, they kept all their yield for the next spring. In 1905, they planted over 1100 acres — one-third of the total field crop acreage in the district.[102] Not since 1891 had growing conditions been so ideal. This colony harvested a bumper crop of almost 35,000 bushels of grain as crop yields in the entire district were the best in the prairie provinces! They increased their acreage almost fourfold in 1906, (see Map 5, p. 98, for trend to farming), and again harvested an excellent crop.[103] It seemed to them that God had bountifully rewarded their devotion and labors in their new home.

MAP 5
Area of Field Crops in Swift Current District 1905, 1906[a]

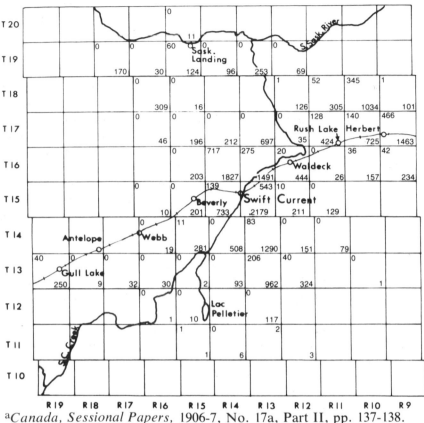

[a]*Canada, Sessional Papers,* 1906-7, No. 17a, Part II, pp. 137-138.
(The top figure shown in each township represents the acreage for 1905, the lower figure that for 1906.)

   The settlement by the second and larger colony of Mennonites on the reserved land south-east of Swift Current during 1905-07 had a more profound impact on the district than had the establishment of the colony around Herbert. In general, the arrival of the bearded men and shawled women, together with their children, all speaking German, and scores of railway cars filled with their effects, was viewed by the Anglo-Saxon community of Swift Current as a mixed blessing. While they welcomed their trade at the local stores, the townsmen found it difficult to converse with the Mennonites, since many of them spoke little English. The store-keepers wished them to succeed in dry-land farming, since they might share in some of the resulting prosperity, but the eight homesteaders who, in error, had been permitted to file during 1905-06 on land reserved for the Mennonites, resented being thrown off this land as squatters when the

UNLOADING SETTLERS' EFFECTS,
SWIFT CURRENT, SPRING OF 1903.

CARLOADS OF SETTLERS' EFFECTS BEING UNLOADED AT SWIFT CURRENT.

Mennonites came to settle.[104] In addition, many new homesteaders from the United States looked enviously upon the dozens of quarter-sections, now realized to be much of the best farm land in the district, that were held in reserve for the Mennonites yet to arrive.

Even those who, on economic grounds, viewed the arrival of the Mennonites as a blessing, saw them as a social, cultural and political threat to the small, young community which treasured British traditions, albeit ones modified by Canadian and American experience. Often, the Mennonites did not want to form or take part in local government bodies or school boards. A minority of them also stoutly resisted the Province's determination to establish and conduct elementary schools in their midst. They rejected attempts by nationalists to make them into "good Canadian citizens". In short, the central question regarding the Mennonites was — would the Anglo-Saxon community be able to assimilate such a large, closely-knit "foreign" population, or would the district become a divided community in the same way that eastern Canada was divided between the French and the English? This was a difficult problem for all parties concerned, and the modification of attitudes on both sides came slowly. Now, more than one hundred years after their arrival in Canada, most of the Mennonites of the district have been assimilated, partly due to schism in their own ranks. But several Mennonite families chose to move to Mexico rather than to submit to Saskatchewan laws, especially on such vital matters as the education of their children.

The Reinland Mennonite Association continued to press for permission to fulfil their homestead duties under the hamlet system.[105] To strengthen their case, they went ahead and formed eight hamlets during the years 1905 to 1907.[106] This left the Dominion with the choice of attempting to force them to obey the law or of recognizing an accomplished fact. The Department of the Interior chose the latter course in April, 1907. Likely the fact that the Mennonites had made a payment of $7,697 on the reserved land in December, 1906 swayed their decision.[107] Neuendorf, Reinfeld, Chortitiz, Reinland, Springfeld, Schoenfeld, Blumenort and Blumenhof came into being south-east of Swift Current.

In all, about two thousand Mennonites from Manitoba and elsewhere came to settle in the Swift Current district between 1904 and 1907. By the spring of 1907, when their migration to the district was almost completed, they not only formed the largest ethnic block in the total population, but they outnumbered all the other residents of the district combined. But for the arrival during these years and later of so many settlers from the United States, from eastern Canada, including Manitoba, from the British Isles and the Scandinavian countries, and other parts of Europe, the Mennonites would certainly have remained the overwhelmingly dominant cultural group in the district. Since the Mennonites neither controlled nor attempted to control any of the institutions in the district, except their own church, they did not use their superior numbers for political advantage. Almost

HARVESTERS CUTTING AND STOOKING THE "BUMPER" CROP OF 1906.

from 1907 onward, their numerical superiority was sharply reduced as an ever-increasing number of English-speaking settlers from eastern Canada, Britain and the U.S. rushed into the district seeking either farm land or business opportunities.

It would not be accurate to say that the district was polyglot by 1907, although there were localities in the district that were settled by some Norwegians and Germans from the U.S., and a few métis still remained. In religion, the district was overwhelmingly Protestant; in race, it was nearly all "white" of north-western European origin. Before the Mennonites' arrival, it had been almost exclusively English in culture, with the British-born being more numerous than the Canadian- born section of the population, due mainly to the influence of the "76" ranch and the settlement by former Mounties. In short, it had been a predominantly "WASP" community. Fortunately, since the cultural diversity between the groups was not great, the chance of serious conflict was slight.

The Mennonites, partly for religious reasons, tended to be slow to establish local government agencies even in heavily populated areas. In the English-speaking parts of the district, once farm settlement had begun, this was not the case. But around the turn of the century, while settlement was sparse, the territorial government, its finances strained from paying much of the cost of local improvements, had to compel the establishment of some form of local government in the district. The early settlers generally opposed local government, since they looked upon it as a device to increase their taxes. The first such form of local government to affect the ranchers was proclaimed May 9, 1899, and covered all of the land area from Herbert to Gull Lake and from Saskatchewan Landing to eighteen miles south of Lac Pelletier. This became Swift Current Local Improvement District (L.I.D.) No. 509. Not included was an area one township in size centred upon Swift Current which had earlier been established as L.I.D. No. 383.[108] William Vaudreuil, an English-born ex-Mountie, became the first Overseer of the new unit of government. The following year the territorial government appointed its own agent from Regina as Overseer, but the local residents, in their annual ratepayers meetings, continued to make the decisions as to the work to be done in the district by their L.I.D. and the disbursement of the small amount of funds raised through local land taxes. Both the assessment and tax revenue in the L.I.D. were low — $2,109 and $570 respectively in 1900 — despite the huge size of the district.[109] The two largest private landlords, the C.P.R. and the Hudson's Bay Company, paid no tax on their lands, the latter company refusing to do so despite local demands that it should. The right to tax the land of both of these corporations was hotly demanded of Ottawa at this time by the non-partisan Territorial Government, led by Frederick Haultain, but the Federal Government, then Liberal, flatly refused. L.I.D. No. 509, already huge, was substantially enlarged in 1902 to include the area south of it to the U.S. boundary and north almost to present-day Rosetown,[110] as a few ranchers began to settle in these regions. Then, as farmers began to fill up the empty lands around Swift Current, a new and much smaller L.I.D., No. 8-J-3, was formed out of part of it on March 7, 1905. It included only four townships, being Townships 15 and 16 in Ranges 13 and 14, all west of the third meridian.[111] Almost all of Swift Current L.I.D. No. 383, at the centre of this new L.I.D., was also included in L.I.D. 8-J-3, except the hamlet and the one-half section of land it occupied, which had been raised to village status just over a year earlier.[112]

No longer was the L.I.D. under the supervision of an Overseer, nor controlled quite as much by the Territorial or, within months, by the newly-formed Provincial Government at Regina. The resident taxpayers in each of the four townships elected one Councillor, who, in turn, selected one of their number to be their chairman. Next, the four-man council hired a secretary-treasurer. The first chairman of L.I.D. No. 8-J-3 was W. P. Bracy, who was succeeded in 1907 by L. A. Sackett. The other members of the first council, besides Sackett and Bracy, were George H. Klemmie and Julius J. Johnson. In 1907 J. E. Snyder and Gus Heden, with Klemmie and Sackett, made up the rural council. James T. Dodds, the local Justice of the Peace and school teacher, was selected to be the first secretary-treasurer. A few months later, Dodds quit to become a homestead inspector. He was replaced by the local barber, H. E. Clinite, in 1905, in whose shop the council met.[113]

Being freed from strict control from Regina did not result in extravagant expenditures by the rural council — quite the contrary. They paid Clinite only $100 per year, and themselves just $2.00 per day salary for their work, with a maximum of four days per year, plus a travelling expense of ten cents per mile, to supervise road work in their townships. By levying a tax of $6.00 per year on taxable quarter-sections, they collected $371.60 in 1905, but kept expenditures down to only $173.00, or less than one-half of their revenue. As settlers flocked into their L.I.D. during the next two years, their tax receipts climbed to $1,612.96 in 1907. While they did spend $1,716.36 that year, almost entirely on road building and maintenance, they still had a reserve left over from the surpluses of the previous two years. Like so many later councillors from the entire district, these first representatives were honest, conscientious citizens who exercised as good or better care over the funds and matters placed in their trust as they did of their own affairs. They never sought financial reward for themselves from their elected office. Nevertheless, on one occasion in 1905, they displayed their wish to achieve some degree of local immortality. In all seriousness, Bracy, Johnson, Klemmie and Sackett voted that henceforth the townships that each represented should be called after themselves, rather than being referred to by location! While in their meetings they used the new names for the townships,[114] the local citizens, some of them residents of much longer standing than they, were amused by their councillors' presumptuousness and did not follow their lead.

The transition from no local government in the district in 1897 to one that ten years later closely resembled a modern rural municipality is some indication of the pace of change from the era of the open range to that of the fenced farm. It was the influx of farm settlers and the changes which they made in the nature of the country that contributed to the curtailment of ranching in the district. In this, the farmers were encouraged and assisted by governmental policies which, apparently, the local ranchers never challenged. Probably the ranchers neither thought that their united opposition would bring a change in these policies, nor realized how vulnerable their industry had become. If 1905 and 1906 had been very poor years for agriculture instead of extremely good ones, possibly financial hardship would have prompted the ranchers to take action to protect their interests — though not by violent or illegal means, for they respected the law too much for that. Yet, even if a few foresaw the ranching era ending, they could not have imagined how swiftly the end would come. Nature had smiled upon the local agriculturalists. Suddenly, without warning, the smile became a snarl.

On November 18 a six-day blizzard swept over the prairies. Snow three to four feet deep on the level blanketed the eastern half of the district, while the bitterly cold wind piled up drifts several feet high. West from Swift Current the snowfall was lighter, but still it locked the range under a blanket of white death. Trains were halted, and telegraph wires were torn down by the weight of the ice and the force of the wind.[115] "Dogies" and weak livestock perished by the hundreds from exposure and hunger. In vain the settlers looked for mild weather to melt the snow which hid the grass and to enable them to travel to their herds and to town. Instead, they were met by repeated snowstorms and abnormally low temperatures. Many of the settlers soon used up their supplies of fuel and food. This forced them to make a now dangerous trip to Gull Lake, Swift Current, Waldeck or Rush Lake for coal and groceries.[116]

As the bad winter persisted, the supply of coal in the district was all consumed — a coal famine set in which lasted for weeks.[117] The rural people were forced to burn their fence posts, corrals, hay racks and every tree, scrap of wood and bit of dried cow dung they could find to keep from freezing to death in the uninsulated frame shacks. The fortunate few who lived in sod houses were warmer. On January 3, 1907, the mercury reportedly dropped to fifty-five degrees below zero (F.) in parts of the district and remained below zero for the next three weeks. A farmer in the small Norwegian settlement just northeast of Swift Current had an experience typical of many:

> One pioneer, Peter Thodeson, sat up all night with his fur coat, mittens and fur cap on to keep the fire going so he wouldn't freeze to death in his single ply board shack.[118]

The pioneers travelled at the risk of their lives. More than one homesteader became lost in the smothering blizzards while tending his livestock or gathering firewood and died. The bodies of the Smith brothers, who

104

farmed south of Gull Lake, were not discovered until the following summer.[119] On January 31, the press reported:

> Campbell McCutcheon, a young Scotsman on the Wayne Ranch, some forty miles north of Swift Current, committed suicide during Wayne's absence. Rumour has it he took his own life when lost on the prairie rather than being frozen to death.[120]

It took Swift Current's Coroner and first physician, Dr. W. H. Field, and its Mountie, Corporal Botteley, four days to travel the forty miles to this ranch to view the remains, and four more days of battling deep snow and bad weather to return to the railway village.[121] Another cowboy, Jim Reagen, from the Kirkaldie Ranch on the river about sixty miles northwest of Swift Current, spent five exhausting, terrifying days on the trail from the ranch to Swift Current. For two days and nights he kept alive without either food or fire. His face frozen and his horse's saddle blanket clutched around him for warmth, he stumbled along through the snow holding on to the tail of his saddlehorse. When he finally reached safety, even his underwear was so frozen that it had to be cut off him.[122]

A few feeble Chinooks arrived late in January, but the intense cold began again in February, turning the surface of the snow into a thick layer of ice. Only the horses could paw through it to reach the grass below. Antelope were so weak from hunger and cold that they could be knocked down with clubs. The cattle drifted ahead of the storms to perish miles away from the feed on their home range. Fences failed to hold them, for the snow had drifted over the top of fence posts and the ice crust formed a pavement over the white drifts. The livestock sought shelter along the river where many either starved to death or drowned by falling through air holes in the river ice near James Smart's ranch — about 500 head had drowned in this way during the last week of January.[123] Early in March, the police patrol reported:

> The river banks on the north side were simply lined with dead cattle; in one small clump of willows alone fifty-six head being counted.[124]

A brief mild spell came about March 20, but more storms followed which took a devastating toll of the much-weakened livestock, especially of new-born calves and colts. Even by June 1, patches of dirty grey snow still dotted the north slopes of hillsides in the district.[125] It had been a terrible ordeal for all the settlers, but for many of the ranchers their fight for economic survival was over, and they had lost.

As one would expect, it was those large ranchers who could not provide feed for their livestock who suffered the heaviest losses[126] — in some instances, when their herds were mainly "dogies" from eastern Canada or the U.S.A., such losses were as high as seventy per cent.[127] Since these stockers had often been purchased with borrowed money, the loss of the cattle was a doubly devastating blow. To make matters worse, especially for those who had invested heavily in stockers, beef prices declined sharply as thousands of poor, thin cattle were dumped upon the market in an effort to raise money to clear off bank loans or just to get out of

ranching. Coming when it did, this terrible winter was mistakenly considered to be the prime cause of all the ranchers' hardships, instead of simply
the death blow to a dying era. The well-established ranchers with seasoned
range cattle and a good supply of feed came through the winter with much
lighter losses, especially those in the Cypress Hills. Horse ranchers lost
only a few head, and enjoyed a good market at high prices in 1907.[128] Still,
when the winter was finally over, not only many of the ranchers but also
some of the newly-arrived farmers who had witnessed their first prairie
winter packed up and left the district.

Beset by unbeatable forces, the ranching industry staged a major
retreat in the district. Still, it was not totally beaten. A few veteran ranchers
continued to raise livestock, but ranching no longer held sway in the field of
agriculture. Some six years afterward, one authority wrote of this rather
abrupt transition from ranching to farming:

> The change, while regrettable in some respects, is altogether desirable.
> The farmer who keeps cattle and feeds them grain before marketing
> does so at a profit, and not only helps to maintain a better market for his
> beef, but furnishes a better quality beef for the consuming public.[129]

Those who remembered the flavor of the beef from a four-year-old, range-
finished steer certainly would not have agreed — especially if they had
been the ones to raise the steer! But for most areas in the district, the
change was for the best. The romantic period in the region's history — the
day of the open range — was over. The era of the ranching frontier was at
an end and the era of the grain farmers and the townsmen had begun.

Chapter VII

TOWN BUILDERS — AND OTHERS

Swift Current had sprung into existence like a prairie mushroom after a summer rain. No sooner had the railway given it life late in 1882 than the trail freighters had transformed it into an important trans-shipping and distributing centre. The C.P.R. navvies had swiftly graded their way westward across the rolling prairie to Medicine Hat by June 10, 1883,[1] then spanned the river and toiled north-west to the Rockies, while the track layers followed relentlessly behind. When winter overtook the railway builders they had spiked the steel rails fifteen miles beyond Calgary, which then became that winter's western railway terminus. Keeping pace, the floating retinue of the railway camps had moved on from Swift Current to harvest the payroll of the construction gangs at the newest end-of-steel. With their passing, the period of hectic growth which had marked Swift Current's first months of existence ceased. During that time this railway divisional point had been transformed from a tent town into a small cluster of falsefronted wooden shops and a handful of modest frame houses, all huddled around the railway depot, dining hall and hotel, freight shed and water tank. The new community formed a tiny island in a vast and vacant sea of grass.

For the next twenty years the citizens awaited a return of the boom conditions that had fostered the rapid growth of the community, all the while drawing sustenance from the railway. Three times in the 1880's their waning hopes were revived: first, when the hamlet became, for ten weeks, a military supply base for the Riel Rebellion in 1885; next, in 1886, when a trading flurry prompted a modest enlargement of the business establishments; and finally, with the development of Sir John Lister-Kaye's huge "76" ranch just south of the trading centre in 1888-89. While Swift Current had benefited from these developments, they were insufficient to cause it to grow even to village proportions.

Still, the 1890's were the most difficult years to bear. They began dismally, for the C.P.R. had greatly reduced its local staff by 1889 and trail freighting to Battleford ended late in 1890. The lost business this caused was accompanied and made worse by the exodus of local population, especially of native peoples who had depended upon trail freighting for their livelihood. Since the métis freighters, as well as the local Indians, customarily exchanged buffalo bones for goods that they needed at the two local general stores, they had provided an important amount of doubly profitable business for the merchants. The devastating hail storm of 1890, which completely ruined the promising crops on the nearby "76" ranch and damaged all the local buildings, further disheartened the community. It especially discouraged the businessmen, whose hope of expanding their trade depended upon the district developing a grain growing reputation that would attract farm settlement. The hamlet's few stores did continue to operate, though the ownership changed as pioneer merchants left for greener pastures and were replaced by men who had more hope and faith in the country than seems warranted. Confidently, and then desperately, these new storekeepers hoped for an end to the conditions which held prairie settlement in check and frustrated the ambitions of all the white residents of the West. They were not alone in experiencing the long deferment of their hopes. Grain farming was the mainspring of urban growth, and economic conditions then were unfavorable to the spread of farm settlement throughout the central prairie region. As a result, none of the villages or towns in what is now Saskatchewan grew very much during the 1890's.

The businessmen of Swift Current were occasionally encouraged by the spasmodic growth of the local ranching industry during the 1890's, as small ranches were begun along the district's waterways. Gradually the ranchers and their families — mostly former "76" employees — replaced the population that had departed with the end of trail freighting. However, such affluence as these ranchers knew was but partly reflected in increased sales of the local merchants. Ranchers such as Robert Cruickshank often drove their livestock to market at Moose Jaw or Medicine Hat[2] or else

A GROUP OF PIONEERS IN FRONT OF CHARLES REID'S STORE, *circa* 1893. The store on the left is owned by William Milburn.

TABLE 1

Swift Current Post Office Transactions from August 1, 1883 to March 31, 1907.[4]

| Fiscal Year Ending | Gross Postal Revenue $ | Money Order Transactions | | | |
		No. Sold	$ Value Sold	No. Cashed	$ Value Cashed
1884	285.81	a	a	a	a
1885	251.17	a	a	a	a
1886	b	127	2,416.08	b	284.08
1887	b	225	5,405.35	b	894.30
1888	1,255.61c	b	b	b	b
1888	b	216	4,175.99	b	689.47
1889	842.52	196	3,116.23	b	700.33
1890	445.05	164	3,195.91	b	330.83
1891	504.76	233	3,578.05	b	184.38
1892	548.79	273	3,377.68	b	1,197.82
1893	511.71	310	3,691.59	b	493.66
1894	758.13	309	3,330.22	b	2,542.29
1895	415.99	255	2,951.98	b	723.38
1896	401.50	151	1,467.85	b	373.67
1897	453.04	156	1,505.12	b	346.44
1898	526.34	160	2,252.85	b	369.98
1899	530.95	152	2,256.87	18	345.75
1900	434.90	93	1,168.74	7	200.65
1901	467.55	167	2,141.70	21	440.70
1902	492.55	218	2,835.27	25	548.11
1903	963.14	248	3,404.39	40	1,083.24
1904	1,465.79	602	10,824.17	99	4,180.87
1905	1,691.00	814	14,439.71	154	4,803.82
1906	2,133.69	1,460	30,645.01	409	14,585.63
1907*	2,321.75	1,665	30,134.98	66	1,890.68

* Nine month period only, ended March 31, 1907.
a Postal Money Order office not yet established.
b No figures given.
c This represents the gross revenue since July 1, 1885.

boarded the train for these bigger towns, where a much larger array of goods awaited their selection. Moreover, in these towns they could find some entertainment and a comfortable hotel with a bar. Many of the railway men also could shop with ease in either Medicine Hat or Moose Jaw, the ends of the railway division west and east of Swift Current. As a result, the volume of business done in Swift Current was barely enough to sustain its few original stores. Under these circumstances, growth of the business community was impossible.

By the spring of 1900, local retail business was at its lowest ebb. However, that summer it began to improve, in pace with the agricultural development of the entire district.[3] The cattle and horse ranching industry entered a prosperous phase in 1900 which reached a climax locally in 1905-06. During these years many new ranches were started and the ranch population increased substantially. Also in 1903, farmers at last had begun to settle the empty prairie around Swift Current. Between 1904 and 1907 some two thousand Mennonites alone flooded into the district. The farmers enjoyed immediate success, and owing largely to the excellent crop years of 1905 and 1906, the district was soon considered to be a highly desirable wheat farming area.

With the arrival of farm settlement, long awaited by the merchants, the business district at once began to thrive and expand at an amazing rate. After being a hamlet for twenty-two years, Swift Current at last became a village in 1904. Spurred on by its newly-found prosperity, within three more years it became a town.

By 1907 the agricultural potential of the district was obvious. Large scale ranching, particularly range finishing of stocker cattle, was rapidly giving way to grain farming, its retreat hastened by the disastrous winter of 1906-07. On every street in the town, the ring of hammers and the hum of saws announced that Swift Current, at last, had come into its own. The building boom had returned, and the long years of disappointment, the years of waiting and doubting, appeared to be at an end. It seemed too good to be true to the few pioneers who had persevered through those difficult years. A prairie boom town was rising from the ancient buffalo grounds.

During the early years of the hamlet, a population of one hundred, predominantly male, lived near the depot — a few more in the good years to 1889, a few less in the depression years that followed. By 1901 the residents of the hamlet numbered just 121.

Since its population in these years was small and less than one-quarter were property owners and entitled to a voice in local government matters, there were too few public-spirited citizens to bring about incorporation. Its mixed-blood and Indian element, all being squatters, had no say, and therefore no interest, in the matter. The bachelor railwaymen living in the C.P.R. bunkhouse, a transient group, were probably as indifferent to the question of local self-government as were the natives. They and the other C.P.R. employees residing on company property could not vote on the question anyway. The remaining group of locally-qualified electors, made up of settled C.P.R. men, merchants and ranchers, held divided opinions. Some saw local government as a step towards higher taxes, others as a move towards much-needed community development. As things stood, the territorial government built and maintained all the roads and bridges in the district without any local tax being levied upon its citizens. This arrangement helped thwart any local agitation for self-government. Even if the long term settlers had been united in desiring to form a village, which they were not, it seems improbable that there were enough dwellings within a prescribed area to meet the territorial government's minimum requirements for such incorporation.

Since local governments were the creatures of the territorial government, a change in the status of Swift Current could be expected to be initiated from the capital at Regina. The depressed conditions of the 1890's provided the catalyst. The territorial government, financially unable to continue providing for local public works throughout much of the N.W.T., began, in 1897, the compulsory establishment of Statute Labour and Fire Districts, thereby thrusting part of the expense of public works onto local tax payers. There were 359 such organizations created within the next two years.[5] One of these, No. 383, was formed on March 25, 1898, and covered an area one township in size with Swift Current at its centre. William Milburn, a merchant and rancher who favored local government, was elected as Overseer.[6] Thus, without any struggle on the part of the citizens of Swift Current, local self-government was established. But since this also meant that they must begin paying a share of the cost of building and maintaining local roads and fire guards, a struggle was soon begun to prevent any more advanced form of local self-government (and more taxes) from being forced upon them.

Only months after Milburn assumed his role as Overseer, the territorial government decided to change the Statute Labour and Fire Districts into Local Improvement Districts. Learning that a huge Local Improvement District to include almost the entire Swift Current district was to be formed the next year, Milburn wrote to the Deputy Commissioner of Public Works in October, 1898. He did not want the small unit of local government of which he was Overseer to go out of existence. To him, the best alternative was for Swift Current to become a village, as Maple Creek had done in 1896.[7] Milburn asked the Deputy Commissioner for a copy of the oridinance respecting villages. The territorial official seized upon the enquiry. He sent Milburn a strong recommendation, almost a directive, that Swift Current should become a village in order to improve its public facilities and to safeguard public health. He went so far as to state that, unless the local citizens objected, he would arrange that Swift Current become a village on December 21, 1898.[8]

A majority of the local citizens quickly reacted to what must have seemed bureaucratic high-handedness from Regina. But most important, they had no wish to pay the higher taxes that would result from incorporation. In indignation, they petitioned against it. Milburn did what he could to rally support for incorporation, even charging that some of those who objected to it were not qualified voters, but he was only upheld in this in one case. The objections caused the Deputy Commissioner to delay the incorporation, but not to give up the idea. On February 23, 1899, he asked

WILLIAM MILBURN, a one-time Mountie, pioneer merchant, rancher, hamlet Overseer, Dominion Lands agent, Justice of the Peace and a popular town Councillor — a "town builder". (Photo *circa* 1929.)

THE HAMLET OF SWIFT CURRENT IN 1903, AT THE START OF THE BUILDING BOOM. Note, on the left, the Imperial Hotel, under scaffolding.

Horace A. Greeley, a newly-elected M.L.A. representing the constituency which included Swift Current, to try to persuade those opposed to forming a village to change their minds. Greeley canvassed the voters of Swift Current on March 6, 1899 and left, like countless other politicians before and since, mistakenly believing that he had switched several votes.

His visit, however, brought the matter to a head, Later that same day a new petition was sent by the citizens to Regina, but it revealed that only one of the opposition group had been won over.[9] That ended the matter of incorporation for the next four years. Thus, the struggle *against* the advancement of responsible self-government at Swift Current was won — for a time.

Swift Current did not rid itself of its small unit of local government, however, for in 1899, when the huge Local Improvement District No. 509 was set up to include the surrounding district, the small Statute Labour and Fire District was transformed by the territorial government into Local Improvement District No. 383 with William Rutherford as Overseer.[10] Yet, the opposition group among the district's citizens found comfort in the fact that local taxes remained unchanged.

It took the construction of two small frame hotels in 1903, first the Reliance and then the Imperial, to revive the move for village status. R. H. Corbett of Medicine Hat, the owner of the Imperial Hotel, arranged first for a lawyer and then for the Moose Jaw Saskatchewan Land Company, who owned land in the district, to write to the territorial government that summer asking if Swift Current could become a village — Corbett could not get a liquor licence for his hotel bar until it did. Again the Deputy Commissioner of Public Works displayed his eagerness to have Swift Current incorporated. He once more asked for Greeley's aid, this time to determine whether there were fifteen dwellings within one section of land at the place. Apparently there were, as an additional half-dozen new businesses had been established there in 1903. As a result, notice was given that the government would raise Swift Current to village status by September 25, 1903.[11] For some reason there was a delay of over four months. The territorial government was then revising its legislation regulating the structure of local government and may have postponed creating new villages meanwhile. Local ratepayers may also have objected, but there is no record of such a protest. Perhaps the prospect of having their first licenced bar-room won support from would-be dissenters. In any event, on February 4, 1904, the new village, encompassing one-half section of land, was established.[12] With the village an accomplished fact, the ratepayers met on March 9 and, by acclamation, elected the popular Wilfred (Fred) Jones as their village Overseer.[13]

At this time throughout the Territories and, until 1908 in Saskatchewan, village Overseers, but no village Councillors, were elected by the ratepayers.[14] The Overseer, meeting with the ratepayers, was to determine what was to be done by the local government. Though the Overseer, then,

WILFRED (FRED) JONES, the first Overseer of the Village of Swift Current, later the first Mayor of the Town of Swift Current — a "town builder".

had less legislative but more executive power than he did after 1908, when he was one of three elected Councillors, the ratepayers, through the democratic forum of the ratepayers' meetings, had direct control in policy matters within the scope of village government. As a result, at least in Swift Current, a clear policy aimed at a planned development of the village's public facilities failed to emerge from these too-democratic meetings. Usually the ratepayers' main aim was to pay as little in taxes as possible, with the result that only problems of pressing urgency were given attention, and then in the most niggardly fashion.

Fred Jones had arrived in the West from Ontario around the turn of the century with the intention of becoming a cowpuncher. After quickly learning the work, he won a foreman's job on Robert Cruickshank's ranch. Always ambitious, Jones took his pay in horses. When, by 1903, he had accumulated five head, he rented a stable in Swift Current and started a livery business. He used his spare time to advantage by taking up barbering and also became the first local agent for the *Swift Current Sun,* then published in Maple Creek. During his initial term as Overseer, when an increasing number of land-seekers began to arrive, he sold his early businesses and opened the first locally-owned real estate and insurance agency. Before long he was also horse ranching.[15] For obvious reasons, Jones was a strong advocate of the economic and political advancement of Swift Current. His future depended on it.

Jones launched the village government with his usual vigor. In less than a month he had arrived at an assessment of $100,000 for the taxable property in the village. The first ratepayers' meeting was held in the village's one-roomed school on April 11, 1904. After much debate, the citizens agreed upon a low tax rate of only four mills on the dollar, which produced a revenue that year of just $400. The assembled ratepayers — almost everyone in the village who was eligible — decided on the levying of various fees and licences and the expenditure of tax revenue. Drainage, sidewalk construction and street improvement received top priority[16] — probably since the spring weather had turned the streets into a quagmire, as usual. To build wooden sidewalks on Railway Street and Eleventh Avenue (the main street), Jones proposed and won approval for the issue of a $700 ten-year debenture. This turned out to be the only long term borrowing that the village ever did for any purpose.

With attention focussed on the village streets, Jones soon discovered that one of the most prominent citizens, Andrew Patterson, had built a fence over twenty feet across a street where he had then planted a garden. Jones asked him to remove the offending fence, but Patterson, at first, refused to do so. Argue and Cooper, general merchants, in building an addition to their store, had likewise intruded on a village street. The offenders were promptly ordered either to put an end to their encroachment or face the cost of having the village hire someone to move the structures. Both trespassers complied with the order. To attempt to placate the disgruntled Patterson, Jones gave up to him his position as village licence inspector. Another matter Jones had to deal with concerned William Sanders, who had started a dairy business in the hamlet in 1890 and later ran a bakery and meat market on Railway Street. He was told to move his slaughter house from behind his shop to some location beyond the village limits,[17] less likely to offend public sensibility.

Such orders from a less diplomatic man than Jones might have resulted in opposition. This was not the case, with the possible exception of the influential Patterson — C.P.R. locomotive superintendent, business proprietor and Justice of the Peace. The fact that Jones was re-elected by acclamation late in 1904 to a second term of one year[18] shows that the ratepayers were well pleased with the way the village was progressing under his leadership — leadership which he continued to give until 1906 when he chose not to seek re-election. Certainly the territorial government was also satisfied, since Swift Current was now giving the attention to its facilities and public health that had been urged by its public works department in 1898.

Until 1903, Swift Current consisted of only the C.P.R. buildings, plus a half-dozen business establishments, a school, two churches and no more than ten houses, some of them mere shacks. All were strung out along Railway Street, north of the tracks. A short distance south of the village stood the home of the meteorological observer and the extensive buildings of the "76" ranch. Many of the village buildings were weather-beaten structures that had been hastily erected when the hamlet was first founded, and had borne without grace the ravages of twenty years. To railway

SWIFT CURRENT, LOOKING NORTH FROM A ROOFTOP DOWN CENTRAL (11th) AVE., *circa* 1904. The Reid store faces the site of the present Pioneer Co-op store.

117

passengers travelling through it must have seemed a drab, lifeless place, unlikely ever to prosper. That its pace of life was quickening by 1903, though, was evident in the N.W.M.P. report of that year, which stated: "Swift Current is a rising place, and requires more than the one constable who has hitherto been stationed there."[19] This recommendation stemmed from an increase in the volume of routine police work, not from rising unruliness, for serious crime was unknown in the district.

The village continued to grow rapidly in 1904. In fact, there was such a demand for building materials during that spring that construction was forced to halt until the community's only building supplies store had replenished its exhausted stock of lumber.[20] Fully sixteen business firms were established in the village by that year, ranging from such modest but essential ones as a dray and water hauling business, to the three-storey, twenty-two room Imperial Hotel complete with bar and dining facilities.[21]

This expansion highlighted the inadequacy of the tax levy. Take, for example, the moving story of the village firehall. This little wooden building had been simply taken over from the previous Local Improvement District and left where it stood, on a side street. The building lots in the village were owned either by individuals, the Anglican or Presbyterian churches, or the Canada Northwest Land Company, a real estate firm formed by C.P.R. magnates.[22] The village government owned only the village streets. At a ratepayers' meeting early in 1905, citizens complained to Jones that the structure was blocking one of their streets. A motion was passed empowering Jones to buy a lot for the firehall, but was hastily amended by the cautious element to the effect that ". . . not over $125 be expended by the Overseer in securing an efficient fire service." Due to the influx of land buyers, vacant lots with just twenty-five foot frontage brought prices of up to $300. Under these circumstances, Jones was unable to buy a site for the firehall.[23] Instead, the village's only public building was moved onto a privately-owned lot. In 1906, William Alexander, the owner of this lot, demanded that the structure be removed.[24] Lamentably, the village still did not have enough funds to purchase a lot for its one public building. J. G. Maxwell, who succeeded Jones as Overseer in 1906, could do nothing more than move the firehall onto yet another vacant lot. Within months the lot's owner, William Vaudreuil, was objecting to its presence on his property. Again, in the spring of 1907, the firehall was moved — to its fourth temporary location within two years! This time the town did exempt from taxation the lot on which it was squatting.[25] No permanent firehall site was purchased until late in 1908. One can imagine the cry of "Fire!" being raised during these years with frantic volunteer firemen dashing about the village in search of the firehall.

The short-sighted and self-defeating attitude which the majority of the ratepayers displayed during this period in not adopting a higher tax rate or borrowing to provide so essential a thing as a good fire-fighting service also manifested itself in several other ways. The fact that the village grew to town proportions within three years was not due to the efforts of the village government. Few public improvements had been made to make the community more attractive to prospective businesses or settlers. Indeed, the village grew almost in spite of itself.

Apart from the tax funds — used mainly to build sidewalks and streets in the business district — and the paltry sums spent for a fire-fighting service, the ratepayers approved only one notable expenditure. Late in 1905, they had empowered Fred Jones to pay $200 for ten acres of C.P.R. land north-east of the village to be used as a cemetery.[26] No doubt it was the prospect of future sales of burial plots that helped to justify this purchase.

The ratepayers, seemingly without confidence in their collective financial ability or in the future, followed a pay-as-you-go policy. But, since they were likewise determined to hold taxes down to the trifling amount of four-tenths of one cent on each dollar of assessed valued, the village's total revenue, including taxes, licences and the income from the sale of cemetary lots, in the peak year of 1906 amounted to only $821. Once the Overseer's salary of $100, plus the debenture payment, was deducted, just $585 was left to cover all other expenses.[27]

It is small wonder, then, that the village of Swift Current in 1907 lacked so many public works and services. The only running water was in the creek. There were no sewers, concrete walks, street lights or road maintenance equipment. The village still did not own a building lot, so naturally it did not have a village hall or administrative office. Instead, meetings were held in the school or in the Overseer's business office. The village government owned no office equipment — not even a safe to hold its tax collections and records. The firehall was a shack with fire-fighting equipment to match. There was no public pest house where those with serious contagious diseases could be quarantined, and the closest hospital was at Maple Creek, almost a hundred miles away. The citizens had neither electric lights nor telephones. When it rained, the numerous low spots in the streets became miniature lakes which were soon churned into a sea of mud by the horse-drawn vehicles. It must have been small comfort to such public-spirited citizens as Fred Jones in those times that Swift Current's taxes and debt were so low.

An explanation for the ratepayers' unwillingness to tax themselves and spend more to improve the public facilities of Swift Current may possibly be found in the long periods of financial depression through which many of them had lived. Perhaps believing that their newly-found prosperity would not last, they were extremely cautious in committing themselves to a tax rate which might become an insupportable burden in future. This "depression phobia" did not die easily.

Early proposals from more optimistic citizens that Swift Current should become a town as soon as it could qualify met with resistance from the majority of the ratepayers. With town status went the right to substantially increase public debt to fund various public works. Higher taxes could

RAILWAY ST. W., SWIFT CURRENT, *circa* 1905, showing both the Reliance Hotel and the Imperial Hotel and other business premises.

RELIANCE HOTEL,

SWIFT CURRENT, ASSA,

STEVENS & FRANKLIN, Proprs.

⸗ Under New Management ⸗

Everything First-class.   Rates 1-50 per day.

GOOD SAMPLE ROOMS.   CHOICE LIQUORS AND CIGARS.

GENT'S YOU'RE WELCOME

We are prepared to furnish you with the very finest cigars and drinks, every minute if desired,, consequently there is no time lost. If you do not get your drink red-hot or ice-cold, as desired, please mention the fact to the proprietor and the barman will be blown to the clouds from the mouth of a cannon.

CAUTION

My kicking machine is run by electricity and the current is always turned on. Persons asking credit will be electrocuted. Advertising fakirs and book agents are shot without mercy. A gallows for hanging dead beats stands ready in the fighting room. Suckers loafers, blowers and common liars will be instantly murdered. Twenty-eight persons who tried to borrow money are dead in the cellar now. My office hours for tramps are only on February 29th at 13 a.m. and 15 p.m. Beggars will get a sound thrashing without warning.   [over]

AN EXAMPLE OF FRONTIER HOSPITALITY AND HUMOR, *circa* 1905
(Reliance Hotel business card)

121

A PANORAMIC VIEW OF THE VILLAGE OF SWIFT CURRENT IN 1906.

be expected, as a result. Continued years of prosperity after 1902, however, coupled with the arrival of hundreds of new citizens not sharing the "depression phobia", swelled the ranks of those who favored the idea of town status for Swift Current. Gradually, this group, led by Fred Jones, overcame the unprogressive element opposing them.

The village of Swift Current was not yet a year old when, in January, 1905, Overseer Jones wrote to the territorial government to learn the procedure whereby the village could be incorporated as a town.[28] He thought that it then had sufficient population to qualify, since 400 persons residing within 1280 acres of land had been fixed as the minimum qualification in the Territories in 1903.[29]

At a special meeting held on incorporation the following month, citizens unfavorable to the step blocked a decision on the issue. They succeeded in having a five member committee formed to explore with the officers of larger towns the advisability of Jones's proposal.[30] The committee was to report its findings at a meeting to be held exactly one month later, but, since the report was not ready, the meeting was cancelled. Not until the December meeting was the report forthcoming. Andrew Patterson, who had defied Jones when first asked in 1904 to stop fencing the street, in speaking for the committee, presented an uninviting view of incorporation. Fred Jones as well as James Stoddart, the village's first jeweller, saw their hopes of town building fading while Patterson spoke. They tried to rally support for their cause, but with little success. The group who opposed them could count on the votes of the conservative-minded citizens who,

like their counterparts everywhere, saw change as a threat rather than as a blessing. Wisely, Jones's supporters did not risk jeopardizing their position by then requesting a vote on the matter[31], for defeat of their proposal was probable.

The citizens at this meeting elected by acclamation John G. Maxwell, a handsome young furniture dealer of only one year's residency, as their Overseer for 1906.[32] During his term of office hundreds of people settled in the village and surrounding district. Even the Medicine Hat newspaper remarked on this inrush of land seekers and cited the land sales of one of the village's newest real estate companies:

> The local office of the Swift Current Land Co. has sold during the past two weeks, land and town [sic] lots amounting to $67,600. Purchasers were mainly from Ontario and the U.S.[33]

During the years 1903 to 1906 about fifty-five new businesses were established in Swift Current, almost one-half of them in the latter year alone.[34] These newcomers soon swelled the ranks of the group desiring town status. Moving cautiously, they succeeded in-having passed an innocuous and therefore unopposed resolution instructing John Maxwell to take the village census.[35] Two months later, a special meeting of ratepayers was called to discuss and pass upon incorporation. Overseer Maxwell reported that a still incomplete census showed that the village had 460 residents, which exceeded the provincial requirements for town incorporation. Believing the time was ripe, Fred Jones, seconded by W. Milwarde

Yates, who had published the local newspaper in the village for one year, proposed that Swift Current become a town. The limits were to be extended to include a newly-developing area on the south side of the C.P.R. tracks bringing the total area of the town to 560 acres.[36] Andrew Patterson, still a property owner but now a resident of Medicine Hat, vigorously attacked the motion. Despite this, when it was put to a vote at the meeting, it passed easily with thirty-two in favor and eleven against it.[37] Soundly beaten, the opposing forces never rallied again, even though this vote on incorporation was later set aside since the required notice of motion had not been given in advance. Obviously, Jones had not mastered the procedural regulations that he had received from Regina a year earlier. However, W. Oswald Smyth, who had arrived in the village in 1905 to become its first lawyer, successfully guided the desired resolution through the proper stages late that summer. A completed census, meanwhile, revealed that the population was 550.[38] So, on March 15, 1907, after not a little difficulty, Swift Current became a town.[39]

The town's first municipal elections called forth an amazing display of public spirit from the citizens. The schoolhouse was filled to capacity for the meeting to nominate candidates for their first town council. Not surprisingly, Fred Jones was the first to be nominated for Mayor. An old-timer, Charles Reid, a local merchant since 1892, was nominated to oppose Jones. No less than thirty-one other citizens were nominated to compete for the six council seats; however, fifteen of the men withdrew their names.[40] One week later, on April 13, 1907, the voters elected Fred Jones as Mayor. Of the five pioneer residents who sought council seats, only William Milburn, a long-time advocate of progress in local government, was successful, and he topped the polls. The remaining five Councillors were I. E. Argue, merchant and rancher, T. W. Hutcheson, druggist, Dr. W. H. Field, Swift Current's first doctor, Edward J. Brown, building contractor, and William W. Marlow, lumber dealer.

Mayor Jones and his six town councillors promptly undertook their duties. Before the month of April was ended they had met three times, passed five by-laws, including fire and building regulations, formed five committees to deal with various aspects of town government, appointed as Secretary-Treasurer and Assessor the town's first dentist, Dr. S. A. Hodgson, ordered 100 dog licence tags to be sold to raise revenue and control stray dogs, borrowed $700 from the local Union Bank of Canada to provide operating capital, written to the City of Moose Jaw for a copy of its by-laws (these puritanical regulations were used as a model), initiated a deal to purchase forty acres of Hudson's Bay Company land just west of the town to be used as a nuisance ground, ordered that the tie posts for horses be removed from the streets and be replaced by tie rings along the outer edge of the wooden sidewalks (the town had just entered the automobile age), and hired the town's first full-time employee, whom they designated as an Inspector.[41] Jones, the man of action, was back in charge,

CHARLES REID, *circa* 1906, a pioneer rancher and merchant who was a "town builder".

and this time supported by a forward-looking council rather than being hampered by an unprogressive group of ratepayers.

The council could not be accused of squandering the public's money, for they assigned enough duties to the Inspector to keep at least two men busy. He was to collect the poll tax from all adult male citizens, sell dog licences and impound stray dogs and other animals running at large in the town, maintain and be responsible for the town's firehall, buildings, equipment and tools, repair the sidewalks, maintain the streets and drainage ditches, cut the weeds and oversee all municipal works. These duties were to occupy him at least ten hours each day. In addition, he was to be the town's constable, keeping a watchful eye for signs of break=ins and fires and aiding the R.N.W.M.P. in enforcing law and order in Swift Current. One further condition of his employment was that he could not leave town without the council's permission. The Inspector was to be always on call, and he was not to take a vacation until he had first hired an acceptable person to take his place.

Amazingly enough, there were four applicants for the position, Paul Henze being the successful candidate. One might suppose that the four men had been attracted by the offer of a high salary, but this certainly was not the case. The Inspector was to receive twenty-five cents for each poll and dog tax he collected, plus a wage of only sixty-five dollars a month. Perhaps the fact that his work day left him with no idle time in which to spend his money helped Inspector Henze to survive.

The town presented a much different view to the new arrival in the spring of 1907 than it had to his counterpart only four years earlier.[42] Approaching Swift Current by train from the east, as most of the land seekers then did, the newcomer's first impressions would have been of the railway itself. The large rail yard, totalling nine miles of track, was filled almost to its 700 car capacity with an assortment of freight cars and yard engines in row after row to the south of the passenger train. There, also, stood the roundhouse and railway shops, like the rail yard addition, newly-built during 1903-04 to handle the ever-increasing volume of traffic.[43] The cluster of dwellings and business premises which comprised Swift Current resembled a semi-circle to the north with a radius of about one-eighth of a mile, its base being the railway. Beyond this stood the occasional house and shack, each with its indispensable privy and often some other outbuilding. The train crossed the bridge over the tree-lined creek, then passed by a small slough which marked the north-eastern boundary of the town. There were hardly any other trees in sight, except for those around the former "76" ranch just south of town. Before the new settler's excursion train hissed to a stop beside the wooden railway station (soon to be replaced by a fine brick one), it slid by the livestock shipping yards, the coal and freight sheds, the water tank and the plank platform piled high with a variety of farm machinery, household effects, building supplies and every manner of goods thought necessary to life. Here the

DOMINION DAY CELEBRATIONS, JULY 1 - 2, 1907 looking north up Central Ave. from Railway St.

farmers often shovelled their grain directly from their wagons into box cars for shipment to market, since there were, as yet, no grain elevators in the town. Let us follow one newcomer on his first day in town.

Alighting at the station, hungry after his trip, he stops at the large, attractive dining hall, just built to replace the old one which had lasted for a quarter of a century. The pleasant lady in charge serves him a full-course meal for thirty-five cents. Outside again, he passes by the two-storey brick C.P.R. telegraph station with living quarters above for the agent. (Swift Current was an important telegraph repeating station, employing several operators.) To his right stands the town pump that has supplied part of the community's water needs for a generation. Leaving the cindered walk, he picks his way between numerous horse-drawn rigs, crossing the rutted, muddy street to the board sidewalk on the west corner of Railway Street and Eleventh Avenue (Central Avenue). He is standing in front of the town's largest building, the Imperial Hotel. From this vantage point, he can look up both of the main streets of the town. In the next block to the west, a shallow slough left behind from the melted snow of the long, deadly winter of 1906-07 encroaches upon Railway Street. Not far north from where he stands, Eleventh Avenue becomes a multi-rutted road which climbs a hill and disappears from view (the old Battleford trail). He sees that Swift Current is not very big (the population was about 800), but it is growing and busy. This encourages him. If others can prosper here, perhaps he can, too. Eagerly he begins to explore the town and meet its citizens.

That evening, his reconnaissance complete, he reflects upon his day's experience. He can choose from no less than seven restaurants, two of them run by Chinese. There are two hotels, both with barrooms, and a third one will be opening soon. There is also a wholesale liquor dealer. Two pool rooms and a bowling alley are in operation (and he was told that to the south and north of the town there are houses of prostitution). In the town's drug store, he has noticed a good selection of popular and classical books for only twenty-five cents each. There is a local newspaper, as well, edited by the town's lawyer. On the east side of town he remembers seeing three Protestant churches, also two schools, one of them a concrete block, two-storey structure, not completely finished. He has not seen a hospital, but there is a nursing home, he was told, and a dentist, as well as three doctors. He has counted four general stores, three butcher shops, two groceries, a bakery and confectionery, two furniture stores, one hardware, with two more under construction, three lumber yards, a coal dealer, a harness shop, two jewellers, a men's wear store, two tailors, a barber, two Chinese laundries, four real estate and insurance agencies, a bank, four farm machinery dealers, two blacksmith's shops, two draymen and four livery, feed and sales stables. He was informed by a local booster that the recent building boom had attracted two tinsmiths and plumbers, two paint-ers and decorators, and four building contractors to the town. He recalls stopping at the little post office on Railway Street to mail a letter and ask directions to the Dominion Lands Sub-Agency office. Later, at the land office, the friendly agent introduced him to the two government land guides and the town's magistrate. They told him of how rapidly Swift Current had progressed in the past few years, and urged him to file on a homestead while choice land was still available. Last year, they said, crop yields in the district were the best in Saskatchewan! Sure, the town was raw and ugly, and there were things it did not yet have, but what else could one expect when it was growing so fast?

Thinking it over, he is convinced that much more business is being done here than in many a larger town back East. Yes, the prairie West is the land of the future, and the future of Swift Current looks bright indeed! All things considered, it is even better than he expected. True, there are not many women here, but there is a girl waiting back home who might be persuaded to come out. That settles it — he must write to her just as soon as he chooses a homestead! He has decided to stay.

Though this new citizen was fictitious, his first impressions were typical of those of many real settlers who arrived in the district during the beginning of the land rush. Swift Current was simply there, and they accepted without question or comment the fact that it was a town. They inherited the fruits of the labors of the town builders, probably without even knowing or caring who their benefactors were. With a rare exception, their interest was only in their own present and future, not in the past. In this, they were no different from those who had come before them. They found a foundation already laid, and they built upon it.

Part of that foundation was made of such readily identitiable things as the physical environment, the economic life of the district and the current stage of local civic development. But there were other dimensions to the foundation which were present and pervasive, if less obvious. They were the political parties, the territorial and the federal government, the law, the church and the schoolhouse. All these helped to shape the life of the people in the district.

Chapter VIII

STATE, CHURCH AND SCHOOL

We hope to see a new Upper Canada in the North-West Territory — in its well-regulated society and government, in its education, morality and religion. Toronto *Globe*, June 2, 1869.

On the Canadian prairies, unlike the American West to the south, government, law and religion long preceded white settlement. These institutions were little, if at all, modified by their new environment. Rather, they greatly moulded the life style of prairie people. It is clear that their existence prevented new and rival social institutions from developing. Once the railway brought white settlement to the Swift Current district in 1882, two other eastern institutions — politics and education — were soon transplanted as well. The history of these institutions locally is an important part of the story of Swift Current pioneers.

Many of the adult male citizens of the Swift Current district took an interest in politics. This was especially so of those who were patronage seekers. Yet, during the district's first quarter-century, no local person ever represented its citizens in either the territorial or provincial legislature or in the Dominion parliament. Nor was a local citizen ever a candidate in these elections. As a result, general interest in politics did not reach the intensity that it did in areas where a local politician sought voters' support. Political activity around Swift Current, then, involved mostly patronage seekers. That is not to say that national or local issues or political ideals had no influence on these people. They did. But to an even greater degree than is generally true of Canadian political parties today, the foundation of the Liberal and Conservative parties of that time rested squarely on the principle of patronage for friends of the party.

In the Swift Current district, despite its small population, there was a surprising number of government appointments that could be made to friends of the ruling party. Presumably, this was also true of other districts. The positions of postmaster, mail contractor, land and immigration agents, homestead inspector and meteorological observer were federal appointments, while those of Stipendiary Magistrate, Justice of the Peace (J.P.), Notary Public, liquor licence inspector and hide inspector were made by the territorial or later the provincial government. Since the Conservatives held sway in Ottawa until 1896 and at Regina until 1897, it was their friends who received the political spoils during most of the years between 1883 and

1897. The local Liberals, long denied the fruits of office, quickly claimed them once their party came to power.

F. Fraser Tims (elected in 1894 as a Conservative M.L.A. from the District of Alberta) became Swift Current's first postmaster and its mail contractor in 1883.[1] He was awarded the government contract to supply 9,000 bushels of oats to the N.W.M.P. in 1886[2] and was also appointed a Justice of the Peace. When he sold his Swift Current store to Neil McDonald, a fellow Conservative,[3] McDonald conveniently succeeded Tims as postmaster and Justice of the Peace.[4] In 1885, Tims had relinquished the Dominion mail contract, and a Conservative newly-arrived in Swift Current, Walter G. Knight, was given the job.[5] Knight also held the posts of Dominion Meteorological Observer[6] and Notary Public[7] at Swift Current and became a J.P. in 1888. He demonstrated both his loyalty to the Conservative party and his gift for oratory when, at the 1891 convention of his party in Moose Jaw, he nominated as candidate for a second term Nicholas Flood Davin, editor of the *Regina Leader* and M.P. for Assiniboia West.[8] The party organization in the North-West was not united at this time,[9] which resulted in Davin being opposed both for the nomination and subsequently for the federal seat by a fellow Conservative, Thomas Tweed, who was a merchant from Medicine Hat and also the Justice of the Peace and postmaster.[10]

Despite Tweed's local popularity (fifteen Conservatives at Swift Current had publicly petitioned him to seek election as their M.L.A. in 1888[11]), Knight and William Sanders used their influence in Davin's favor. While Tweed easily won almost every poll from Moose Jaw west, Davin won the eastern and larger polls in the constituency — and the election. At Swift Current, due mainly to the efforts of Knight and Sanders, Tweed's majority was held to only three votes.[12] Soon afterward, Sanders was appointed J.P.[13] — a position unsuited to his temperament. Sanders never presided over a court case, but was involved in several. He was successfully prosecuted for assault in 1893[14] and for wounding a horse in 1896.[15] He prosecuted section foreman William McTaggart for shooting his pigs which had broken into the C.P.R. garden in 1893[16] and also prosecuted James Shouldice, C.P.R. telegraph repairer, for assault.[17] Early in 1896 he was made Licence Commissioner.[18] Knight also received his reward on being elevated from Justice of the Peace to Stipendiary Magistrate,[19] later being also made Inspector of Fisheries for the district.[20]

Several other appointments, some minor, others not, were made to the party faithful during these years. When Neil McDonald, Justice of the Peace, left Swift Current in 1892, Andrew Patterson, staunch Conservative and C.P.R. locomotive foreman, received the appointment of Justice of the Peace.[21] Later, in 1897, he also became Commissioner of Oaths.[22] William Rutherford, a fellow Conservative, held the post of Liquor Licence Commissioner from 1893 to 1895.[23] To promote settlement during the mid-1880's in what became south-western Saskatchewan, the Conservative government at Ottawa appointed as Immigration Agent at Swift Current a party supporter named J. A. Grant.[24] In view of the extent of patronage in the civil service at this time, it is probable that the first Dominion Lands agents at Swift Current were also political appointees. Certainly this was the case when the Laurier Liberal government placed William Milburn, their supporter, in charge of the newly-opened sub-agency office in 1903.[25] James T. Dodds, who was made a J.P. in 1903[26] and a Homestead Inspector in 1906[27] by the federal Liberals, was a prominent supporter of that party.[28] The federal positions of mail contractor, meteorological observer and later postmaster at Swift Current would certainly have changed hands after the federal Liberals defeated the Conservatives in 1896, but for another development. Walter G. Knight, the Conservative appointee, had died in 1895. His widow carried on his jobs, but then, early in 1897, married a declared Liberal, the Mountie, William Vaudreuil.[29] As the wife of a Liberal supporter, Mrs. M. Vaudreuil was safe in her positions.

Perhaps the most interesting example of political activity and patronage in the district concerned the beginning of the local newspaper. The *Swift Current Sun* first appeared late in 1903.[30] B. F. Merton, a Liberal who edited and published this paper from Maple Creek, also published the *Maple Creek Signal*.[31] The building which housed these two newspapers was owned by John Dixon,[32] merchant and Liberal postmaster at Maple Creek, who ran as Liberal candidate in the 1905 Saskatchewan election.[33] Walter Scott, Liberal M.P. for Assiniboia West in 1904, had promptly arranged a place for the *Swift Current Sun* on the government patronage list for future advertising.[34] At the Dominion Day celebration in Swift Current in 1904, Merton met a young Boer War veteran, Milwarde Yates, then ranching near the village. In conversation, Merton told Yates that he wanted to go to Banff with his "sister" for a long overdue vacation, but had no one to edit the two newspapers in his absence. He offered the job to Yates who impulsively accepted.[35] Soon after his vacation, Merton left the area and Yates continued as editor. A Liberal himself, he threw all the influence of both newspapers behind Walter Scott in the federal election campaign of 1904. In addition, he made several trips on horse-back to round up more Liberal votes. That fall, Scott handily defeated his Conservative opponent, George M. Annable.[36] Always mindful of past favors, Scott then wrote to Clifford Sifton, minister in charge of the R.N.W.M.P., recommending that Yates be given an Inspectorship in the Mounties,[37] but Sifton could not grant this request.

Yates, meanwhile, had taken in George W. Bilbrough, a Liberal friend[38] and former ranching companion, to act for a time as representative of the *Sun* in Swift Current. The village was then growing rapidly. This, plus the urging of Charles Reid, who offered space above his newly-built store to house the printing plant, persuaded Yates to leave Maple Creek in the spring of 1905 and begin to publish the *Sun* in Swift Current.[39] That

Col. William Milwarde Yates, as a junior officer before leaving Swift Current to go overseas to the First World War in 1914.

year, with the creation of the Province of Saskatchewan, another election loomed to fill its first legislature. Yates's continued loyalty to the Liberals was rewarded by Walter Scott, M.P., arranging that the federal government would continue to place Homestead Regulation advertisements in his paper.[40] But Yates, tiring of the newspaper business, was formulating a scheme to sell the *Sun* at a good profit.

Swift Current had a small but zealous Conservative group, determined to elect their candidate, David J. (Joe) Wylie, a Maple Creek rancher, as their first provincial M.L.A. Yates knew that his newspaper (there were only two others in the constituency) would have a significant local influence in the campaign and that its value to the politically-minded would be increased as a result. In June, soon after Wylie's nomination, Yates wrote an editorial calling for the fielding of an Independent candidate to oppose him.[41] In view of the traditional lack of solidarity among the Conservatives, this would probably have resulted in a serious split in their vote. The Liberals, more united on the prairies in these years, had nominated John Dixon. Fearing the loss of support, local Conservatives asked Yates to sell the *Sun* to them, but he refused their offer. Instead, he fixed an exorbitant price at which they balked. Carrying out his plan, Yates continued his newspaper campaign against Joe Wylie. He climaxed it early that fall with a blistering attack on the Conservatives (Provincial Rights Party), led by Frederick W. G. Haultain[42] and a renewed call for an Independent candidate. This turned the trick. The local Conservative group decided that they must meet Yates's price. With pretended reluctance, Yates accepted, but not before stipulating that he be permitted to hold some stock in the company to be formed.[43] As a result, that fall The Sun Printing and Publishing Co. Ltd. was incorporated.[44] Besides Yates, its shareholders included Charles Reid, Andrew Patterson, William Sanders, W. H. Patterson, George Webster, and the Conservative candidate himself, Joe Wylie.[45] Yates had achieved his purpose, but the Conservatives soon realized theirs. The *Swift Current Sun,* now under new editorship, campaigned hard for Joe Wylie, who won the seat in the election on December 13, 1905, despite a Liberal victory in the province. In revenge, the new premier, Walter Scott, wrote to Ottawa to have the *Sun* immediately taken off the federal Liberal government's patronage list.[46] Thus, in the first two years of its existence, the *Sun* had helped to elect first a Liberal M.P. and then a Conservative M.L.A.

The fact that civil servants of the large governments — federal, territorial and provincial — owed their positions to political patronage seemingly did not bother the average citizen of the Swift Current district — at least, no more than it did Canadians generally. Perhaps they realized that political patronage had existed in some form since man first devised government. They may also have known that there were advantages to the public in having patronage dispensed by an elected governing party, rather than by one that was neither responsible to, nor elected by, the people. At least the democratic process held forth the promise to supporters of major rival political parties that they could hope for a share in the fruits of office. Some citizens may have felt that a reward was due to those who gave their time and money to elect a party to power and who thereby risked losing trade in their business or profession from others who championed a rival cause. Whatever may have been their reason for acquiescence, there is no record of any local protest against the "spoils system". Apparently, it was enough that their political appointees had been selected by the party in office as being the most suitable of the available supporters desiring a minor local position. However, even the senior government posts beyond the district, which required skill, experience and impartiality, were usually filled by political appointees, and there were frequent complaints that these people were incompetent and sometimes corrupt, as well. But, possibly because the local government jobs were minor in nature and required little skill or ability, this sort of complaint was not heard in the district. Efforts had been made at Ottawa as early as 1882 to reform the civil service, but patronage was not reduced. The most forward step towards reform came in 1908, in the form of a Civil Service Commission that provided for competitive examinations before appointments to many positions in the federal civil service.[47] Still, until 1908, and for some time afterward, civil servants locally and elsewhere received their appointments through patronage. Under these circumstances, it may seem surprising to those opposed to political patronage that so sensitive and important a service as law enforcement and the administration of justice, locally, was successful. The explanation may be that political appointees in this field were especially well chosen by the government party, or perhaps it was only the absence of serious crime in the district before 1907, as well as the law-abiding character of the citizens, which made law enforcement relatively easy.

Enforcing the law in this sparsely-settled prairie region required many of the same qualities in the Mountie as were needed by a pioneer settler. As with the rancher and cowboy, a Mountie had to be able to withstand the long, lonely hours of riding patrol. He needed a rugged constitution, a responsible attitude, a willingness to endure discomfort, and at least enough courage to face up to fighting a prairie fire or forcing his way through a blizzard. And like the cowboys, he had to enjoy the demanding life he led, for his pay was no better. Every pioneer community had its misfits and the Force was no exception. Two such constables deserted from Swift Current in April, 1905, and headed for New Zealand ". . . in search of a better climate."[48] But generally, the Swift Current district and the Canadian West were fortunate in the calibre of Mountie which they had in these years. Many of them, upon receiving their grant of a quarter-section of land when their term of service ended, settled in the country they had come to love.

A Mountie's life, in this district at least, was not glamorous. In fact, most police duties were dull routine. For example, soon after the 1885 rebellion, it was ordered that a Mountie must escort the mail over the Swift Current-Battleford trail.[49] Constable William Milburn often handled this uneventful task until the authorities, realizing that the Indians and half-breeds were no longer a threat, withdrew the mail guard. Another Mountie, William Vaudreuil, who, like Milburn, finally quit the force to settle locally, was stationed along the trail at Saskatchewan Landing until that police post was closed in 1891 as being no longer necessary.[50] By this time, even the most panicky white settler had ceased to fear another native uprising.

The ordinary duties of the police included checking for prairie fires (two Mennonite farmers were fined in 1905 when they refused to help fight a prairie fire[51]), keeping an eye on the Indians locally (they only once gave trouble when, in 1886, the police had to use force to get a wandering group to return to their reserve[52]), handling minor cases of theft, enforcing the game act, ordering the destruction of diseased livestock, apprehending those who stole rides on the C.P.R. (especially during the Klondike gold rush in 1897), and meeting all passenger and freight trains to search for illegal drugs or liquor. Once, in May, 1891, the Mounties seized and destroyed at Swift Current a huge underworld drug shipment — almost two hundred pounds of opium,[53] possibly destined for Butte, Montana, then an American sin-city. Some of the N.W.M.P. also presided over court cases. The legendary Mountie, Sam Steele, later knighted, reported that on several occasions during and soon after the building of the C.P.R. through the district, he judged court cases at Swift Current while seated on a Red River cart. He placed a plank across it to serve as a bench and took down the evidence from the trial on the flap of his despatch bag.[54]

Police duty in the Swift Current district had its occasional exciting moments, despite the fact that no serious crimes involving local settlers are reported to have occurred in the first quarter-century of the community's existence. However, on five occasions in these years the Mounties were required to apprehend livestock rustlers near Swift Current — in all but one of these cases they were American thieves who had stolen horses in Montana.[55] The most dramatic incident of the four occurred in 1884 when three supposedly dangerous Montana cowboys with a band of horses made camp near Swift Current. Corporals Fyffe and Davidson of the local N.W.M.P. detachment decided to investigate the ownership of the horses, despite the cowboys' threats warning everyone to stay away from their camp. Unperturbed, the two Mounties rode in and seized twelve horses that appeared to fit the description of animals reported missing from Montana. Returning to Swift Current, they telegraphed to Montana, where the suspected identity of the animals was verified. At once, they galloped back to arrest the leader of the gang, an outlaw named Sam James. Seeing the corporals coming, this horse thief, despite his earlier bravado, chose to flee rather than fight. Hot in pursuit, the two policemen caught him after an hour's race across the prairie, disarmed him, and took him to divisional headquarters at Maple Creek.[56]

On another occasion, this time in the winter of 1898, the local Mounties captured an American couple who were wanted by the police at Boston, Mass., for grand larceny. Acting on information from the U.S., the two Mounties who made up the Swift Current detachment boarded the passenger train when it stopped at the station. The suspects were in one of the staterooms, possibly armed. When called upon by the police to open the door to their compartment, the Americans refused. Without hesitation, the Mounties broke open the door. Inside, they found Abraham Tibbitts, a woman supposed to be his wife, and $30,000 worth of stolen money, bonds and jewelry. The culprits and their loot were promptly taken into custody and returned to the U.S. authorities.[57] Thanks to the Mounties, the Canadian West was not to become a safe haven for American criminals.

The single incident where the police arrested district citizens who were convicted of livestock rustling occurred in April, 1907. A group of half-breeds living around Lac Pelletier were caught stealing and killing cattle by the Mounties' "flying patrol". The gang leader was none other than Solomon Pritchard, the half-breed who had been a witness of the Frog Lake Massacre and, afterwards, a prisoner of the Cree chief, Big Bear, during the 1885 rebellion. Pritchard was sentenced to three years in Edmonton Penitentiary, while his métis confederates received shorter prison terms.[58]

In dealing with the liquor problem, the police had only modest success. Virtual prohibition prevailed in the Territories until 1892 and in the Swift Current district until its two new hotels opened licenced barrooms in 1904. However, some special permits were issued by the Territorial Government entitling the privileged holder to import liquor for his own use. This system of quasi-prohibition was fraught with difficulties. It was easy enough to arrest a drunk, but it was much harder to prevent people from drinking illegally. In 1890, C. C. McKenzie, a Scot in the employ of the "76" and a man with a thirst for his native whisky, was prosecuted by Hubert Pelham Clinton, the local "76" ranch manager, for stealing coupons from Clinton's permit book.[59] Several arrests and heavy fines, especially of métis, for illegally selling or possessing liquor were meted out from 1884 to 1887 at Swift Current in an attempt to enforce prohibition.[60] Determined violators merely became more crafty. For example, in January, 1884, the Mounties seized a suspicious looking barrel, allegedly containing onions, which was consigned to an unknown W. Wilson of Swift Current. Inside the barrel was a partly full keg of whisky which at once explained the recent boisterous behavior of a certain C.P.R. section foreman and a fellow employee. Both men were promptly fined and fired.[61] The police destroyed a whisky distillery in the Cypress Hills in 1885,[62] and another twenty-two gallons of illicit liquor at Swift Current in 1886.[63] Despite these actions by the Mounties, those who sought liquor in order to escape the loneliness and drudgery of their lives frequently found means of getting it. A tragic example was the ex-Mountie named Jamieson who committed suicide in the coalshed behind the C.P.R. dining hall at Swift Current in 1891 after a drinking bout.[64]

The people of the district were generally divided into two groups, those that championed temperance (which meant prohibition) and those who opposed it. The fact that liquor was both illegal and scarce, caused even those who might otherwise have been moderate drinkers to drink to excess whenever the opportunity to do so presented itself. Sometimes the hard liquor that they got was cheap "home-brew" of dubious quality. Since a man faced a stiff fine if caught possessing illegal liquor, he often resorted to destroying all the evidence in one drunken binge. In a frontier community where women were few and rarely drank, their moderating influence was absent from these drinking parties. Those men who possessed only a thin veneer of civilization shed it on these occasions and violence frequently occurred, often ending with police arrests. The resulting notoriety provided the advocates of temperance with powerful ammunition to fire at any who proposed liberalizing the drinking laws of the Territories. Sixteen such "prohibitionists" formed a Royal Templar Council in Swift Current in 1894 which they named after the recently deceased Alfred Fenton, C.P.R. agent and member of the Methodist Church, who had championed the cause of temperance.[65] The Protestant churches, generally, led the forces in the Territories that were opposed to the liquor trade. But during most of these years a large number of the people, including many of those responsible for enforcing the law, were unfavorable to prohibition.

The beliefs and attitudes which the first settlers brought with them to the district were perhaps more important in the shaping of the nature of their new society than were either their skills or their material possessions. That was evident in their attitudes to the institutions of government, politics and law, and was reflected as well in their attitude to religious matters.

A profile of the religious affiliation of residents of the district may be sketched in a general way from figures given in the census reports.[66] In 1885, the total population of the huge region in the electoral district of Assiniboia West lying between the third and fourth meridians (including all of south-western Saskatchewan) of which the Swift Current district forms the nucleus, was 828. Of these, the largest group was Roman Catholic, numbering 283. Of the six Protestant groups then present, the Church of England (Anglicans) were the largest, with 213 adherents, followed by the Presbyterians with 133 and the Methodists with sixty-six.[67] The other Protestant denominations numbered only a few each — Lutherans with twenty-four, Baptists with seven and Congregationalists with only four adherents. Except for the Lutherans, the latter were never numerically significant before 1907 either in this vast south-western region or in the Swift Current district. The 1885 census listed ninety-seven "heathens" in this region;[68] apparently they were non-Christian Indians residing, for the most part, in the Wood Mountain area south-east of Swift Current.

The Roman Catholics were probably made up of almost all of the 139 half-breeds or métis, as well as the majority of the ninety-nine Indians[69] listed as Christians, plus about fifty white settlers. Neither the Roman Catholic nor any other religious organization had built a church with a resident priest or minister in the entire region or in the Swift Current district by 1885.[70] For the Catholics living around Swift Current, services were conducted among them from 1884 to 1890 by travelling priests from St. Mary's in Regina. Then, from 1890 until 1905, when their first resident priest arrived, they received visits from the Fathers at Medicine Hat. The first Christian baptism in the district was performed by Father Larche when on May 7, 1884, he baptized Marie-Emilie Desjarlais, a métis. Father Graton presided at the first Christian burial, that of a seventy year old métis, Jean-Baptiste Adam, at Swift Current on May 14, 1887. A Catholic couple were married and six others were confirmed when they came to meet their travelling priest at the railway hamlet in 1887.[71]

The Roman Catholic population in the region, and presumably in the Swift Current district, declined slightly between 1885 and 1891. The birth rate and Catholic immigration during these years apparently was not quite sufficient to offset the exodus of Indian and métis Catholics. By 1901, the Catholics in the district were still the numerically largest Christian group,[72] but they had maintained their positon mainly through natural increase, rather than through immigration. Moreover, only a few of the new settlers who arrived in the district during the following few years were Roman Catholics. While Father Claude Passaplan arrived in Swift Current in 1905 as resident pastor of the tiny congregation, he left that fall for Lac Pelletier, where he spent the winter living in a cave on the east side of the lake and ministering to the métis nearby. The following spring he began building a chapel in the hamlet on Railway Street property that his church had acquired earlier, but he was unable to complete the structure that year. Once again, he spent the winter in his cave at Lac Pelletier, returning to the town the following spring to hold regular services in the old school, for he still lacked support to complete the chapel.[73] Had he and the other priests who had served the area spoken English rather than French as a mother tongue, possibly the support from the few English-speaking Catholics in the town would have matched that of the métis in the countryside. But during these years English-speaking priests for the new Western settlements could not be secured in sufficient numbers by the Catholic hierarchy.[74] This factor may partly explain why it was 1912 before the Catholics succeeded in building a church in the town.[75]

Even in 1885, when the Roman Catholics were the largest group in both the region and the district, the Protestant Christians were over half again as numerous. This ratio increased until there were two and one-half times as many Protestants as Catholics by 1891, and it remained constant through the 1901 census,[76] due mainly to the small number of new Roman Catholic settlers arriving. Part of the reason for this was the departure of many métis and Indians both from the area and the district when hunting, cart freighting and bone gathering declined. Between 1901 and 1907, though, some Catholics did settle around Swift Current and Gull Lake, which offset the continued departure of the Catholic natives in these years. Still, the overwhelming majority of the thousands of settlers arriving in these years was Protestant.

The dominant Protestant church during the first quarter-century of the district's existence was the Presbyterian. While it is true that in 1885 there were a few more Church of England (Anglican) supporters in the region and district than Presbyterians, by 1891 their position had reversed. Part of the reason for this was probably the new trend to hiring Scots rather than Englishmen by the "76" ranch. But more important would have been the erection of the first church in the Swift Current district by the Presbyterians in 1889.[77]

The first Christian churchman to visit Swift Current was Dr. James Robertson, Superintendent of Missions for the Presbyterian Church. He visited the hamlet one day in May, 1883,[78] less than one month after the railway had begun to carry passengers over the newly-built line. By early 1886, Dr. Robertson had appointed Swift Current's first resident preacher, the Presbyterian missionary, W. Malcolm, of the Regina presbytery. Malcolm held a total of forty-five regular services, usually in the C.P.R. dining hall, for the eleven families in his congregation who, in turn, contributed the niggardly sum of $29.00 towards his support.[79] As was the case with the Roman Catholics, Anglicans and Methodists in the district during those years, the Presbyterians continued to receive the services of a travelling minister without contributing sufficient to maintain him. Perhaps it was as a result of this that in 1888-89 the Presbyterian missionary, W. A. Markley, helped support himself by teaching school at Swift Current.[80]

The local Presbyterians were the first to succeed in building a church in the district. This was also the first Presbyterian church between Moose Jaw and Medicine Hat. Six C.P.R. employees donated their labor and, with the help of a local merchant, raised the $700 which the frame church cost to build. On July 3, 1889, the 200 seat capacity Knox Church was dedicated by the pastor in charge, Rev. William Moffat.[81] Before long, funds were raised locally to buy for the church an organ costing $350.[82] In addition to the weekly services, prayer meetings, Sunday school and Bible classes were held in the new house of worship. The congregation that year contributed $89 of the $134 yearly stipend raised for their minister, who also served a congregation at Maple Creek.[83] Support for Knox Church continued to grow in the community, partly because it was the only church that a Christian could attend, but also because by 1892 it had become the centre of its own mission field, with its resident minister regularly preaching at four other railway points from Rush Lake westward almost as far as

Maple Creek.[84] Despite the prevailing economic depression in these years, the congregation, which numbered seventy, now paid the full stipend of $250 a year to their minister.[85] Since the total population living in Swift Current, or close enough to it to easily attend church services, was probably close to one hundred at this time, it is evident that people of many Christian backgrounds attended Sunday services to worship in this, the only church available. By coming together in a church of any denomination, the pioneers were able to stave off a measure of loneliness. Rumor has it that there were even English-speaking Roman Catholics singing in the Presbyterian church choir! In any event, an ecumenical spirit did prevail for a time in Swift Current. This, like the pioneer's willingness to help his neighbor, stemmed partly from necessity and self-interest. It was also an early indication of the strong support prairie Protestants would give to the church union movement already gaining momentum in 1902.

By 1907 Knox Church was still the biggest at Swift Current and had the largest congregation.[86] Moreover, this church group was in the best financial position, for in 1899 they had received patent to a forty acre gift of land which adjoined the townsite on the east side.[87] By 1907, this property was well within the town limits and was rapidly increasing in value.

Like the Presbyterians and Catholics, the Anglicans in the Swift Current district received visits from a missionary for several years before they built their own church and were given a resident priest. In 1884, the Diocese of Assiniboia (later Qu'Appelle) was established, and the Reverend J. P. Sargent of St. John the Baptist Church in Moose Jaw began conducting Anglican services on alternate Sundays at Swift Current, either in the C.P.R. dining hall or in private homes.[88] The 1885 census shows that there were 213 Anglican adherents living in what is now south-western Saskatchewan, making them the next largest denomination to the Catholics.[89] By 1891, as a result of immigration and an excess of births over deaths, the Anglicans numbered 250.[90] However, in the Swift Current district it is doubtful that the Anglicans did more than maintain their 1885 membership level, for the Presbyterians had the only church building at Swift Current and were recruiting new members. The fact that Anglican church work in the West was still under the direct control of the Church of England in Britain and was short of men and money was probably another factor which limited the size of the Church of England congregation.[91] The Anglicans were granted permission to hold services in Knox Church during most of the 1890's. Like the Presbyterians, they also received as a private donation a parcel of forty acres of land beside the townsite. It was patented to the Synod of the Diocese of Qu'Appelle in 1896.[92] Two years later, the local Anglicans, led by the Reverend T. W. Cunliffe, began to build at Swift Current a small frame church which cost almost $700.[93] The finished church building, named Saint Stephen's, was dedicated on April 25, 1899.[94] By 1901, the Anglicans had increased in numbers throughout the Swift Current district until they were slightly more numerous than the Presbytcrians (127 to 120).[95] This was in marked contrast to the entire federal electoral district of Assiniboia West, where Anglican numbers declined from being the second largest religious group in 1891 to the fourth largest in 1901, while the Presbyterians were the largest group in both periods.[96] Still, the Anglicans by 1901 were beginning to improve their position throughout western Canada. This was a result of the formation in 1893 of a General Synod of the Church of England in Canada, followed by the creation of their new Missionary Society in 1901 which was charged with vigorously campaigning in the Canadian West.[97] The combination of these factors brought about the appointment in 1903 of a priest, the Reverend G. Stillwell, as Vicar of Swift Current. He helped to build his own vicarage and organized the first Anglican Sunday school, also finding time to homestead south of the village. He was succeeded in 1906 by the Reverend Charles Wright, who travelled extensively with horse and buggy throughout his huge parish to hold services and establish new missions.[98]

Of the four major church groups holding services in Swift Current before 1907, the Methodists were the smallest until about 1905, when their numbers increased dramatically due to the start of the land settlement boom which brought many Methodists, mainly from Ontario. The local Methodists were served by a travelling missionary from 1883[99] until 1903 when they received their first resident minister, the Reverend G. W. Laverick.[100] Records indicate that the number of Methodists in the Swift Current area more than doubled between 1885 and 1891, then gradually increased to fifty-seven by 1901.[101] Immigration to the district from eastern Canada and England may account for the rapid increase during the early period. However, by 1901 there were only eighteen Methodists living in or close to Swift Current, while thirty Methodists resided on the eastern edge of the district in the Chaplin census area.[102] At Swift Current itself, it appears that during these years the Methodists lost numbers to the Presbyterian congregation. In the whole of Assiniboia West the Methodists had risen from being the third largest religious group in 1891 to that of second largest in 1901.[103]

Soon after the Presbyterians built Knox Church in 1889, the Methodists, like the Anglicans, were granted permission to hold fortnightly services there. This led to the establishment of a Union Sunday school in Knox Church, supported by the local Presbyterians and Methodists, as well as some Anglicans. Christmas concerts and special functions were jointly conducted in this way. For example, on July 1, 1893, the Union Sunday school sponsored a large picnic and sports event ending with a fireworks display. It attracted 400 people[104] — much more than the entire population of the district! This is the first recorded celebration of Dominion Day at Swift Current. It is also evident that the western leaders, Dr. James Robertson and Dr. James Woodsworth of the Presbyterian and Methodist churches, had brought to the local level their belief that their churches should promote, along with religious ideals, the development of Canadian identity among the diverse peoples in the West.[105]

This demonstration of the ecumenical spirit, partly born of necessity, ended when the Anglicans built their own church in 1899. At about the same time, the Methodists also withdrew from the Union Sunday school to establish one of their own under the leadership of Andrew Patterson, who became the choirmaster.[106]

The Methodists received the leadership of a dynamic resident minister in 1904, when the Reverend William K. Allen of Ontario arrived to take charge of the Swift Current mission. Property had been purchased on the corner of Railway Street and Thirteenth Avenue (Second Avenue North-East) late in 1903, and an unsuccessful effort had been made to raise funds for a church building. Finally, the Reverend Allen was able to arrange a small loan, and a tiny frame church with a capacity of only 100, and costing $900, was dedicated in January, 1905. Under their new minister's guidance, the Methodist congregation increased from twenty members in 1904 to seventy in the spring of 1907, by which time it was also free of debt.[107]

The Mennonite farmers who arrived in the district between 1904 and 1907 quickly demonstrated the priority which they gave to their church and religion. Barely two months after the arrival of the first fifteen Mennonite settlers in the spring of 1904, this little group had built and dedicated a small frame church.[108] Similar rural churches were quickly built by the hundreds of Mennonites who followed them into the district in the next three years. These people, mostly members of the strongly evangelical Mennonite Brethern group, were generally devout and strict in the observance of their faith. By the spring of 1907, they were easily the largest church group in the district, and they represented almost one-half of the total population, though they lived exclusively on farms in two main settlement areas.

In the town of Swift Current, meanwhile, there were only three churches, with a combined capacity of about 400 people. The town's population, made up mainly of adherents to these churches, was double this figure, while the surrounding district contained a great many more Presbyterians, Anglicans, and Methodist adherents than these churches could possibly hold — if all the people wished to attend. Just as the Swift Current citizens, through their local governments from 1897 to 1907, refused to spend sufficient money to provide themselves with so many important public facilities, so, too, were they unwilling to either donate or borrow enough to erect adequate church buildings. They seem to have lacked sufficient faith in the district or in themselves, or perhaps did not take too seriously their responsibility as Christians to practise and propagate their faith.

Just as one can only speculate as to how much religious instruction and worship was carried on in the home, one is similarly left to guess at the extent to which district children were educated in school subjects by their parents. Before the fall of 1886 — more than three years after a substantial white settlement had begun at Swift Current — there was still no school for the district children.[109] For these local youngsters, there were only two alternatives. Either they received some formal education at home or they went without it. Some of the parents — the few non-treaty Indians, and to a lesser extent, the métis — can be excused for not providing a school for their children on the grounds of poverty or tradition. The federal government cannot so easily be forgiven, for it did not provide aid to make it possible for these native people to attend school without requiring them to exchange their freedom for the confinement of a reserve. As for the white citizens, apparently they believed that the education of the young was the sole responsibility of their parents, for publicly-supported public education was successfully opposed by a group of local taxpayers until as late as 1889.[110]

A private school, receiving supplementary aid from the territorial government,[111] was opened at Swift Current in the fall of 1886. The children of the C.P.R. employees made up nearly all of its first enrolment; the teacher was the wife of Thomas Rooks, the C.P.R. baggageman;[112] the C.P.R. provided the school building, a railway box car set upon the ground[113] — probably the same one used by the Canadian Militia for a temporary base hospital during the Riel Rebellion. The closing exercises of this school, held on July 4, 1887, were marked by the awarding of prizes for good conduct, spelling, reading, writing and arithmetic, followed by a lively program of entertainment that involved most of the adult population of the hamlet as well as guests from Medicine Hat.[114] The recitations, songs and dancing were interrupted at midnight when young and old sat down together to a fine meal, after which the happy gathering danced until three in the morning.[115]

This private school continued until a public school district was finally formed at the end of 1889. Miss Martha Kerr, who was also vice-president of the Teachers' Association of Western Assiniboia, taught in this school from the fall of 1887 until the summer of 1889.[116] She was followed by the Presbyterian missionary, W. A. Markley, in the autumn of 1889. That same year, local citizens attempted to organize a school district, but in doing so they made some technical error which enabled a rival group opposed to taxation for school purposes, possibly led by Sir John Lister-Kaye's company, to have the proceedings set aside for a time. However, on December 24, 1889, those residents desiring a tax-supported Protestant public school succeeded in passing a motion requesting the territorial government to establish a school district with boundaries extending to the section lines one mile north, two miles east and west and four miles south of the hamlet. By extending the boundaries much more to the south than to the north, most of the land near Swift Current that was owned by Lister-Kaye's "76" ranch was subject to school tax. As a result, the "76" company had to pay a large part of school taxes levied. The Christmas Eve meeting elected as trustees William Smillie, of the C.P.R. section house, Samuel J. Curry, a pioneer merchant, and Alfred E. Fenton, the C.P.R. agent. The latter became the first secretary-treasurer of the newly-created Swift Current School District No. 167.[117] A tax rate of three mills on the $74,295 of assessable property provided a revenue of $105.06 in 1890.[118] Markley, who held a third class teaching certificate, continued as teacher until the summer of 1890. His school inspector reported that the subjects of reading, spelling, arithmetic and ethics were being offered to all of the dozen or so students, while composition, writing, grammar, geography and history were given to only some. Markley was rated as only a "fair" teacher.[119] He was replaced in 1890 by Mrs. Elgan McCargar, who held a second class teaching certificate, taught an improved and much expanded curriculum of thirteen subjects, had a student enrolment that had increased by over one-half and received a rating of "good" from her inspector. Yet, she was paid only $45.00 a month, while Markely had received for his teaching a monthly salary of $58.33.[120]

Around this time, the school trustees enlarged the old railway car to a size of sixteen by twenty-four feet, added a peaked roof and a tiny porch and painted it brown. It looked like a granary with windows. A student of the 1890's stated that the half-breed children attended this school only irregularly, for their families moved to Lac Pelletier for part of each year.[121] Another former student of the school recalls that there were no more than thirty pupils in attendance and that the school was not crowded until the wave of settlers began to arrive in 1903.[122] By the spring of 1904, there were fifty-nine students enrolled in the one-room school, although, because of crowding, they could not all attend.[123]

The rural school district had become a village district on May 14, 1903, several months before Swift Current was incorporated as a village. The rapid growth in population, beginning in the spring of 1903, had prompted the school trustees to consider building a new school house.[124] A ratepayers' vote on the issue of building a $3,000.00 school was held that summer, but no one voted — not even the trustees, for they thought that they were ineligible to do so![125] Consequently, the entire procedure had to be gone through again early in the next year. Meanwhile, the district was beginning to be settled by farmers. This time by a unanimous vote, the ratepayers approved in principle the trustees' plan to spend up to $6,500.00 to construct an even better school than the one proposed the year before. If the N.W.T. government gave the necessary permission, W. H. McLean, the chairman, and Donald Coons, the treasurer of the school board, advised that the board would borrow the entire sum by issuing a debenture, and the old C.P.R. box car school would be replaced by a fine, two-storey, four room, brick veneer school with a stone foundation, measuring thirty-six by fifty-eight feet.[126] The lower two rooms would be immediately used for school purposes and the other two would serve, temporarily, as a public hall. Plans and specifications were drawn for the building, and public tenders were invited.[127]

At this point, D. H. Andrews, manager of the Canadian Land and Ranche Company ("76"), launched a successful protest to the territorial Department of Education which, together with the unfavorable recommendations of the school inspector from Maple Creek, caused the government to withhold its consent to the issue of the required debenture. Andrews pointed out that when the school district had been formed it had included a square block of twenty-five sections with Swift Current situated in the middle of the most northerly row of five sections, rather than in the geographic centre of the district, as he and the original opposition group felt it should have been. Andrews urged that the north and south boundaries be moved two miles north, which would free ten sections of his company's land from school tax. Furthermore, he declared that the cost of the new school was at least twice too much.[128] The school inspector, William Rothwell, in his report of April 29, 1904, agreed that some type of new school house was needed at Swift Current, but in all other respects, his report supported the arguments put forth by Andrews. He stated that the trustees felt that if they lost the right to continue taxing most of the "76" ranch, then the ratepayers would not wish to construct the fine building as planned. Rothwell's short-sighted view was that it would be many years before Swift Current would need more than two school rooms.[129] As a result, the N.W.T. Department of Education failed to approve the $6,500.00 loan, and further advised the school trustees to scale down their plans and to revise the school district boundaries (in line with Andrews' recommendation) before requesting further permission to borrow for school construction purposes.[130]

To those trustees who had hoped to secure the proposed school (which would have been the finest building in the village) and to have almost one-quarter of its cost paid for by taxing the "76" ranch, this must have been a keen disappointment. Still, they recognized the need for prompt action, so they quickly altered the school district boundaries, as outlined.[131] Next, they drew plans for a cheaper, one-storey, metal-clad frame school, with cottage roof and a stone foundation, measuring only twenty-two by thirty-six feet. J. T. Dodds, the school board secretary, informed the Department of Education that the ratepayers had approved the expenditure of $2,000.00 for construction, so the government sanctioned the necessary loan.[132] This building was then promptly built, but, as the trustees and the ratepayers had correctly foreseen, within a year this structure, plus the old box car school which was still in use, were totally inadequate to accommodate the school population that had grown to 115 pupils. The school inspector was forced to recommend the hiring of a third teacher, just as soon as space permitted.

For a fourth time within three years the Swift Current School Board was obliged to draw up proposals, hold a ratepayers' meeting and formulate plans for a new school. On February 15, 1906, the ratepayers were almost unanimous in approving the building of a two-storey, concrete

SWIFT CURRENT'S EARLY SCHOOLS. On the left, the one-roomed school built in the early 1890's from part of the first school house (a railway boxcar). At the right, the two-roomed school built in 1904. In the centre, the concrete block school with four classrooms, opened in 1907, and which, until 1975, was part of the W. A. Beatty Collegiate.

block school, measuring sixty feet square. Initially, only four classrooms on the ground floor were to be equipped; the upper floor was to be rented as a hall until required for school purposes. Donald Coons, the secretary, who advised the Saskatchewan Minister of Education of the proposals, stated that the debenture debt of the school district was only $1,800.00 and asked to be assured that the board would be allowed to borrow up to $12,000.00 to construct and equip the school.[133] Again, as in 1904, opposition to the project developed, this time from a local merchant, W. W. Cooper, who was chairman of the school board! Not satisfied that his proposal to build a school only half as large had been rejected by the ratepayers' meeting held the previous month, he wrote to the Minister of Education on March 3, 1906, urging that the size of the proposed school be only sixty by thirty feet, with four classrooms. An addition increasing the school's size to sixty feet square could be added later, he argued, for it would be at least four or five more years, he confidently (and wrongly) predicted, before more space would be needed.[134] Despite all that had gone before, it was this private advice that the new provincial government acted upon! A debenture for only $10,000.00 was authorized on April 24, 1906.[135]

TABLE 3

School Districts Formed in the Swift Current Region[a]
1904—Spring, 1907[b]

Year	Name	No.	Location
1904	Eby	1026	near Swift Current
1904	Herbert	1075	Herbert
1904	Enz	1099	near Herbert
1904	Prairieville	1115	five miles north of Swift Current
1905	Beverley	1172	Beverley
1905	Lobethal	1290	near Main Centre
1905	Turnhill	1470	north-east of Rush Lake
1906	Reed Valley	1522	near Herbert
1906	Flats	1602	near Success
1906	Bethania	1626	near Herbert
1906	Pleasant Hill	1665	near Swift Current
1906	Rockside	1689	in the Rush Lake-Herbert area
1907	Waldeck	1718	Waldeck
1907	Gull Lake	1748	Gull Lake
1907	Cut Bank	1822	close to Burnham

[a]Area defined by Map 1, p. 4.
[b]A. S., Chronological Roll of School Districts.

Once new plans were drawn and a contractor's bid for $17,000.00 was accepted, construction got under way late in 1906. Meanwhile, crowding in the two small frame schools was so acute that the local school board had to adopt the half-day system for some of the classes.[136] Late in the spring of 1907, the new building, called Central School (later the front portion of the Swift Current Collegiate Institute), was ready to receive its first students.[137] Among the members of its first teaching staff was Miss Annie Jackson, who had begun teaching in Swift Current in 1905.[138]

In the surrounding district, with the upsurge in settlement, a similar need for schools arose. To meet this need, from the beginning of 1904 to the spring of 1907, no less than fifteen new school districts were formed in the Swift Current region (see Table 3 on page 149). Yet only about one-third of these school districts, among them Bethania, Turnhill[139] and Prairie-ville,[140] had their one-room schoolhouses built and operating by the spring of 1907.

On the western edge of the Swift Current district, at Gull Lake, a village was rapidly developing on a part of the former "76" ranch property that had been purchased in 1905 by the Gull Lake Land and Townsite Company.[141] School was held there during 1906 in one room of the big, old "76" ranch house until a two room school was built the following year. Miss Sarah Pennock, who had for several years worked in the C.P.R. station at Gull Lake, became its first school teacher.[142]

In the rural areas especially, the school house quickly became the centre for all community activities. These included church services, Sunday schools, dances, concerts, meetings of various organizations, funerals,

GULL LAKE, SASK

PART OF THE BUSINESS DISTRICT OF GULL LAKE *circa* SPRING, 1907.

weddings and receptions, bridal showers, farewell parties and patriotic observances.

The school, and to an even greater extent, the churches, taught brotherly love and helpfulness, which fostered a sense of community spirit. In this, these institutions were aided by the prairie environment which obliged a man to help his neighbor, if only to earn help in return. But there were other forces which opposed the development of this sense of community. The local agricultural economy was based upon the profitable production of livestock or grain for an export market. This drew each farmer and rancher into the *laissez-faire* capitalistic system of the day. The law supported and encouraged the institution of private property. It and the capitalistic system promoted within these people the philosophy of individualism. This, however, manifested itself almost exclusively in economic matters. In social matters, these pioneers of the ranching frontier displayed the practical, homespun virtue of Christian neighborliness. The highest praise one could win in the district went not to the wealthiest man but to the man who was known as a good neighbor.

From this survey of the major institutions in the district, it is clear that the citizens tended to be passive in their attitude to politics, government and law, and more actively involved in their church and school. As a consequence, they exercised more influence on the latter institutions than on the former. Those few people who were most aggressive and able were usually prominent both in the local Protestant churches and in politics. Their political activity, when their party was in power, often brought them patronage. In contrast, whether by design or otherwise, no Catholic resident ever received a political appointment during the district's first quarter-century. Possibly few, if any, district residents saw anything immoral in political patronage. If the local churches spoke out against it, then their criticism went unheeded and unrecorded.

One cannot know whether religion had a greater influence upon the daily lives of these people than had secular education, but it appears that their church building was less of a community centre than was the schoolhouse. The pioneers felt that the school belonged to all the citizens in the district. In addition, there was less restriction over its use. The school, itself, was a melting pot which helped to blend persons of diverse religions, languages and cultural backgrounds into a new people. Together with environmental forces and the law, with economic and political institutions and the Christian Church, the school fashioned Canadians with a prairie outlook.

Chapter IX

LIVING

The history of any region is the story of people — how they lived or died. Their endurance is the endurance of a district. If life is bearable, and offers hope and occasionally joy, they and it go on. If not, slowly or quickly, both die. In the study of a community, an historian — if his subjects are to be more than shadows in a dim past — must be concerned with the way in which people transcended the daily round of toil; how they worked out the closer relationships of life; and how they played. The statistical outlines of the population can be drawn — race, language, sex ratios, ages, marriages, births, housing, but these bold strokes need the color and highlighting of daily events and relationships to achieve a picture that is not of units but persons, and not of a collectivity but a community.

The best way to begin to gain some understanding of how the people in the Swift Current district lived in these early years is to start on the firmest ground possible — by analyzing census data. Yet even these records do not afford precise information about the people of the Swift Current district during the years before 1901, for the district then formed only the centre of two huge census districts encompassing all of what is now south-western Saskatchewan (see Note 66 for Chapter VIII for the methodology used in applying census data). Still, it is possible to generalize about many aspects of life in the Swift Current district from analyzing these data, for other records support the view that the district possessed an analogical character closely parallelling that of the huge region of which it was the central part.

In 1885, a total of 828 people lived in the huge area included in the Swift Current and Maple Creek census districts, and by 1891 their numbers had increased to 1009.[1] About one-quarter of these people in these years lived within the Swift Current district of this history. By 1901, the population of this district had reached just 400,[2] with practically all of these people living beside either the railway or the waterways (see Map 2, p. 4). About a half-dozen Indians were all that remained around Swift Current of the earlier Indian population.[3] The others had been driven inexorably to the reserves by an increasing scarcity of fish, game animals and buffalo bones, as well as the accelerating trend to ranch settlement. However, this exodus of Indians was more than offset by the trickle of white immigration after 1891 and by natural increase, which had also accounted for the gradual growth in population during the decade ending in 1901. Thereafter, the pace of local settlement quickened, until by 1906 there were 3,516 people residing in the district[4] — a phenomenal 879 per cent increase in five years!

Saskatchewan, meanwhile, had experienced a remarkable but much smaller increase of 282 per cent (see Table 4, below).

TABLE 4

Comparison of Population Increase and Sex Ratios of Swift Current District [a] and Saskatchewan (as part of the N.W.T.),[b] Census Years 1901, 1906[c]

	1901		1906		
	Males to 100 Females	Total pop.	Males to 100 Females	Total pop.	% Increase
S.C. District	153	400	155	3,516	879.00
(N.W.T.) Sask.	120	91,279	145	257,763	282.39

[a] Area defined by Map 2, p. 4.
[b] *S.P.,* 1907, No. 17a, Part I, pp. xi-xii.
[c] *S.P.,* 1906-7, No. 17a, Part I, pp. 28-31.

In language, from the beginning, both the surrounding region and the district had a polyglot nature. While in 1885 most of the people spoke English as a mother tongue, a substantial minority spoke French or an Indian language, with a few others speaking one of the Scandinavian languages. Almost one-half of the population then had been born in what later became Canada, while those born in Britain, followed by the U.S.-born, accounted for almost all the remainder.[5] In the decade closing in 1901, despite the decline in the small Indian population, language diversity continued, due to the arrival of a few settlers speaking Dutch or German.[6] At this point, two languages prevailed — English and French — with English being the language of business. Though both language groups in the district had grown in size (in the case of the French-speaking métis solely as a result of natural increase), by 1901 the English-speaking group was twice as large as the French.[7] However, so many German-speaking Mennonites arrived from 1904 to 1907, that German was, for a short time, the first language of the largest group in the district. It was closely followed by English, with French and Scandinavian languages being spoken by a small minority.

The frontiers of North America had always called loudest to young men; consequently throughout the huge region and in the district, as with other frontier communities, there were always more males than females. In the combined census districts of Maple Creek and Swift Current in 1885 there were 1.86 males for every female[8] and this disparity increased slightly until by 1891 there were 1.91 males to every female.[9] Fortunately for the men of the Swift Current district, the ratio improved locally to 1.53 to 1.00 in 1901, and 1.55 to 1.00 in 1906 (see Table 5 below). These more balanced ratios were not entirely due to the arrival in the district of women who either were, or soon became, the wives of local men, but to the settlement of the Mennonites in family groups. The typical settler in the entire area of Assiniboia West in these years, and presumably in this district also, was a single man between the ages of twenty and twenty-nine.[10] As a result, in 1885 there were almost three times as many men as women (289 to 99) in the nineteen to thirty-five year age bracket within the combined census districts,[11] and this situation prevailed for many more years.

TABLE 5

Population and Sex Distribution of the Swift Current District, Census Years 1901, 1906[a]

| | 1901 | | | 1906 | | |
	Male	Female	Total	Male	Female	Total
Rural	168	111	279	1776	1186	2962
Hamlet						
or	74	47	121	363	191	554
Village						
Total	242	158	400	2139	1377	3516
Sex Ratio	153:100			155:100		

[a]Population in area defined by Map 2, p. 4.
Source: *S.P.,* 1906-7, No. 17a, Part 1, pp. 28-31.

It was a young population, even in 1885 when the native Indians and métis made up over forty per cent of the region's people. At this time, over one-third (256) of the 828 people in this vast, almost vacant, region were under nineteen years of age, while most of the remainder (480) were between the ages of nineteen and forty-four. Of the balance, only thirteen were over sixty and just three of these had passed seventy.[12] If the local native population was typical of prairie Indians and métis generally, then it is clear that longevity was extremely rare among them.

It is, perhaps, unusual in such a young population composed, as it was in 1885, of so many métis and Indians, that teenage marriage was so uncommon — only ten girls and two boys younger than twenty-one had married, and just one — a girl — under sixteen years old had done so.[13] Apparently, the Roman Catholic natives and the pagan Indians living in the region and, in turn, in the district, did not favor early marriage. Among the non-Christian Indians, the men preferred to have several mature wives. As for the young, single white men, there is an obvious reason why they had not married — there was a scarcity of single white women of marriageable age locally. Marriage between the local whites and either the half-breeds or the Indians was rare and probably frowned on socially, at least by the whites. Consequently, in 1885 just over one-half the adult males (who were mostly white men) had spouses.[14]

This situation would seem to be ideally suited to a white woman seeking a husband in this prairie frontier. A single white woman or a widow of marriageable age was fairly certain to be promptly sought after as a wife, regardless of how little charm or beauty she possessed. She could take her pick locally from a wide range of young, virile men, and the trains paraded an even broader selection daily. Eastern spinsters would have done well to follow this modified version of the oft-quoted advice to "go west, young woman, go west."

Since, in 1885, the married couples throughout the region were practically all of a productive age, one would expect that the average size of the family group would have been fairly large. Surprisingly, it was not, for it averaged less than two children per family.[15] The latent reproductive potential revealed itself six years later, however, when in 1891 the average number of children per family reached three.[16] This natural increase, which apparently the Swift Current district shared in, was fortunate, for it, along with the establishment of the three "76" ranch-farms there, was partly able to offset the sharp decline in local population when many of the Indians and C.P.R. employees left the district. While no statistics exist to indicate exactly how large the average family unit in the district was in 1901 and 1906, it is probable that it exceeded five persons. This assumption is based upon several factors — the trend to larger families among the earliest settlers, already evident by 1891, the marriage of and the resulting birth of children to several former local bachelors between 1891 and 1906, and the fact that the Mennonites, in particular, usually had large families.

Throughout the quarter-century after 1882, nearly every local family had a home. However, these "homes" were often cold in winter, hot in summer, and cramped, drafty and dark in all seasons. A person's dwelling denoted his position on the economic scale. Moreover, the location of this dwelling, at least in or near Swift Current, was a good indication of his racial origin. The whites worked and lived in their community, which was clustered around the railway facilities. The few métis lived a half-mile away along the creek (between Elmwood Park and Sixth Avenue North-East).[17] When the Indians made camp near the hamlet,[18] they often selected a knoll about one-half mile north-east of the C.P.R. depot (the Swift Current Union Hospital property), or they camped south-east of the hamlet (near the C.P.R. dam).[19] In 1885, when Indians and especially métis were numerous, several of the occupied dwellings were simply wigwams, tents or shanties.[20] While the wigwams and tents may have had the advantage of being cool in summer, they were frigid during the prairie winter. By 1891, the majority of the few Indians who remained had given up their wigwams and moved into shanties abandoned by earlier white residents. As for the white and métis population, every family was living in a frame house.[21] Yet, as was typical of the entire region, many had only one room, although an even larger number of the more affluent families lived in two-storey houses with over six rooms.[22] Presumably, by 1901 the size and quality of housing for the average family in the district was as good as, or better than, it had been before, or was to be later when the land rush began, for at the turn of the century the local residents were mostly long-established settlers. Once large-scale farm settlement began around 1906, with the typical homesteader hastily building his cheap one-roomed shelter from prairie sods or single ply lumber covered with tarpaper, the average dwelling was more like the inferior ones of 1885. Sod houses were almost non-existent locally before 1904, since they were typical of a prairie farming rather than a ranching frontier. The "soddies", while having the advantage of being warmer in winter and cooler in summer than frame houses, had numerous drawbacks. Most of the sod houses were small, dark, one-roomed structures, many with only a dirt floor, with mud falling at any hour from the underside of the sod roofs after heavy rains, necessitating repairs above and clean-up below. Moreover, field mice found them quite comfortable, much to the dismay of the human occupants.

There was as much variation in the amount and quality of furnishings in these pioneer homes as there was in the houses themselves. Except in the Indians' wigwams, there would usually be, in even the poorest house, a bed, chairs, table, cooking stove, water barrel and a food container, plus cooking and eating utensils. Candles or a kerosene lamp lit up these frontier homes. Possibly the pioneer ranchers made some of their own furniture, just as they built a few of their own houses, from logs cut along the waterways. Certainly many of the farm homesteaders who arrived early in the twentieth century built much or all of their first wooden furniture from bits of lumber and packing cases. These home-made furnishings soon gave way to better things, once the settlers were established and could afford to purchase them. And at that point, if they could not find a suitable item locally or in neighboring centres, then the T. Eaton Company catalogue brought the world to their door.

Just as there was a wide range in the quality of housing for the district people before 1907, so was there a similar variation in their diets. The Indians fared the worst in both respects. In the aboriginal state they had usually been better off than they soon were after the railway and the new regime drove the buffalo from the plains. The Indians had traditionally depended upon the native prairie to supply their wants. They picked wild saskatoons and chokecherries, killed "prairie chickens", rabbits, antelope, deer and bear and hunted both waterfowl and their eggs. When hunting failed, as it increasingly did after white settlement began, they had to supplement their food supply by gathering buffalo bones and trading them at the stores for such staples as ammunition, flour and other neces-

TWO BACHELOR "SODBUSTERS" NORTH-EAST OF GULL LAKE PREPARING CHRISTMAS DINNER, 1907. Note neckyoke used for hauling water.

sities. When the buffalo bones became almost as scarce as the game animals, they were reduced to starvation and quit the district to search for a livelihood elsewhere.

The métis, standing between Indian and Caucasian in race and culture, similarly occupied a middle position in income, food and housing between the frequently dreadful plight endured by the red man and the fairly good living conditions enjoyed by the whites. Like the Indians, the métis engaged in hunting and food gathering on the prairie, but they also fished and cultivated small garden patches, mostly raising potatoes. The mixed-bloods were more fortunate than the Indians in many ways, especially since they were more willing and able to adapt to the new civilization which the whites had introduced to the district. Many of the métis worked for the whites, mainly in freighting, and when these occupations ended, some of those who stayed on in the district began to raise a few livestock. In this way, they were able to buy some essential food items which they could not themselves produce. Yet, it was a marginal existence. The location of their main settlements, north from Swift Current along the river, southwest along the creek south of Gull Lake, and south at Lac Pelletier, reveals that they were living on the fringes of white society in more ways than one.

Another cultural difference between the white settlers and the Indians and métis is revealed in their attitude to hunting and gathering. To the whites, these were enjoyable outings or "sports" which merely yielded a pleasant change in their diets, whereas the natives were often dependent for survival itself upon these pursuits. Generally, the pioneer townsmen and ranchers atc better during these early years than did those who arrived after 1903 to begin farming. Not only that, but they had a better water and fuel supply than those who later settled out on the dry, treeless prairie. The pioneer farmers, during their first years in the district, generally lived on — or died from — an insufficient and unhealthy diet that was largely made up of starchy foods. Until a well was dug, their water often had to be hauled from a great distance, and many at first had only dried cow dung, called "buffalo chips", for fuel. The established ranchers fared much better.

There were many reasons for this disparity in diet and comfort between the old and the new white rural settlers. The district ranchers lived along the treed coulees beside the river or creek, and they rarely had the problem of a shortage of water or fuel. Often they could irrigate a garden patch on bottom land and thus produce some of their food, whereas many of the local farmers made no attempt at gardening until they had a well to supply water. Furthermore, the ranchers, unlike the majority of the early farmers, had saddle or driving horses, which made it relatively easy for them to travel for groceries to the nearest store. And by making regular shopping trips to Swift Current, as most of the ranchers did, they could share in such bounties as the townsmen enjoyed as a daily fare. Here they could buy fresh dairy produce and eggs, pick up a supply of baked goods and fresh meat, and, if they could afford it, purchase a fairly wide variety of dried, cured, bottled or canned goods at the general stores. Finally, the C.P.R. dining hall, as well as later restaurants, provided a good meal to those who had grown tired of home cooking.

Despite a less than ideal diet, the early citizens of the district were generally healthy. There were few old people and nearly everyone led an active life. However, lack of proper sanitation in Swift Current did cause disease and death. Typhoid fever broke out several times in the 1880's. In the fall of 1888 there were fifteen cases of it at one time in the hamlet[23] — a veritable epidemic considering the small population. Frank Elliot, a young farm laborer who had come from England only months before to work for the "76", died of typhoid in January, 1889.[24] This prompted the N.W.M.P. surgeon from Maple Creek, together with the C.P.R. district superintendent and Sir John Lister-Kaye, to investigate the cause of the disease. It was traced to the water supply, and steps were promptly taken which succeeded in stamping out this scourge.[25] Once again in 1889, poor sanitation led to an outbreak of disease — this time diphtheria. It claimed the lives of the two small children of Mr. and Mrs. J. T. Barker, managers of the C.P.R. dining hall.[26] Other than the 1903 outbreak of smallpox among the métis living around Saskatchewan Landing, which was kept from spreading by a police-imposed quarantine,[27] most of the other health problems among the citizens were of a fairly minor nature. Yet there were numerous accidents, especially to C.P.R. employees, many of them fatal. Between 1903 and 1907 six railwaymen were killed in accidents at work — all of them during the winter months.[28]

Medical help during the earliest years was provided by a doctor from Medicine Hat whose services were under contract by the railway company. The first C.P.R. medical doctor was Dr. Oliver, who made numerous trips to Swift Current in 1887 and 1888 to treat patients there.[29] The following year, those needing hospital care could go to the Medicine Hat Hospital which was opened in 1889.[30] This arrangement continued until 1903, when the C.P.R. engaged Dr. W. H. Field to act as its resident physician at Swift Current.[31] Before the hamlet became a town, two other medical doctors, Louis Hoppin (1905) and E. A. Kelly (1907), and a dentist, S. A. Hodgson (1906), had begun practices in Swift Current. All these medical men had been born in Ontario.[32] Dr. Field opened the first drug store in the hamlet in 1904[33] and also acted as Coroner. Still, there was no hospital in the district (although a Mrs. Warn operated a nursing home), so patients were usually treated either in their homes or in the doctor's office. Frequently, the country wife was helped with childbirth by a neighbor acting as midwife. By 1904, hospital facilities had crept closer — Maple Creek now had a hospital[34] — but many of the local people who sought hospitalization continued to go to Medicine Hat or Moose Jaw, as they had done for years.

Undoubtedly one of the reasons why so many of the district pioneers enjoyed good health was that they usually led a vigorous outdoor life. Their work day was long and physically demanding. The railwaymen's shift was ten or twelve hours a day — frequently at dangerous tasks, while carpenters and similar tradesmen worked two hours longer, six days a week. Merchants opened for business regularly at 7:00 A.M. and closed at 7:00 P.M., except, of course, on Sunday. Hardship was a trail freighter's daily fare. The stockman often left his bunk before dawn to start his day and ended it that night doing barnyard chores by lantern light. Especially from spring thaw until "freeze up" in the fall, the farmer labored industriously to transform his prairie acreage into a productive farm. A fortunate few had, or could hire, a steam engine pulling a many-shared plough to "break" their tough grassland. As many more had horses and a sulky plough on which they could ride. But the great majority of the early farmers possessed only a team of oxen, a single furrow walking plow and harrows with which to till their land. Behind these crude implements they trudged mile after dusty mile over the rough, freshly-turned sod. The pioneer women in the district, particularly those making their homes on ranches or farms, matched their men side by side and often hour for hour at such tasks as seeding, tending poultry and livestock, hauling or pumping water, gardening and many other outdoor chores. In addition, they had their usual duties of cooking, sewing, housekeeping and motherhood to perform — mostly without the aid of a single labor saving machine. It has often and truly been said of the frontier woman that her work was never done. These people had no need for physical fitness programs to keep their muscles from turning to flab.

Not surprisingly, people such as these who led an active life at work, were usually also active at play. Their environment, their need to do something useful, even at play, or merely their need to justify the time taken from work, made hunting in the countryside surrounding Swift Current a natural sport for many men. Besides, fresh, wild meat was always a welcome change in one's diet — particularly if the alternative was no meat at all. Hunting gave the men a chance to demonstrate both their prowess with a gun and their ability as providers in the age-old tradition. Hunters seldom returned empty handed, for in the early years wild animals were fairly plentiful locally and not especially wary.

The most sought after game animal on the prairies had always been the bison or buffalo, and residents of the area played a part in its near extinction. By October, 1881, when the C.P.R. survey crew was staking out the projected line for the railway across the Swift Current Creek, there were only a few stragglers left from the millions of buffaloes that had roamed these plains. They were now so scarce locally that a party which sighted four of these animals along the survey line near Swift Current in 1881 believed that they were the last buffaloes in Canada.[35] This was a false conclusion. H. A. Starkey, a Dominion Lands Surveyor, came across a large number of dead buffaloes scattered over several acres north-west of Saskatchewan Landing in 1883, and concluded that they had died of some disease. Not long afterward he saw about six to ten buffaloes grazing together.[36] A traveller on the Battleford trail during June, 1883, also reported that he had seen one old buffalo south of Saskatchewan Landing,[37] and Hillyard Gregory, a pioneer resident of Swift Current, declared that local Indians occasionally brought in fresh buffalo meat to sell to the C.P.R. construction crews in 1882 and 1883.[38] This may well have been true, for in March, 1883, Pascal Bonneau, a Regina grocer, offered twenty tons of buffalo meat for sale.[39] This meat was brought in by métis hunters from near Willow Bunch.[40] The last few wild bison roaming freely over the plains ranged along the south bank of the South Saskatchewan River between its junction with the Red Deer River and its northward bend at the Elbow. In mid-August, 1886, a Cree Indian came across a herd numbering eighteen and shot two of the bulls and two cows. This led the *Medicine Hat Times* to urge that whatever buffaloes remained be preserved, since the species was almost extinct.[41] Apparently no one in authority, and few others, heeded this advice, for the slaughter went on. In November, 1887, a party of métis from Saskatchewan Landing, led by Jean Nolan, came across eleven of the animals near present-day Empress, Alberta, and shot a magnificent big bull, two cows and a calf from the herd. They brought the heads and hides from these animals to Swift Current where they sold them to J. A. Grant and the Curry Brothers, who in turn sent them to a taxidermist in Winnipeg. The mounted bull's head was later loaned by Grant to the Canadian government, which displayed it at the Chicago World's Fair as being the head of the last of the big buffalo bulls shot on the Canadian

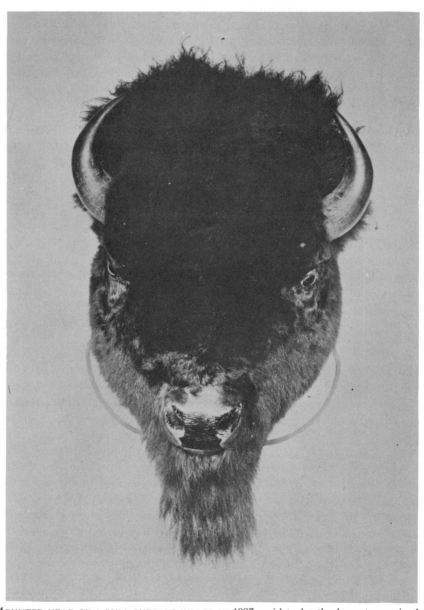

MOUNTED HEAD OF A BULL BUFFALO KILLED IN 1887, said to be the largest seen in the Swift Current district.

THREE PIONEER HUNTERS FROM SWIFT CURRENT, *circa* 1884. From the left: Hillyard Gregory and Wm. C. Tims (employees of F. Fraser Tims), and N.W.M.P. constable, Frank Goodwin.

prairies.[42] Still no move was made by the authorities to protect and preserve the remaining buffaloes. In July, 1888, a half-breed named Sanderson shot two more buffalo bulls that he found in the same vicinity.[43] One month later an Indian named Joe killed six buffloes out of a herd of seven in the same area.[44] That December, buffalo meat was advertised in the *Saskatoon Herald* by Mahaffy and Clinkskill of Battleford.[45] This was probably the last advertised sale of wild buffalo meat in the North-West Territories of animals shot roaming the plains, and it marked the end of these wild animals on the Canadian prairies.

The same disregard for the preservation of the buffalo was shown towards other lesser species of game animals. In 1886, four men were using a swivel gun at Rush Lake to slaughter and export waterfowl in immense numbers.[46] This practice was later prohibited by the government. But again at Rush Lake, in 1890, the general manager of the "76", Thomas Stone, and two of his friends shot sixty-one geese in one day.[47] And in the same area in a single day in 1906, James Woods of Swift Current bagged ninety ducks.[48] Under these circumstances, it is small wonder that the game animals upon which the native depended were soon scarce.

The Indians, métis and whites did not hunt together, nor is there evidence to indicate that in the early years they met and mixed in social gatherings. Each group in the district tended to remain aloof from the other two, making contact only when there was some business to be done. How the Indians entertained themselves is not recorded. In view of their unfortunate plight, they probably had little occasion for celebration. The local métis engaged in festivities during the winter months,[49] much as their ancestors had done. Their amusements consisted of gathering in one another's homes to chat, feast, sing, dance, play games and often drink wine or liquor which they had made themselves.

The entertainment of the whites was as broad in range as possible, given the basically English cultural heritage of these people, their training and ability, their small numbers and the physical environment in which they lived. They were sociable among themselves and were generally willing to give freely of their talents for the sake of entertaining one another. Because their work was hard and, for the ranchers and farmers, lonely as well, they missed few opportunities to get together socially. Often this involved nothing more than a visit with a neighbor, a game of cards (if one's religion permitted it), a shared meal or just a lengthy chat in the general store when one went for mail and supplies. Since they were literate, reading was also a common pastime. As there was no local newspaper until late in 1903, the district people read the news of the region in newspapers published at Battleford, Medicine Hat, Maple Creek or Moose Jaw. Probably some also subscribed to a newspaper from their former homes in Eastern Canada, Great Britain or the United States. A wide variety of inexpensive books and novels could be ordered by mail, if the local store or an obliging neighbor could not provide what one sought.

Besides these casual pastimes, more formal, planned entertainments were regularly held in the district. Community picnics at some wooded spot near the water in summer, such as Fenton's Grove, featuring foot and horse races and ending with a dance in the evening, were always popular. So were debates, readings, lectures, skits, plays, musical concerts and banquets. Local events, such as the transfer of a well-liked C.P.R. employee, a wedding anniversary, a religious or national holiday, were frequently occasions for social gatherings that generally concluded with a dance. Either because these celebrations were too infrequent or because those fond of uproarious amusements felt restricted by the presence of children or staid fellow citizens, the occasional party of Homeric proportions took place. Such was the case in 1901 when James Robinson, a bachelor and an employee of the C.P.R. at Swift Current since 1885, married Florence Frow who worked in the dining hall. The wedding was held on December 23, but the party held in the dining hall continued until after Christmas. Everyone could agree that:

> It was a great wedding, lasting three whole days of 24 hours each, and no one thought of overtime. The road crews joined the party as they reached the end of their run, and the ranchers came and stayed — it was the event of the period . . .[50]

The churches and the school frequently sponsored some local entertainment, often with a patriotic theme,[51] the proceeds going to aid the Medicine Hat Hospital,[52] or some local church project.[53] Several Dominion Day celebrations were sponsored by private groups of citizens before Swift Current became a village and took over such official functions.[54]

The first recorded formal celebration to take place at Swift Current

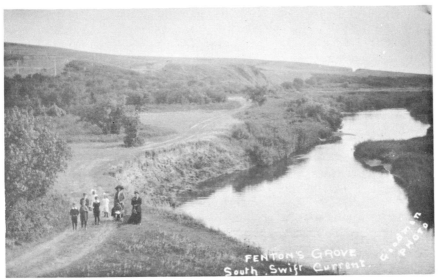

FENTON'S GROVE, a favorite recreation spot (now the site of the Swift Current dam).

was held in the C.P.R. dining hall on Christmas Eve, 1885. Nearly every white resident of the district attended, and a good many of them took an active part in the program. They were a talented, musical group, made up of people born in Canada, Great Britain and the United States. Their patriotism to Canada and the British Empire, their appreciation of talent and their love of good fun is evident from the enthusiastic description of this celebration in the *Medicine Hat Times*:

> An entertainment was given consisting of instrumental and vocal music & C., and it must be admitted, even by an outsider, that it was a marked success. The large hall, which was tastefully decorated with flags and evergreens, and presented a very pretty appearance, was kindly loaned for the occasion by Mr. Allden. The entertainment was commenced with a suitable address by the chairman, Mr. R. Clarke, followed by "This Canada of Ours" sung very effectively by Mr. Fenton, the chorus being well rendered by Miss Fenton, Messrs. Cox, Baker and Knight. E. Baker satisfactorily gave "The Red, White and Blue". A reading by Mr. S. Currie, "Why She Didn't" produced uproarious laughter. Instrumental music by R. Clarke exhibited careful training. W. G. Knight, in the most amusing manner, gave "The Sailor's Consolation". "The Hunting Day" by Mr. Cox was well received. Mrs. W. G. Knight's rendering of "Beautiful Star" was thoroughly appreciated and loudly applauded. Mr. Knight assisted in the chorus. Mr. Pearce's fine tenor voice showed to great advantage on the well known and popular melody, "Gathering up the Shells on the Sea Shore", and in response to a well deserved encore he gave

165

"When the Leaves Begin to Fall". The industrious way in which Mr. Wynn worked while singing "The Village Cobbler", caused roars of laughter. A part song, "Ye Mariners of England", by Mr. and Mrs. Knight and Mr. C. Baker was given in good style and was followed by a very important part of the proceedings, consisting of a very elaborate and substantial spread, provided by the ladies. Too much praise cannot be given for the very excellent arrangements made for serving the repast, and as to the viands, they could not be surpassed. On beholding the elegant designs and the taste displayed in the production of some of the articles of cuisine, one would almost suppose they were works of art to be admired, and not food for mortal man. In connection with this part of the entertainment, the names of Mrs. Powell, Mrs. Pitt, Mrs. Fenton, Mrs. Fothergill and Mrs. Currie, must be mentioned. Immediately after the refreshments had been done justice to, "two strangers" were introduced (Messrs. Baker & Cox), and from the color of their faces, they might have come direct from a very warm place! One was armed with a banjo and the other with some "bones". After discussing the politics of Swift Current and other matters, they commenced to sing and caper in a most alarming way, much to the delight and amusement of everybody. They were heartily cheered and deserve great credit for their performance. Miss Smillie then sang "The Old Wooden Rocker", her sweet voice commanding every attention. Mr. Baker's "Strangers Yet" was a happy hit. A. C. Cox's "I'm Gwine Back to Dixie", was encored and he replied with the "Midship Mite". A reading by the chairman was followed by Mr. Knight's "Sussex Whistling Song", causing great amusement, and for an encore, which would not be denied, he gave "Alonzo the Brave". A comic song by Mr. J. Ashbury, "All's Well" by Messrs. Knight and Baker, and the National Anthem completed the program. Mrs. Fothergill kindly presided at the organ during the evening. The proceedings then terminted amidst mutual good wishes and congratulations.[55]
It could have been the report of many an evening of entertainment picked at random over the next twenty years.

Formal structures regulating various aspects of entertainment soon appeared in the district. Shortly after the first successful entertainment at Swift Current, cited above, a Musical and Debating Society was formed,[56] which planned and directed several succeeding programs.[57] The churches and the school sponsored various others. As the local population grew and became more stable, other organizations soon appeared. In 1894 a Debating and Literary Society was formed.[58] A Bachelor's Club, which sponsored dances and card games, began functioning in 1899.[59] In 1906 a Rifle Association with free rifles and subsidized ammunition supplied by the government attracted several members. Late in 1906 a brass band made up of twelve experienced bandsmen was organized under the able direction of W. A. Stephenson, the local harnessmaker. Also, before Swift Current

THE SWIFT CURRENT BAND, SPRING 1907. Left to right: foreground, H. Smith (drummer boy), A. Furnis; front row, W. Hodges, H. Benson (?), J. G. Maxwell, W. A. Stephenson (the Bandmaster), V. Clinie or L. Talman (?), Fred Jones; back row, Charles Reid (Honorary President), William Marlow (President), W. R. Dick (?), A. S. Moote, C. Williams (?), A. Webber (Sec./Treas.).

became a town in 1907, the Foresters, Orangemen and Masons had formed local lodges, and the Oddfellows were busy organizing. Finally, such trade organizations as the Ancient Order of United Workmen and the Board of Trade were formed early in 1907,[60] but still no Agricultural Society existed in the district.

The white pioneers were generous and hospitable, at least to others of their race. Houses in the country area were rarely locked, especially during the winter, for a wayfarer might need shelter. The ranchers, in particular, usually stabled a traveller's horses, and gave him a place at table and a bed. Moreover, these rural people helped one another in time of need, demonstrating a spirit of charitable co-operation. It can fairly be said that they were generally prudent, law-abiding, thrifty, hard-working people. These qualities enabled them to survive and often to prosper in this frequently harsh environment.

Chapter X

SOME REASONS WHY

Understanding of why a community came to exist or why it then developed as it did is never complete. Complex phenomena are never fully explainable by simple answers. None the less, the historian endeavors to comprehend the past as best he can, and to make his knowledge of it meaningful and useful to those in the present. This requires the logical postulation of generalizations based upon a careful analysis of such facts as he has marshalled in his research. In this way, the historian can and does achieve relative certitude in his work. This chapter presents what, in this writer's opinion, are the major reasons for the birth and the nature of the early growth of the community centred on Swift Current — factors which also serve to place its history in the context of national and international influences and events.

In part, Swift Current was a by-product of the process of nation building. It is obvious that the establishment of Swift Current and its neighboring railway points during 1882-83 was entirely the work of the C.P.R., itself a product of the national policy of John A. Macdonald's federal Conservative government. The main purpose of the railway, as seen by Macdonald's government, was to promote the settlement and development of the Canadian West — primarily for the benefit of central Canada. In turn, economic and geographic factors caused the railway to be built by the southern, prairie route between Moose Jaw and the Rockies, rather than by way of Battleford. Again, a combination of these two factors prompted the C.P.R. syndicate to make Swift Current a divisional point. The steam trains needed water from the Swift Current Creek, and the creek was almost equidistant from the other divisional towns of Moose Jaw and Medicine Hat, which were likewise favored with a suitable water supply. With the outbreak of the North-West Rebellion in 1885, once more geographic and economic considerations — rail, water and trail transportation — combined to cause the Canadian militia to establish its main supply base and communications centre in the hamlet.

From the beginning, the prairie environment, as determined by climate and geography, dictated that agriculture was the economic key to the development of the Swift Current region. While trail freighting did help to promote the early growth of the tiny hamlet, the extension of rail lines into the West made this a transient business which attracted and developed a transient people — the métis. Agriculture, in contrast, meant permanent settlement. Environmental factors virtually dictated the type of agricultural economy that could exist locally. The region was almost exclusively suited to either livestock production or grain farming, although the recognition of even these two potentials came slowly to prospective settlers and others. Gradually, stockmen realized that the range along the district's waterways was suitable for ranching. Years later, those intent on farming concluded that grain would grow on its open grasslands.

In the semi-arid prairie regions of Canada where farm settlement became established earlier than it did around Swift Current, it was the adoption of technological developments, mostly of American origin, which made dry-land farming possible. Such inventions as windmill pumps, barbed wire, breaking plows with chilled steel plowshares, steam-powered tractors, seed drills, flexible harrows, grain binders, threshing machines and a host of other mechanical devices for coping with the prairie environment were invaluable to these prairie settlers. Without exception, all of these technological developments existed before Swift Current did. But, except for a select few of these inventions which were introduced and used locally by ranchers, these implements were rarely to be found in the region before the year 1905. Moreover, whatever sound, dry-land farming techniques that may have been used elsewhere on the semi-arid plains, they were not in common use around Swift Current until years after 1905. It was not the lack of dry-land farming technology which delayed large-scale agricultural settlement in this region, nor was it primarily the local introduction of this technology which changed the agricultural pattern from range to tillage. Indeed, most farmers who lived in the district during the time-span of this history possesed few, if any, suitable implements for farming in this semi-arid region. The reason was economic in nature — they simply could not afford to buy them.

The basic reasons for the trend to grain farming locally were the prospect of profitably growing wheat for export and the scarcity of free or cheap farm lands in less arid prairie regions elsewhere. Two other factors combined to force a rapid transformation of the district's grasslands from a ranching frontier to a farming frontier early in the twentieth century. This change locally from ranching to farming, given the conditions just cited, was inevitable. It was hastened by the unusually severe climatic conditions of the winter of 1906-07, followed by the sharp decline in livestock prices in 1907. These dual hardships ruined many local ranchers.

Immediately after the railway established Swift Current and trail freighting began, it became a tiny service centre providing a frontier hinterland with marketing and transportation facilities. The hamlet, dominating a frontier hinterland, had some of the characteristics of a metropolis in embryo — but all the while Swift Current felt the rival influences of several distant metropolises. Montreal, the C.P.R.'s financial and management centre, as well as being a major port for trans-shipment by water, was the most dominant of these metropolises, for it greatly benefited from Canadian tariff protection afforded by the National Policy. Not only was much of Swift Current's livestock production channelled through Montreal, but the railway employees of the district (who bulked large in the total population) and the local railway facilities fell under the ultimate control of transportation interests located in Canada's largest city. In addition, most of the district's imports came either from or through that centre. Montreal had rivals who vied with it for the control of this hinterland. The "76" ranching enterprises were financed and directed from London, England; the Matador ranch was owned and controlled by investors in Glasgow, Scotland; and the Turkey Track ranching company was a United States firm with offices in Pueblo, California. While the "76" often marketed its livestock in Liverpool, *via* Montreal, the Matador and the Turkey Track, as well as some smaller local ranches, usually shipped their livestock to the Chicago market. Nor was this flow only an outward one from the district. The "76", once it had purchased its basic herds in the U.S., brought in capital, purebred stock and employees from Britain, while the Matador and the Turkey Track brought in livestock and men from the United States. Other, though less important, market centres for district livestock producers, were Winnipeg, Calgary and Vancouver. With the rapid expansion of local grain production during 1905 and 1906, Winnipeg — long the chief wholesale supply point for the district — also became the most important agricultural market centre. In the early years, before either livestock or grain were exported from the district, the abundant harvest of buffalo bones found a ready market in Minneapolis and St. Paul — a trade that was aided somewhat by the construction in 1893 of a railway linking Moose Jaw to North Portal. Although the flow of trade was mainly east and west, as the National Policy intended, there was a strong north-south pull as well.

The Swift Current region, like the prairie West in general, could only develop if profitable export markets expanded for its staple products. Economic and technological developments in the U.S. and Europe resulting in cheaper water transportation to distant markets, plus rising demand and prices in American and European markets, were largely responsible for both expanding and changing the nature of local agricultural production from livestock to grain. It was in response to these changes that Swift Current attained town status by 1907, when it elected its first urban government comprised of a mayor and councillors. And for the same reasons, many sleepy railway sidings throughout the district quickened with new life.

While the basic causes of Swift Current's founding and development were, in the broadest sense, economic and geographic, the role played by key entrepreneurs, naturally, economically motivated, was important. Three men, in particular, stand out in this regard. F. Fraser Tims deserves the title of "Mr. Pioneer Businessman of Swift Current"; Sir John Lister-Kaye obviously was the father of the ranching industry in the region; and Fred Jones, Swift Current's first Overseer and Mayor, was the most influential town builder during the early part of the twentieth century,

171

although William Milburn and Charles Reid also deserve honorable mention here.

The role of the federal government in the settlement process which occurred in the Swift Current region was certainly important, although less so than those external economic forces already cited. Initially, the land settlement policies of the Dominion encouraged the growth of the ranching industry, but almost as soon as ranchers settled in the district the federal government began to withdraw its earlier support until by 1903, when many local ranch leases were opened for homesteading, the government had all but abandoned the ranchers in its apparent willingness to encourage farmers to settle upon even the poorest of the grazing land in the district. The callous indifference with which the federal government had treated the local native people years before obviously was, in turn, displayed in a modified form to the locally-established ranchers.

Just as there was diversity in the economic influences impinging upon this district, so, too, was there variety in the social and cultural influences. The ideas which the settlers had brought with them from Manitoba, Ontario and other provinces in eastern Canada, from the United States, Britain and other European countries, plus the customs of the existing native people, created a cultural mosaic. This was gradually changed by the "melting pot" influence of the school system, the communications media, and business and governmental institutions. These forces, in concert with local environmental influences, produced English-speaking Canadians in the area — although with a prairie outlook which set them somewhat apart in culture from that which emanated from the metropolises.

Institutions can help to shape the history of a people. In turn, some institutions are created by the people of a region, while others, responding to local economic and environmental pressures, are modified from the form that they possessed when first implanted there. The institutions of law, government, church and school were all transplanted into the Swift Current district. The law, which enshrined the institution of private property, was partially challenged by the Mennonites, who defied the government by settling in hamlets rather than on individual homesteads. Many of the ranchers also flouted the law by freely grazing their herds on the unfenced Dominion, C.P.R. or Hudson's Bay Company lands. Seemingly, no effort was made by the N.W.M.P. to confine these or other extra-legal practices. As for the institution of government, the only instance where a federal policy was changed to suit local conditions was the liberalizing in the 1880's of homestead requirements in the district which permitted settlers, for a time, to grow trees rather than raise crops as a condition of "proving up". As a result of economic and environmental forces, the local churches did experience a period of enforced co-operation, but reverted to individualistic denominationalism once the congregations felt that they could operate on their own. However, the early ecumenical experience gained during this period of co-operative church work was not forgotten, but re-emerged early in the twentieth century to help foster, in 1925, the union of Methodists, Congregationalists and Presbyterians in the United Church of Canada. Finally, the school was modelled upon the schools of Ontario in the academic sense, and in this respect this institution was hardly altered by the environment of this ranching frontier. Yet the functions performed by the school house, serving as it did as the community centre, changed the attitudes of many settlers from older societies towards the school and its proper role in a community. Thus, in many ways, the school became a culturizing influence among the adults in the community, just as it was to a greater extent among the local children.

The people of the district did not noticeably demonstrate the traits of rugged individualism reported to be common to the frontiersmen of the American West. While the institution of private property clearly pointed the settlers in that direction, their own recognition of their mutual need for helpful co-operation, if they were to survive in this often-harsh environment, thwarted the growth of such anti-social attitudes.

The environment worked other changes on the minds of the district people, in this case on their political views. As a result of the growth of the ranching industry, by the turn of the century the C.P.R. employees, who were mainly Conservatives, no longer comprised the majority of the local population. The increasing agricultural population, reflecting its own economic interests, demonstrated its approval of the Liberal government's policy of reduced and preferential tariffs (in defiance of the Conservatives' high tariff National Policy) by helping to elect a Liberal, Walter Scott, rather than a Conservative, to represent them in Ottawa. Twice more before 1907 the majority cast their votes federally for the Liberals and these same favorable trade policies. On the provincial level, many of these voters changed their political allegiance and revealed their general sympathy for the grievances of prairie people by electing a Conservative in 1905 who, with his Provincial Rights Party, had campaigned for such western causes as local taxation of C.P.R. and Hudson's Bay Company lands, and the ending of federal control over crown lands and natural resources in the prairie provinces — to them an odious reminder of their colonial status within Canadian federation.

Sometimes chance seems to change the course of history, and probably chance was a factor in Swift Current's early development. Had the C.P.R. syndicate selected a more scientific and less enthusiastic person than John Macoun to report on the agricultural potential of this semi-arid region, perhaps the railway would have by-passed the region far to the north. If there had been a crop failure at Balgonie in 1887, it is probable that Sir John Lister-Kaye would never have launched his grand ranch-farm scheme in 1888. Had drought and hail not devastated the crops on the local "76" estates in 1890, there is a good chance that the district would have acquired a reputation for grain growing much earlier than it did, and

173

consequently the era of the farming frontier probably would have begun during the 1890's, instead of a decade later. But for the disastrous winter of 1906-07, the ranching frontier might have persisted a few years longer in the district. Clearly, chance (or Divine intervention) is not to be casually dismissed as an unimportant historical determinant.

In conclusion, of all the influences which shaped the early years of Swift Current, the physical environment, together with the institutions of law, government, church and school, exerted the greatest guiding force. Yet these were not the catalysts which engendered most developments. Typically, these were but agents acting upon a process set in motion by economic factors.

But even this certainty of the primacy of economic forces in promoting the region's development is made relative by the acknowledgement that individuals do not always recognize what is in their economic interests, and that their conduct is not consistently motivated by such considerations. Free will is an inevitable factor in determining individual action, and men are not all or always motivated by material considerations. Also, it is clear that many settlers came to the region for economic and material purposes which they were unable to achieve, but decided to remain in the community primarily because they either had come to like the prairie environment or felt that they had no other choice.

*   *   *

By 1907, Swift Current and the surrounding district was entering a seven year period in its development in which rapid growth in almost every measurable sector of its life would far surpass all that had gone before. Those who came to settle the virgin plains during this next phase considered themselves the pioneers. Indeed, in many ways they were, for they transformed the district from a prairie thinly dotted with settlers' houses into a farming community with homes on most of its thousands of quarter-sections. They ploughed up its grasslands, obliterated its old trails, built fences, planted shelter belts and harvested millions of bushels of grain from its fields. These "late pioneers" changed the old main line railway sidings into thriving villages and towns and built dozens of communities along the new branch lines of the C.P.R. They also caused Swift Current to become a city by 1914. These were the boom years which were just beginning almost twenty-five years after the C.P.R. first bridged the Swift Current Creek in 1882.

By early 1907, Swift Current was no longer a ranching frontier. Government, law and order had come many years before; the arrival of the railway had marked the end of the old order based upon barter and the buffalo hunt and had ushered in the order of the capitalist market economy: the pioneer ranchers, great and small, had first proven the district's worth; then the farmers at the end of this first quarter-century of Swift Current's history had shown that its plains could yield grain crops to rival those anywhere on the Canadian prairies; the institutions of church and school were well-established; and, in addition to the tiny hamlets which were emerging along the C.P.R. and elsewhere in the district, Gull Lake, a town in embryo, was rising up to challenge the bustling market and service centre of Swift Current.

The prospects of Swift Current and district in 1907 rested on the efforts of many a pioneer, unsung, and now forgotten. But they rested, too, on the attrition of the local natives and many of the early ranchers, as well as the heedless onslaught upon all the local wild creatures and their habitat. Swift Current was part of the frontier saga of westward expansion, and for her, as for the rest of the plains, triumph was purchased with tragedy.

NOTES

CHAPTER I
THE LAND

[1]W. L. Morton, *Manitoba, A History* (Toronto: University of Toronto Press, 1957), p. 104.

[2]Isaac Cowie, *The Company of Adventurers, a Narrative of Seven Years in the Service of the Hudson's Bay Company during 1867-1874 on the Great Buffalo Plains* (Toronto: William Briggs, 1913), pp. 289-292.

[3]John Warkentin, *The Western Interior of Canada, A Record of Geographical Discovery, 1612-1917* (The Carleton Library No. 15; Toronto: McClelland and Stewart Limited, 1964), pp. 146, 187, 229, 232.

[4]Robert Bell, "Report on the Country between Red River and the South Saskatchewan, with Notes on the Geology of the Region between Lake Superior and Red River," A Report to Alfred R. C. Selwyn, Director of the Geological Survey of Canada, *Report of Progress for 1873-74* (Montreal: Dawson Brothers, 1874), pp. 70, 74. Bell mentioned that a friendly Indian had told him of the presence of lignite coal along the banks of the Swift Current Creek, but after being warned by the local Indians not to enter the Swift Current district, he wisely did not attempt to investigate the report. Years later white settlers found small, scattered outcroppings of soft coal in the district. This they promptly dug and used for fuel — a welcome find in a district where firewood was scarce.

[5]John Peter Turner, *The North-West Mounted Police, 1873-1893*, 2 vols. (Ottawa: King's Printer, 1950), Vol. I, p. 142.

[6]One was the old Montana-Elbow trail connecting the trading post, Fort à la Corne, at the junction of the North and South Saskatchewan rivers, to the Missouri River in Montana. The other was the Cypress Hills-Fort Qu'Appelle trail. Until 1874, all known traffic over the portion of these trails lying within the Swift Current district, except for the previously mentioned Cowie, was that of Indians or métis hunters and traders.

[7]J. B. Campbell et al., *Range Management of Grasslands and Adjacent Parklands in the Prairie Provinces* (Ottawa: Canada Department of Agriculture, Queen's Printer, 1966), pp. 8-9.

[8]Canada Department of Agriculture, Research Branch, *Research Report, 1955-1960, Experimental Farm, Swift Current, Saskatchewan* (Ottawa: Queen's Printer, 1963), p. 9.

CHAPTER II
RAIL AND TRAIL

[1]Frank Gilbert Roe, "An Unsolved Problem of Canadian History", *Report of the Canadian Historical Association, 1936* (Toronto: University of Toronto Press, 1936), pp. 70-77. In recent years, two writers have adopted F. G. Roe's views on the matter of the C.P.R.'s selection of this portion of the southern route, but neither have credited Roe as being the source of their ideas. They are: Don W. Thomson, *Men and Meridians: the History of Surveying and Mapping in Canada, 1867-1917* (Ottawa: Queen's Printer, 1967), Vol. II, p. 91, and Pierre Berton, *The Last Spike; The Great Railway, 1881-1885* (Toronto: McClelland and Stewart Limited, 1971), pp. 12-19.

[2]John Macoun, *Autobiography of John Macoun, M.A., 1831-1920* (Ottawa: The Ottawa Field-Naturalists' Club, 1922), p. 171.

[3]John Macoun, *Manitoba and the Great North-West* (Guelph, Ontario: The World Publishing Company, 1882), pp. 78-80.

[4]Macoun, *Autobiography of John Macoun*, pp. 183-185.

[5]Turner, *The North-West Mounted Police*, I, p. 611.

[6]On March 11, 1882, the Dominion Government reserved from homestead entry all of its even-numbered sections next to or along both sides of the C.P.R., creating a mile-wide belt of reserve land for the purpose of forestalling land speculation. Once the railway station sites were selected, some of this land was sold, and, by 1884, the remainder was opened for entry. See: Don W. Thomson, II, p. 91.

[7]Thomson, II, pp. 96-97. A site just west of where the C.P.R. crossed the Swift Current Creek, section 25, in township 15, range 14, west of the third meridian, had been selected to be the townsite.

[8]*The Saskatchewan Herald* (hereafter cited as *S.H.*) (Battleford, North-West Territories), September 2, 1882, and September 30, 1882.

[9]*Ibid.*, December 9, 1882.

[10]J. W. Morrow, *Early History of the Medicine Hat Country* (Medicine Hat, Alberta: The Medicine Hat News, 1923), p. 54.

[11]*The Morning Leader* (Regina), September 15, 1923.

[12]*Golden Furrows, An Historical Chronicle of Swift Current*, ed. Dave Belbeck and Alice Belbeck (Swift Current: The Local Council of Women, 1954), p. 2.

[13]Canada, *Sessional Papers* (hereafter cited as *S.P.*) 1888, No. 25B, p. 174.

[14]Archives of Saskatchewan (hereafter cited as A.S.). Regina, H. Kerr Papers, File no. 248.

[15]*S.H.*, August 16, 1886.

[16]The C.P.R. secured patent to this section on June 24, 1884 — the first issued in the district. See: Saskatchewan, Department of Agriculture, Lands Branch, *Records of Township 15, Range 14, West of the 3rd Meridian.*

[17]Apparently this street was named in honor of Dr. Walter Butler Cheadle, the rugged tutor-physician-companion to Viscount Milton. Together, these two had wandered through the North-West during 1863-64. As in Regina, also planned by Hamilton, the future main street was called 11th Avenue. In Swift Current the only avenue west of main street was 10th Avenue West.

[18]This dam was built on the N.W. ¼ Sec. 19, Twp. 15, Rge. 13, W. 3rd, which adjoins the southeast corner of the original townsite. See Saskatchewan, Department of Agriculture, Lands Branch, *Records of Township 15, Range 13, West of the 3rd Meridian.*

[19]Arlene Esther McPherson, "A History of the Battlefords to 1914," unpublished M.A. Thesis (Saskatoon: University of Saskatchewan, 1966), p. 62.

[20]*S.H.*, January 20, 1883. This crossing is referred to on a Dominion Lands map dated December 1, 1878 (*The Sun,* (Swift Current). June 13, 1951).

[21]*Ibid.*, April 28, 1883. The Battleford merchant, Alexander Macdonald, later rose to prominence by establishing the Winnipeg-based grocery wholesale firm of Macdonald's Consolidated. See McPherson, "A History of the Battlefords to 1914," pp. 79-80.

[22]*Ibid.*, May 26, 1883.

[23]*Ibid.*, February 12, 1890. This private mail service began in 1883. Battleford citizens repeatedly urged the government to make this the Royal Mail route, instead of continuing the mail route through Saskatoon. Not until April, 1887, was this done, but this route was abandoned in November, 1890.

[24]*Ibid.*, June 1, 1885. Tims had sold his Regina store business shortly before buying this freighting and ferry business (*The Regina Leader,* April 7, 1885).

[25]Committee of the Historical Association of Saskatoon, *Narratives of Saskatoon, 1882-1912, by Men of the City* (Saskatoon: University Book Store, n.d.), p. 48.

[26]*The Sun* (Swift Current), 25th Birthday Number, June 1929.

CHAPTER III
SWIFT CURRENT — THE MILITARY BASE

[1]*S.P.*, 1886. No. 8, pp. 50-51.

[2]McPherson, "A History of the Battlefords to 1914", p. 98.

[3]Glenbow-Alberta Institute, Calgary, "Telegrams relating to Riel Rebellion, 1885", news reporter McKinnon at Swift Current to the *Witness* at Montreal and the *Sun* at Winnipeg, April 9, 1885.

[4]*Ibid.*

[5]Public Archives of Canada (hereafter cited as PAC), *Caron Papers,* Vol. 199, p. 167, telegram from John Cottingham to A. P. Caron, April 5, 1885.

[6]*S.P.*, 1886, No. 8, pp. 50-51.

[7]Glenbow-Alberta Institute, Calgary, "Telegrams Relating to Riel Rebellion, 1885", McKinnon to *Witness and Sun,* April 9, 1885.

[8]PAC, *Caron Papers,* Vol. 199, pp. 236-237, telegram from Major General F. Middleton, Fort Qu'Appelle, N.W.T. to A. P. Caron, April 2, 1885.

[9]*Ibid.*, pp. 123-124, telegram from A. MacDonald, Edouard Richard, Robert Young, Winnipeg, to Robert Watson, M.P., April 2, 1885.

[10]*S.P.* 1886, No. 6, Folder.

[11]Reverend Ralph E. R. Howell, *The Parish of Swift Current, 1885-1949, Commemorating the Fiftieth Anniversary of the Dedication of Saint Stephen's Church, Swift Current, by the Right Reverend John Grisdale, D.D., Lord Bishop of Qu'Appelle, on Saint Mark's Day, April 25th, 1899,* n.p., May 1, 1949.

[12]R. H. Roy, "Rifleman Forin in the Riel Rebellion", *Saskatchewan History,* XXI, 3, Autumn, 1968, p. 101.

[13]*S.P.*, 1886, No. 8, p. 51.

[14]*S.P.*, 1886, No. 6, p. 45.

[15]R. H. Roy, "Rifleman Forin", *Saskatchewan History,* XXI, 3, Autumn, 1968, p. 101.

[16]"When Swift Current was an armed camp", diary of Geo. B. Murphy (hereafter cited as Murphy's Diary), Brigade Transport Officer for Battleford column, 1885, *The Sun* (Swift Current), April 2, 1909. The *Northcote* arrived thirteen days before the first of Galt's steamers, the *Minnow,* because its crew were aboard it when orders came despatching the boat to the Landing. Three days passed before Galt's steamers left Medicine Hat, and by this time the water level of the river, as is usual just after the ice goes out, was falling rapidly (PAC, *Caron Papers,* Vol. 199, p.277, telegram from A.T.Galt to A.P.Caron, Apr. 15, 1885).

[17]Murphy's Diary (*The Sun*), April 2, 1909.
[18]*Ibid.*
[19]*S.P.*, 1886, No. 8, p. 51 and Turner, *The North-West Mounted Police, 1873-1893*, II, p. 156.
[20]Middleton was reluctant to have Laurie involved in the campaign. However, by posting him as commander of the Swift Current supply base, he apparently hoped to avoid any possible challenge to his command on the battlefield. Middleton's opinion of Laurie is revealed by his message to A. P. Caron at this time: "He (Laurie) will, I am afraid, be a nuisance and troublesome but I will try him." (PAC, *Caron Papers*, Vol. 199, p. 270, telegram from Middleton to Caron, April 14, 1885).
[21]*S.P.*, 1887, No. 9, Appendix No. 4, "Report of Major General Laurie, Commanding Base and Lines of Communication upon matters in connection with the suppression of the Rebellion in the North-West Territories," p. 6.
[22]*Ibid*, p. 4.
[23]*Ibid*, pp. 4-5.
[24]*The Sun* (Swift Current), June 25, 1958.
[25]*S.P.*, 1887, No. 9, Appendix No. 4, "Report of Laurie", p. 9.
[26]*Ibid.*, pp. 4-20.
[27]R. H. Roy, "Rifleman Forin", *Saskatchewan History*, XXI, 3, Autumn, 1968, pp. 101-102.
[28]*S.P.*, 1887, No. 9, Appendix No. 4, "Report of Laurie", pp. 7-8.
[29]*Ibid.*, p. 20.
[30]PAC, *Caron Papers*, Vol. 199, p. 141, telegram from Galt to Caron, April 2, 1885, and p. 119, telegram from Van Horne to Caron, April 2, 1885, and pp. 162-163, telegram from Van Horne to Caron, April 5, 1885 (in this last telegram the confusion was cleared up as to whether a temporary railway line was intended instead of a telegraph line).
[31]Murphy's Diary (*The Sun*), April 2, 1909.
[32]*S.P.*, 1887, No. 9, Appendix No. 4, "Report of Laurie", p. 5.
[33]*Ibid.*, p. 6.
[34]George F. G. Stanley, *The Birth of Western Canada: A History of the Riel Rebellions* (Toronto: University of Toronto Press, 1966), p. 371.
[35]*S.P.*, 1886, No. 5, p. 361.
[36]*Ibid*, 1887, No. 9, Appendix No. 4, "Report of Laurie", pp. 6-7.
[37]The *Minnow*, owned by Galt's firm, the Northwest Coal and Navigation Company, had a gross tonnage of only 20.05. Its stern paddle wheel was powered by a 5.79 horsepower steam engine. The *Northcote*, operated by the Winnipeg and Western Transportation Company, a subsidiary of the Hudson's Bay Company, was 150 feet long, 28.5 feet wide and had a draft of twenty-six inches. Its gross tonnage was 461 tons and its stern paddle wheel was powered by twin steam engines producing a total of 39 79/100 horsepower (A.S., "Early Steam Vessels on the Saskatchewan River").
[38]PAC, *Caron Papers*, Vol. 199, p. 345, telegram from Laurie to Caron, May 1, 1885. Clarke's Crossing was located just north on the South Saskatchewan River from Saskatoon.
[39]*S.P.*, 1887, No. 9, Appendix No. 4, "Report of Laurie", pp. 8-9.
[40]PAC, *Caron Papers*, Vol. 199, p. 437, telegram from Laurie to Caron, May 16, 1885, and *S.P.*, 1887, No. 9, Appendix No. 4, "Report of Laurie", p. 12.
[41]Desmond Morton and Reginald H. Roy, *Telegrams of the North-West Campaign, 1885* (Toronto: The Champlain Society, 1972), p. lxxxvii.
[42]*S.H.*, May 25, 1885.
[43]PAC, *Caron Papers*, Vol. 199, p. 355, telegram from Laurie to Caron, May 16, 1885.
[44]*S.P.*, 1887, No. 9, Appendix No. 4, "Report of Laurie", p. 12.
[45]PAC, *Caron Papers*, Vol. 199, p. 355, telegram from Laurie to Caron, May 3, 1885.
[46]*S.P.* 1887, No. 9, Appendix No. 4, "Report of Laurie", pp. 9-10.
[47]PAC, *Caron Papers*, Vol. 199, pp. 378-379, telegram from Laurie to Caron, May 8, 1885.
[48]*S.P.*, 1887, No. 9, Appendix No. 4, "Report of Laurie", p. 13.
[49]PAC, *Caron Papers*, Vol. 199, p. 283, telegram from D. Bergen, Surgeon-General, to A.P. Caron, April 17, 1885.
[50]*S.P.*, 1886, No. 5, p. 361. No tents had been provided for the teamsters, so they had to seek shelter from the heavy snowstorm early on April 17 by huddling beneath their carts or wagons (Murphy's Diary, *The Sun*, April 2, 1909).
[51]*Ibid.*, p. 378.
[52]*Ibid.*, No. 6, p. 45.
[53]PAC, *Caron Papers*, Vol. 199, p. 464, telegram from Middleton to Caron, May 22, 1885.
[54]*Ibid.*, p. 553, telegram same to same, June 24, 1885.
[55]*S.P.*, 1886, No. 8, Part II, Appendix B, p. 54. Late in July a small group of Indians from Battleford were sent to Regina via Swift Current. They were escorted by a whole regiment of militia who were returning to Winnipeg. (PAC, *Caron Papers*, Vol. 199, p. 594, telegram from Middleton to Caron, July 21, 1885).
[56]PAC, *Caron Papers*, Vol. 199, p. 633, telegram from E. Whitehead to Caron, October 13, 1885.

CHAPTER IV
THE AFTERMATH OF THE REBELLION
AND THE END OF TRAIL FREIGHTING

[1]*S.H.*, May 17, 1886, and Turner, II, p. 305.
[2]Turner, II, p. 358.
[3]*Ibid.*, pp. 347-348.
[4]Col. S. B. Steele, *Forty Years in Canada* (Winnipeg: Russell, Lang & Co., 1915), p. 247.
[5]*Ibid.*, p. 390.
[6]*S.P.*, 1890, No. 13, 119.
[7]*Ibid.*
[8]*Ibid.*, 1887, No. 7, Part I, p. 79.
[9]PAC, *Caron Papers,* Vol. 199, p. 526, telegram from W. H. Jackson to Caron, June 21, 1885.
[10]*S.H.*, September 17, 1887.
[11]*Ibid.*, June 18, 1887.
[12]Jackson, Whitehead and Forrest reported: "It cannot be denied, however, the people generally in that part of the country (N.W.T.) adhered to the time-honored practice of getting all they possibly could out of the Government." *S.P.*, 1886, No. 6A, Appendix IV, "Preliminary Report of the Commission on War Claims, February 25th, 1886."
[13]*S.H.*, June 21 and November 8, 1886.
[14]*Ibid.*, March 8, 1884.
[15]*Ibid.*, May 17, 1884.
[16]*Ibid.*, July 4 and September 27, 1886.
[17]*Ibid.*, March 20, 1885.
[18]*Ibid.*, June 4, 1890 and *Swift Current Sun,* June 29, 1910.
[19]*S.H.*, November 22, 1886. These large freighting outfits generally used wagons pulled by horse teams rather than carts drawn by a single ox, since they could haul loads at least twice as heavy and cover about half again as many miles per day. The superiority of the freight wagon over the Red River cart, when used on a well-developed trail, hastened the end of cart freighting.
[20]*Ibid.*, August 23, 1886.
[21]*Ibid.*, February 2 and September 24, 1890. Probably Tims sold this business to Russell expecting that the railway would soon be built to Battleford, as announced in 1887, but in 1888 the promoters changed their plans and surveyed a line between Regina and Prince Albert instead.
[22]*S.P.*, 1893, No. 15, p. 107.
[23]Marjorie Wilkins Campbell, *The Saskatchewan* (Toronto: Clarke, Irwin & Company Limited, 1965), p. 233.

CHAPTER V
THE NOBLE "76"

[1]James B. Hedges, *Building the Canadian West, The Land and Colonization Policies of the Canadian Pacific Railway* (New York: The Macmillan Company, 1939), p. 49. Adverse weather conditions after 1885 persuaded the C.P.R. to abandon the farms (*Ibid.*).
[2]A.S., "William Pearce Manuscript," index and vol. 1, p.23.
[3]*S.P.*, 1886, No. 8, p. XI.
[4]*The Medicine Hat Times* (hereafter cited as *M.H.T.*), May 11, 1889.
[5]*The Moose Jaw News and Qu'Appelle Record,* October 10, 1884.
[6]PAC, Department of the Interior, Dominion Lands Branch (Lister-Kaye Papers), volume 93, file no. 80274, correspondence related to Order-in-Council dated October 4, 1884.
[7]"Report on the Cypress Hills, Wood Mountain and Adjacent Country to Alfred R. C. Selwyn, Director of the Geological and Natural History Survey of Canada, from R. C. McConnell," *Geological Survey of Canada, Annual Report for 1885* (Montreal: Dawson Brothers, 1886), Part C, pp. 7-8.
[8]Interview with Contessa de la Feld, May 13, 1971, Victoria, B.C.
[9]Lister-Kaye had hoped to buy all of the 100,000 acres from the C.P.R. with the railway company exchanging their odd numbered sections outside of the blocks with the Dominion for even numbered sections within it. The government, eager to sell its own land, refused to make this trade and offered instead to sell him the even numbered sections at the same price as the C.P.R. wanted for its land. "Lister-Kaye Papers," letter from John R. Hall, Secretary, Department of the Interior, to Sir John Lister-Kaye, December 13, 1886.
[10]*S.H.*, November 22, 1886.
[11]"Lister-Kaye Papers", vol. 93, file no. 80274, Order-in-Council, January 24, 1887, and correspondence related thereto.

[1]-*Ibid.*; Lister-Kaye acquired the mineral rights on the land and planned to develop the coal deposits near Medicine Hat.

[13]*M.H.T.*, October 27, 1887.

[14]*The Weekly Times*, Medicine Hat, Assiniboia, N.W.T., June 14, 1888.

[15]*M.H.T.*, February 9, 1888, and A. S. Ranch file No. 170077.

[16]*M.H.T.*, August 24, 1888.

[17]A.S., Ranch file no. 170077.

[18]*M.H.T.*, August 31, 1888, and *The Daily Times* (Medicine Hat, Assiniboia, N.W.T.), July 21, 1888.

[19]A.S., Ranch File No. F, and "Lister-Kaye Papers", vol. 123, File No. 131787-3, Lister-Kaye to Burgess, August 23, 1888, and same to same, July 13, 1889, and *S.P.*, 1889, No. 15, pp. XXIII-XXIV.

[20]*Medicine Hat News*, August 31, 1888.

[21]*S.P.*, 1889, No. 15, pp. XIII-XXIV.

[22]"Lister-Kaye Papers", vol. 93, File No. 80274, King to Tupper, August 2, 1888.

[23]A.S., Ranch File No. 175823, and *The Sun*, 25th Birthday Number, June 1929.

[24]"Lister-Kaye Papers", vol. 123, File no. 131787, letter from William Pearce to Hon. E. Dewdney, February 12, 1889.

[25]*The Broadview Express*, Grenfell, Saskatchewan, Golden Jubilee Edition, 1955, and *The Sun*, 25th Birthday Number, June, 1929.

[26]*The Daily Times*, July 21, 1888.

[27]"Lister-Kaye Papers", Pearce to Dewdney, February 12, 1889.

[28]Great Britain, *Parliamentary Papers*, Emigration, Sessions 1889-91, No. 9 (London: Henry Hansard and Son, July 31, 1890), p. 158.

[29]*S.H.*, July 24, 1889.

[30]*M.H.T.*, January 17, 1890.

[31]*Ibid.*

[32]Great Britain, *Parliamentary Papers*, Emigration, 1889-91, No. 9, p. 158.

[33]A.S., Ranch File No. 175823.

[34]*The Sun*, 25th Birthday Number, June, 1929.

[35]*S.P.*, 1890, No. 13, p. 119.

[36]*S.H.*, May 8, 1889, and *M.H.T.*, May 18, 1889.

[37]*M.H.T.*, October 17, 1889.

[38]*Ibid.*, September 12, 1889, and *The Sun*, June 25, 1958.

[39]*M.H.T.*, April 6, 1889, and *S.P.*, 1890, No. 13, p. 110.

[40]*M.H.T.*, July 27, 1889, and November 9, 1892.

[41]Great Britain, *Parliamentary Papers*, Emigration, 1889-91, No. 9, p. 159.

[42]*S.H.*, August 7 and September 8, 1889.

[43]Keith Dryden, "The Historic Knoll", *The Western Producer* (Saskatoon), December 12, 1968.

[44]*S.H.*, February 19, 1890.

[45]*Ibid.*, January 22, 1890.

[46]Marjorie Wilkins Campbell, *The Saskatchewan*, p. 251 and Hillyard Gregory, "Swift Current in the Early Days", unpublished article, n.d., pp. 6-7.

[47]*S.H.*, February 26, 1890.

[48]*M.H.T.*, May 1, 1890.

[49]*Ibid.*, July 31, 1890.

[50]*Ibid.*, April 24, 1890.

[51]*S.H.*, April 16, 1890.

[52]*Ibid.*, April 2, 1890.

[53]*M.H.T.*, March 20, 1890, and Great Britain, *Parliamentary Papers*, Emigration, 1889-91, No. 9, p. 153.

[54]*M.H.T.*, July 10, 1890.

[55]*S.H.*, July 23, 1890.

[56]*S.P.*, 1891, No. 19, p. 103.

[57]*M.H.T.*, May 15, 1890.

[58]*Ibid.*, December 18, 1890.

[59]*The Sun*, June 25, 1958.

[60]*Census of Canada, 1890-91*, Vol. 1 (Ottawa: Queen's Printer, 1893), Table II, pp. 112-113.

[61]*S.P.*, 1903, No. 25a, p. 22.

[62]*M.H.T.*, May 4, 1893.

[63]*Ibid.*, May 7, 1891 and *S.P.*, 1892, No. 15, p. 94.

[64]James Shaver Woodsworth, *Thirty Years in the Canadian North-West* (Toronto: McClelland, Goodchild & Stewart, 1917), p. 151.

[65]*M.H.T.*, June 2, 1892.

[66]*The Acts & Proceedings of the Twentieth General Assembly of the Presbyterian Church in Canada, St. John, N.B., June 13-21, 1894* (Toronto: Press of the Canada Presbyterian, 1894), Appendix No. 1, pp. X-XI.

⁶⁷*M.H.T.*, May 11, 1893.
⁶⁸*Ibid.*, January 5, 1893 and February 15, 1894.
⁶⁹*Ibid.*, August 2, 1894.
⁷⁰*The Commercial* (Winnipeg), July 23, 1895.
⁷¹*S.H.*, July 30, 1890.
⁷²PAC, "Lister-Kaye Papers," Vol. 123, file 131787, letter dated July 6, 1895 from A. F. Eden to Minister of the Interior.
⁷³*S.P.*, 1896, No. 15, p. 33.
⁷⁴PAC, "Lister-Kaye Papers", vol. 123, file 131787, A. F. Eden to Clifford Sifton, April 22, 1897.
⁷⁵*Ibid.*, J. Oulet to Clifford Sifton, November 25, 1896.
⁷⁶*Ibid.*, A. F. Eden to C. Sifton, April 22, 1897.
⁷⁷*S.P.*, 1898, No. 13, p. 30.
⁷⁸*Ibid.*, No. 15, p. 83.
⁷⁹*Ibid.*, 1899, No. 15, p. 54.
⁸⁰*M.H.T.*, January 11, 1900.
⁸¹*Ibid.*, 1900, No. 15, p. 39.
⁸²Interview with Alexander Oman, June 20, 1968.
⁸³*M.H.T.*, July 18, 1901.
⁸⁴*Ibid.*, August 5, 1901.
⁸⁵*Ibid.*, August 15, 1901.
⁸⁶Reverend P. M. MacDonald, *Letters from the Canadian West* (Picton, Nova Scotia: Advocate Print, 1903), p. 13.
⁸⁷Jim Greenblat, "Those Were the Days", *The Sun,* October 30, 1970.
⁸⁸*M.H.T.*, August 15, 1901.
⁸⁹*Ibid.*, November 28, 1901.
⁹⁰*Ibid.*, August 15, 1901.
⁹¹*Ibid.*, September 19, 1901.
⁹²*Ibid.*, August 15, 1901.
⁹³*Ibid.*, March 13, 1902.
⁹⁴*Ibid.*, May 1, 1902.
⁹⁵*S.P.*, 1903, No. 28, pp. 13-17.
⁹⁶*Ibid.*, 1893, No. 13, p. 22.
⁹⁷*Ibid.*, No. 25a, p. 22 and *Eighth Annual Report of the Department of Agriculture of the Province of Saskatchewan* (Regina: Government Printer, 1913), pp. 296-303.
⁹⁸*S.P.*, 1904, No. 28, pp. 13-17.
⁹⁹*M.H.T.*, February 25, 1904.
¹⁰⁰Interview with Colonel William Milwarde Yates, May 4, 1970.
¹⁰¹*M.H.T.*, August 27, 1903 and October 29, 1903.
¹⁰²*Ibid.*, April 21, 1904.
¹⁰³*Ibid.*, October 26, 1905.
¹⁰⁴*Ibid.*, November 10, 1904.
¹⁰⁵*Ibid.*, February 25, 1904.
¹⁰⁶*The Gull Lake Advance,* July 1, 1965.
¹⁰⁷*M.H.T.*, October 19, 1905.
¹⁰⁸*Ibid.*, February 25, 1904.
¹⁰⁹The editor of the *Medicine Hat Times* reported that Andrews drew a salary of $50,000 a year — a fabulous and probably exaggerated sum. *Ibid.,* May 18, 1905.
¹¹⁰*M.H.T.*, February 25, 1904.
¹¹¹*Ibid.*, October 19, 1905.
¹¹²Harry Otterson, "Thirty Years Ago on the Whitemud River, or The Last of the Open Range", n.d., p. 22.

CHAPTER VI
SETTLING A BUFFALO PASTURE

¹*S.P.*, 1907, No. 17A, p. 101.
²*The Sun,* 25th Birthday Number, June, 1929.
³*The Gull Lake Advance,* July 5, 1967.
⁴*Henderson's North-Western Ontario, Manitoba & Northwest Directory & Gazetteer, including the City of Winnipeg for 1887* (Winnipeg: James Henderson, Winnipeg Directory Publishing Co., 1887), p. 461.
⁵"Lister-Kay Papers", Vol. 93, file no. 80274, letter by R. A. Ruttan, Homestead Inspector, to H. H. Smith, Dominion Lands Commissioner, Winnipeg, May 6, 1887.
⁶Knight filed on the S.E. ¼ of Sec. 24, Twp. 15, Rge. 14 on August 24, 1885. One week later Fenton applied for two homesteads on the N.W. ¼ of Sec. 18, Twp. 15, Rge. 13 and on the S.W. ¼ of Sec. 18, Twp. 15, Rge. 13. On September 8, 1885, Powell filed upon the S.E. ¼ of

Sec. 30, Twp. 15, Rge. 13. Though Julian was the first settler of the four, he was the last of them to file on a homestead. On September 17, 1885, Julian filed upon the S.W. ¼ of Sec. 30, Twp. 15, Rge. 13 (Saskatchewan, Department of Agriculture, Lands Branch, *Records of Township 15, Range 13, West of the 3rd Meridian and Records of Township 15, Range 14, West of the 3rd Meridian*).

[7]*S.H.*, November 16, 1885.
[8]*The Sun*, 25th Brithday Number, June, 1929.
[9]*S.P.*, 1891, No. 19, p. 104.
[10]*M.H.T.*, August 17 and August 28, 1893.
[11]*S.P.*, 1887, No. 7, pp. 8-9.
[12]*M.H.T.*, March 29, 1900.
[13]*S.P.*, 1895, No. 15, p. 111.
[14]*Ibid.*
[15]Nicholas Flood Davin, *Home for Millions, The Great Canadian North-West, Its Resources Fully Described* (Ottawa: printed by Brown, Chamberlin, Printer to the Queen's Most Excellent Majesty, 1891), pp. 56-57.
[16]*S.P.*, 1903, No. 25a, p. 22.
[17]*The Commercial*, Winnipeg, July 23, 1895.
[18]Saskatchewan, *Annual Report of the Department of Agriculture, 1905* (Regina: Government Printer, 1907), p. 26.
[19]*S.P.*, 1887, No. 34, p. 34 and *S.P.*, 1888, No. 25a, p. 50.
[20]*S.P.*, 1891, No. 17, p. 52.
[21]The river ranches were established by Robert Cruickshank, George Webster, George Smith, Hillyard Gregory, William Openshaw, Louis Guige, James and William McNee, George Howlett, Robert Wayne and William Kirkaldie. The ranchers along the creek, in addition to William Milburn, were William Rutherford, Edward Hogg, William McTaggart, and William and F. McDonald. See: *The Sun*, 25th Birthday Number, June, 1929, and *Henderson's Manitoba and North-West Territories Gazetteer and Directory for 1899* (Winnipeg: The Henderson Publishing Co. Ltd., 1899), p. 407 and p. 413.
[22]Jones and Smart irrigated 210 acres of rye and native grasses at Saskatchewan Landing in 1896, 35¾ acres of timothy, bromus, native grasses and vegetables in 1900, and 104½ acres of similar crops in 1901. Except for the first year, the yields were good. The Canadian Land and Ranche Company ("76") began to irrigate native grasses at Gull Lake in 1897, but abandoned this in later years since abundant rainfall made it unnecessary. See: *S.P.*, 1903, No. 25a, pp. 48-58.
[23]*S.P.*, 1897, No. 13, pp. 37-38.
[24]*S.P.*, 1892, No. 13, p. 54 and *S.P.*, 1895, No. 13, p. 80.
[25]*S.P.*, 1911 No. 25, p. xvii.
[26]*S.P.*, 1898, No. 13, p. 42.
[27]They were Edwin Cooper and John Howlett. See: *The Sun*, 25th Birthday Number, June, 1929.
[28]*Ibid.*, April 23, 1907 and November 14, 1913.
[29]*S.P.*, 1909, No. 25, p. 21.
[30]*The Sun*, June 13, 1951.
[31]*Ibid.*, 25th Birthday Number, June, 1929, and *M.H.T.*, March 29, 1900.
[32]*M.H.T.*, January 13, 1898.
[33]*Ibid.*, August 5, 1901.
[34]*Ibid.*
[35]*The Sun*, June 13, 1951.
[36]*Ibid.*
[37]*The Canada Year Book*, 1914 (Ottawa: King's Printer, 1915), p. 530.
[38]*S.P.*, 1897, No. 15, p. 176 and *S.P.*, 1898, No. 15, p. 83.
[39]*M.H.T.*, April 15, 1897.
[40]*S.P.*, 1897, No. 15, p. 84.
[41]*S.P.*, 1900, No. 15, p. 39.
[42]*S.P.*, 1901, No. 28, p. 31.
[43]*S.P.*, 1900, No. 15, p. 38.
[44]*M.H.T.*, April 19, 1900.
[45]*Ibid.*, February 8, 1900 and *S.P.*, 1901, No. 25, pp. 22-23.
[46]*S.P.*, 1901, No. 28, p. 37.
[47]*S.P.*, 1900, No. 15, p. 39.
[48]*S.P.*, 1902, No. 28, p. 31.
[49]*The Sun*, 25th Birthday Number, June, 1929.
[50]*S.P.*, 1904, No. 25, p. 68.
[51]The Students and Staff of Henry Kelsey Public School, Saskatoon, *What's in a Name?* (Saskatoon: Western Producer Prairie Books, 1968), p. 48.
[52]*S.P.*, 1904, No. 25, p. 68.
[53]*M.H.T.*, August 20, 1903.

[54]*M.H.T.*, September 6, 1906.

[55]Harry Otterson, Thirty Years Ago on the Whitemud River'', n.d., p. 21.

[56]J. W. G. MacEwan, "Matador — A Famous Ranch", *The Family Herald and Weekly Star* (Montreal), September 23, 1942. During 1902-03, Frank G. Bloom and J. C. Huddleson of Trinidad, Colorado, each had leases for 32,800 acres and 87,360 acres respectively in the N.W.T. Probably they were associated with the Matador. *S.P.*, 1904, No. 25, pp. 71-72.

[57]J. W. G. MacEwan, "Matador", *The Family Herald*, September 23, 1942.

[58]Grant MacEwan, *Between the Red and the Rockies* (Toronto: University of Toronto Press, 1952), pp. 222-223.

[59]*M.H.T.*, June 23, 1904.

[60]*Ibid.*, July 13, 1905.

[61]*Medicine Hat News, January 31, 1907.*

[62]*M.H.T.*, June 30, 1898, June 28, 1900, October 8, 1903 and December 15, 1904, and also *Medicine Hat News*, March 7, 1907.

[63]*M.H.T.*, November 26, 1896, January 13 and 27, 1898, and May 24, 1900. Also see *The Sun*, June 25, 1958.

[64]*M.H.T.*, May 24, 1900.

[65]*S.P.*, 1904, No. 28, p. 21.

[66]*M.H.T.*, May 28, 1903.

[67]*S.P.*, 1904, No. 28, p. 16.

[68]*M.H.T.*, October 13, 1904, and *Golden Furrows*, p. 8.

[69]Grant MacEwan, *Between the Red and the Rockies*, p. 132.

[70]*S.P.*, 1906, No. 28, pp. 22-25, and *Annual Report of the Department of Agriculture of the Province of Saskatchewan*, 1905 (Regina: John A. Reid, Government Printer, 1907), p. 25.

[71]*S.P.*, 1907, No. 17a, pp. 104-108.

[72]*Ibid.*, and *Annual Report of the Department of Agriculture of the Province of Saskatchewan*, 1907 (Regina: Government Printer, 1908), p. 26.

[73]*Annual Report of the Department of Agriculture of the Province of Saskatchewan*, 1907, p. 26.

[74]*S.P.*, 1903, No. 25a, pp. 22-26, and *Eighth Annual Report of the Department of Agriculture of the Province of Saskatchewan*, 1912 (Regina: Government Printer, 1913), pp. 290-303.

[75]*The Sun*, June 4, 1909.

[76]Arthur S. Morton, "History of Prairie Settlement", Part I, Vol. II, *Canadian Frontiers of Settlement*, edited by W. A. Mackintosh and W. L. G. Joerg (Toronto: The Macmillan Company of Canada Limited, 1938), p. 125.

[77]*The Farm Business in Saskatchewan, Survey of the Swift Current-Gull Lake District*, by Department of Farm Management, College of Agriculture, University of Saskatchewan (Saskatoon: University of Saskatchewan, July, 1931), p. 14.

[78]*S.P.*, 1915, No. 25, p. 140.

[79]A.S., Papers of the Honourable Thomas Walter Scott ("Scott Papers"), General, 1905, No. 62751.

[80]*M.H.T.*, May 31, 1906.

[81]*Annual Report of the Department of Agriculture of the Province of Saskatchewan*, 1905 (Regina: Government Printer, 1907), p. 26.

[82]*S.P.*, 1908, No. 25, p. 91.

[83]*Fourth Annual Report of the Department of Agriculture of the Province of Saskatchewan*, 1908 (Regina: Government Printer, 1909), p. 91.

[84]A.S., "Scott Papers", No. 631576, Scott to the Department of the Interior, May 9, 1901.

[85]*S.P.*, 1904, No. 25, p. 8.

[86]*S.P.*, 1905, No. 25, p.8.

[87]*S.P.*, 1906, No. 25, p. 8.

[88]*S.P.*, 1906-07, No. 25, p. 8.

[89]*S.P.*, 1907-08, No. 25, p. 7.

[90]*Swift Current Sun*, April 21, 1904.

[91]*M.H.T.*, August 27, 1903.

[92]*Golden Furrows*, p. 8.

[93]S. Delbert Clark, "Settlement in Saskatchewan with Special Reference to the Influence of Dry Farming", unpublished M.A. Thesis, Saskatoon, University of Saskatchewan, 1931, p. 129, and A.S., *Scott Papers*, pamphlet No. 56, 530.

[94]*The Sun*, 25th Birthday Number, June, 1929.

[95]*Scott Papers*, pamphlet No. 56, 530.

[96]*S.P.*, 1904, 1905, 1906, 1906-07, 1907-08, No. 25, pp. 7-8.

[97]A.S., Canada, Department of the Interior, Dominion Lands Branch, Memorandum dated January 27, 1906, microfilm.

[98]*Ibid.*, Memorandum to Privy Council from Clifford Sifton, July 14, 1904, and James G. Gibson, Homestead Inspector, Brandon, to the Secretary. Department of the Interior, August 17, 1904, microfilm.

[99]*Ibid.*, Department of the Interior, Memorandum dated January 27, 1906; microfilm.

[100]*History of Rural Municipality of Excelsior, No. 166* (Swift Current: The Reeve and Council of the R.M. of Excelsior, 1967), p. 19.

[101]S. D. Clark, "Settlement in Saskatchewan with Special Reference to the Influence of Dry Farming", p. 129.

[102]*S.P.*, 1906-07, No. 17a, pp. 137-138.

[103]*Ibid.*, p. 108.

[104]A.S., Canada, *Department of the Interior, Dominion Lands Branch*, Memorandum, Ottawa, July 30, 1906, and letter, P. G. Keyes, Secretary, Department of the Interior, to Dominion Lands Agent, Regina, December 10, 1906, microfilm.

[105]A.S., *Department of the Interior, Dominion Lands Branch*, letter from McLaren, McLeod and Black, Barristers of Morden, Manitoba, to the Honourable Clifford Sifton, Minister of the Interior, December 28, 1904, microfilm.

[106]*Ibid.*, McLaren, McLeod and Black to the Secretary of the Department of the Interior, December 4, 1906, microfilm.

[107]*Ibid.*

[108]*North-West Territories Gazette* (Regina: Government Printer, 1899), May 9, 1899, p. 10, and *Ibid.*, February 28, 1898, p. 4.

[109]*Annual Report of the Department of Agriculture of the North-West Territories, 1900* (Regina: Queen's Printer, 1901), pp. 67-68.

[110]*North-West Territories Gazette*, January 31, 1902, pp. 7-8.

[111]*Ibid.*, March 7, 1905, p. 5.

[112]*Ibid.*, February 15, 1904, p. 4.

[113]A.S., Department of Municipal Affairs, Administrative Services Branch, Municipal Corporation Files, *Rural Municipality No. 137.*

[114]*Ibid.*

[115]*M.H.T.*, November 22, 1906.

[116]*50 Years Along the Cutbank* (Swift Current: Burnham Homemakers Club, Burnham, Saskatchewan, 1955), p. 3, and *The Sun*, June 22, 1955.

[117]"Souvenir Album" (Swift Current: Swift Current Rotary Club, 1955), p. 20.

[118]*History of Rural Municipality of Excelsior No. 166*, 1910-1967 (Swift Current: History Committee of the Rural Municipality of Excelsior, No. 166, 1967), p. 29.

[119]*Medicine Hat News*, July 11, 1907.

[120]*Ibid.*, January 31, 1907.

[121]*Ibid.*

[122]*Ibid.*, March 14, 1907.

[123]*Ibid.*, February 7, 1907.

[124]*Ibid.*

[125]Otterson, "Thirty Years Ago on the Whitemud River", p. 16.

[126]*S.P.*, 1908, No. 28, p. 69.

[127]*Golden Furrows*, pp. 8-9.

[128]*Medicine Hat News*, April 4, 1907.

[129]W. J. Rutherford, "Economic Resources of Saskatchewan", *Canada and Its Provinces*, Volume XX, Adam Shortt and Arthur C. Doughty, general editors (Toronto: Glasgow, Brook & Company, 1914), p. 571.

CHAPTER VII
TOWN BUILDERS — AND OTHERS

[1]*M.H.T.*, November 6, 1885.

[2]*M.H.T.*, May 3, 1900.

[3]This is borne out not only by the account of the agricultural development of the district presented in chapters five and six, but by an analysis of the accounts of the Swift Current post office from its establishment August 1, 1883, through to March 31, 1907, as recorded in the *Sessional Papers* of Canada. Since Swift Current did not have a bank until 1906, its postal money order transactions are the best available indicator of local economic conditions. See Table 2, p. 109.

[4]Canada, *Sessional Papers*, 1885-1908, Reports of the Postmaster General, June 30, 1884-March 31, 1907.

[5]George F. Dawson, *The Municipal System of Saskatchewan* (Regina: The Department of Municipal Affairs, 1955), p. 33.

[6]*North-West Territories Gazette*, February 28, 1898, p. 4.

[7]*Ibid.*, June 1, 1896, p. 76.

[8]Department of Municipal Affairs, Administrative Services Branch, Municipal Corporation Files, Cities: Swift Current, File No. 1.

[9]*Ibid.*

[10]*Annual Report of the Department of Agriculture of the North-West Territories*, 1900 (Regina: Queen's Printer, 1901), p. 48.

[11]Department of Municipal Affairs, *Swift Current,* File No. 1 and *M.H.T.,* August 27, 1903.
[12]L. A. Hamilton's 1888 plan of the townsite was followed but was expanded. The area of the village was the S.E. ¼ of S. 25, T. 15, R. 14 and the S.W. ¼ of S. 30, T. 15, R. 13, both W. 3 (*North-West Territories Gazette,* February 15, 1904, p. 4.).
[13]*Swift Current Sun,* April 23, 1907.
[14]Archibald B. Clark, "Municipal Institutions", *Canada and Its Provinces; A History of the Canadian People and their Institutions by One Hundred Associates,* Adam Shortt and Arthur Doughty, general editors, Volume XX (Toronto: Glasgow, Brook and Company, 1914), p. 399.
[15]*Swift Current Sun,* April 23, 1907.
[16]Village of Swift Current, Village Council Minutes, April 11, 1904.
[17]*Ibid.,* May 23, 1904 and Department of Municipal Affairs, *Swift Current,* File No. 1.
[18]Department of Municipal Affairs, *Swift Current,* File No. 1.
[19]*S.P.,* 1904, No. 28, p. 21.
[20]*Swift Current Sun,* April 21, 1904.
[21]*Henderson's Manitoba, North-West Territories and Western Ontario Gazetteer and Directory for 1904* (Winnipeg: Henderson Directories Limited, 1904), p. 454.
[22]Hedges, *Building the Canadian West,* pp. 85-86.
[23]Village of Swift Current, Village Council Minutes, January 26, 1905.
[24]*Ibid.,* August 23, 1906.
[25]Town of Swift Current, Town Council Minutes, May 28, 1907.
[26]Department of Municipal Affairs, *Swift Current,* File No. 1.
[27]*Ibid.*
[28]*Ibid.*
[29]George F. Dawson, *The Municipal System of Saskatchewan,* p. 32. The minimal requirements were raised by the Saskatchewan provincial acts of 1908-1909. See *ibid.*
[30]Village of Swift Current, Village Council Minutes, February 27, 1905.
[31]Department of Municipal Affairs, *Swift Current,* File No. 1.
[32]*Ibid.*
[33]*M.H.T.,* July 19, 1906.
[34]*Henderson's Manitoba, North-West Territories and Western Ontario Gazetteer and Directory for 1904,* p. 454, *Henderson's Manitoba and North-West Gazetteer for 1905,* pp. 1035-1036. *Henderson's North-West Gazetteer for 1906,* pp. 1128-1129.
[35]Village of Swift Current, Village Council Minutes, March 7, 1906.
[36]*Ibid.,* May, 1906.
[37]*Ibid.*
[38]*Ibid.,* August 23, 1906 and September 10, 1906.
[39]*Swift Current Sun,* April 23, 1907.
[40]Village of Swift Current, Village Council Minutes, April 6, 1907.
[41]Town of Swift Current, Town Council Minutes, April 23, April 25, April 30, 1907.
[42]The information given in the following description of Swift Current, except for note 43 below, was compiled from an analysis of the *Swift Current Sun,* April 23, 1907, *Henderson's Gazetteers* for 1906, pp. 1128-1129 and 1907, p. 1601, an interview with W. M. Yates, May 4, 1970, and from photographs of the period.
[43]*M.H.T.,* July 9, 1903, November 19, 1903 and February 11, 1904.

CHAPTER VIII
STATE, CHURCH AND SCHOOL

[1]*S.P.,* 1885, No. 6, p. 135 and p. 145.
[2]*S.H.,* October 11, 1886.
[3]*The Daily Times,* Medicine Hat, June 23, 1888.
[4]*Ibid.,* July 26, 1888.
[5]*S.P.,* 1887, No. 10, Part 1, p. 141.
[6]*M.H.T.,* December 10, 1885.
[7]*S.P.,* 1886, No. 8, p. 7.
[8]*M.H.T.,* February 19, 1891.
[9]Party affiliation in the N.W.T. became stronger after the grant of responsible government in 1897 which placed patronage under the control of the elected governing party.
[10]*Ibid.,* and *Ibid.,* March 19, 1891, and *Journals of the Council of the North-West Territories of Canada, 1887* (Regina: Government Printer, 1888), Appendix E, p. 98.
[11]*The Daily Times,* Medicine Hat, June 23, 1888.
[12]*M.H.T.,* March 19, 1891.
[13]*S.P.,* 1892, No. 13, p. 6.
[14]*S.P.,* 1895, No. 15, p. 209.
[15]*S.P.,* 1897, No. 15, pp. 258-260.
[16]*S.P.,* 1894, No. 15, p. 211 and *M.H.T.,* August 31, 1893.

[17]*S.P.*, 1896, No. 15, p. 215.

[18]*M.H.T.*, February 13, 1896.

[19]*Ibid.*, February 15, 1894.

[20]*Ibid.*, April 19, 1894.

[21]*North-West Territories Gazette,* Regina, August 15, 1892.

[22]*Ibid.*, April 30, 1898, p. 2.

[23]*M.H.T.*, March 8, 1894.

[24]*S.H.*, May 31, 1886. Grant was suggested as a replacement for Davin as Conservative candidate should Davin lose the 1896 election. See: *M.H.T.*, May 14, 1896.

[25]*Scott Papers,* No. 56, 608.

[26]*M.H.T.*, December 17, 1903.

[27]*Swift Current Sun,* April 23, 1907.

[28]*Scott Papers,* No. 31, 535.

[29]*The Sun,* 25th Birthday Number, June, 1929, and *Scott Papers,* No. 39, 179.

[30]*Swift Current Sun,* April 23, 1907, and Department of Municipal Affairs, *Swift Current,* File No. 1.

[31]*Scott Papers,* No. 62,045.

[32]Interview with Colonel W. M. Yates, May 4, 1970.

[33]*Directory of Saskatchewan Ministries, Members of the Legislative Assembly, Elections 1905-1953* (Regina and Saskatoon: The Saskatchewan Archives Board, 1954), p. 92.

[34]*Scott Papers,* No. 62, 904.

[35]Interview with Colonel W. M. Yates, May 4, 1970.

[36]*Directory of Members of Parliament and Federal Elections for the Northwest Territories and Saskatchewan, 1887-1966* (Regina and Saskatoon: The Saskatchewan Archives Board, 1967), p. 27.

[37]*Scott Papers,* No. 62, 434.

[38]Bilbrough acted as Scott's official agent in the Saskatchewan provincial election held August 14, 1908. See: *Scott Papers,* No. 39, 197.

[39]Interview with Colonel W. M. Yates, May 4, 1970.

[40]*Scott Papers,* No. 62, 904.

[41]*M.H.T.*, June 29, 1905.

[42]Interview with Colonel W. M. Yates, May 4, 1970.

[43]*Ibid.*

[44]*Swift Current Sun,* April 23, 1907.

[45]*Golden Furrows,* pp. 42-43.

[46]*Scott Papers,* No. 62,945.

[47]J. H. Stewart Reid, Kenneth McNaught and Harry S. Crowe, *A Source Book of Canadian History* (Toronto: Longmans, Green and Company, 1959), p. 376.

[48]*S.P.*, 1906, No. 28, p. 25.

[49]*S.H.*, August 23, 1886.

[50]*The Sun,* 25th Birthday Number, June 1929.

[51]*S.H.*, May 17, 1886.

[52]*M.H.T.*, May 21, 1884.

[53]*Ibid.*

[54]Steele, *Forty Years in Canada,* p. 172.

[55]*The Moose Jaw News and Qu'Appelle Record,* June 20, 1884; *S.P.*, 1890, No. 13, pp. 109-110; *The Ranching News and Cypress Hills Gazette,* Maple Creek, Assiniboia, N.W.T., May 19, 1904; *M.H.T.*, April 12, 1906.

[56]*The Moose Jaw News and Qu'Appelle Record,* June 20, 1884.

[57]*M.H.T.*, February 3, 1898.

[58]*S.P.*, 1908, No. 28, Appendix E, p. 71.

[59]*S.P.*, 1891, No. 19, p. 185.

[60]*S.H.*, June 28, 1884 and *Journals of the Council of the North-West Territories of Canada, 1887,* Appendix E, p. 98 and p. 100.

[61]*The Moose Jaw News and Qu'Appelle Record,* January 18 and February 15, 1884.

[62]*M.H.T.*, November 19, 1885.

[63]*S.P.*, 1887, No. 7, p. 25.

[64]*M.H.T.*, May 14, 1891.

[65]*Ibid.*, April 5, 1894.

[66]The census districts of Swift Current and Maple Creek, as they were defined for the 1885 and 1891 census years, almost evenly bisected the Swift Current district — the boundary line between the two census districts being the line dividing ranges thirteen and fourteen, less than a half mile east of Swift Current. Curiously, Swift Current, itself, was within the Maple Creek census district in these years. The two districts encompassed all of present southwestern Saskatchewan from as far east as the third meridian (which intersects the C.P.R. just east of Mortlach), and extended as far north as the boundary line which separates townships thirty-four and thirty-five (a line running east and west some eleven miles south of Saskatoon). Together, these two census districts included all the area of the

first Swift Current Dominion Lands Agency and more. Since the Swift Current district of this history comprises only a portion of this huge region, albeit one of the two main areas of settlement during these years — the other being Maple Creek — no accurate statistics can be given about the people or about agriculture within the district based solely on these two censuses. Yet, it is fair to assume that in many ways the picture of the entire region which emerges from these census reports also mirrors the Swift Current district at its centre. The census districts in this region were increased in number and greatly reduced in size before the 1901 census was taken. Moreover, the 1901 and 1906 censuses published data about each populated township in the region. By transferring these data to a map comprising the 121 townships surrounding Swift Current (an area almost seventy miles square), a detailed statistical profile of the district is achieved. For the years from 1901 to 1906 it is possible to be certain about many aspects of life in the district which can only be postulated as logical probabilities for the earlier years. Most references to census data in this and the succeeding chapter are based upon the above rationale.

[67]*Census of the Three Provisional Districts of the North-West Territories, 1884-5* (Ottawa: MacLean, Roger and Co., 1886), Table II, pp. 6-7.

[68]*Ibid.*

[69]*S.P.*, 1886, No. 36, p. 1.

[70]*Ibid.*, Table XIII, pp. 58-59.

[71]*Historical Sketches of the Parishes of the Diocese of Gravelbourg, Saskatchewan, on the Occasion of its Silver Jubilee, 1930-1955* (Winnipeg: The Diocese of Gravelbourg, Sask., 1956), p. 97.

[72]*Census of Canada, 1890-91*, Vol. 1, Table IV, pp. 328-329, and *Census of Canada*, 1901, Vol. 1 (Ottawa: King's Printer, 1902), Table X, pp. 276-279.

[73]*Historical Sketches of the Parishes of the Diocese of Gravelbourg*, pp. 97-98.

[74]H. H. Walsh, *The Christian Church in Canada* (Toronto: The Ryerson Press, 1968), p. 266.

[75]*Historical Sketches of the Parishes of the Diocese of Gravelbourg*, p. 98.

[76]*Census of Canada*, 1890-91, Vol. 1, Table IV, pp. 328-329 and *Fourth Census of Canada*, 1901, Vol. 1, Table X, pp. 276-279.

[77]*Swift Current Sun*, June 11, 1909.

[78]J. W. Morrow, *Early History of the Medicine Hat Country*, pp. 52-53.

[79]*The Acts and Proceedings of the Thirteenth General Assembly of the Presbyterian Church in Canada, Winnipeg, June 2-17, 1887* (Toronto: Presbyterian Printing and Publishing Company, 1887), Appendix No. 1, p. xii and Appendix No. 28, p. lxxxii.

[80]*Sixteenth General Assembly of the Presbyterian Church in Canada, 1890* (Toronto: Press of the Canada Presbyterian, 1890), Appendix No. 1, p. xxvi.

[81]*Ibid.*, and *Ibid.*, Appendix No. 24, pp. civ-cv and *Swift Current Sun*, April 23, 1907 and June 11, 1909.

[82]*Swift Current Sun*, April 23, 1907.

[83]*Sixteenth General Assembly of the Presbyterian Church in Canada, 1890*, Appendix No. 24, p. civ-cv.

[84]*Eighteenth General Assembly of the Presbyterian Church in Canada, 1892*, Appendix No. 1, p. xxxii.

[85]*Twentieth General Assembly of the Presbyterian Church in Canada, 1893*, Appendix No. 26, pp. cxx-cxxi.

[86]*Swift Current Sun*, April 23, 1907.

[87]This was parcel No. 2 of the S.W.¼ of Sec. 30, Twp. 15, Rge. 13, W. 3rd Meridian. This quarter-section had been filed on by Robert Julian in 1885. See: Saskatchewan, Department of Agriculture, Lands Branch, *Records of Township 15, Range 13, West of the 3rd Meridian.*

[88]*The Moose Jaw News and Qu'Appelle Record*, August 1, 1884.

[89]*Census, 1884-5*, Table II, pp. 6-7.

[90]*Census, 1890-91*, Vol. 1, Table IV, pp. 328-329.

[91]Walsh, *The Christian Church in Canada*, p. 271.

[92]Saskatchewan, Department of Agriculture, Lands Branch, *Records of Township 15, Range 13, West of the 3rd Meridian.*

[93]*M.H.T.*, October 6, 1898.

[94]Reverend Howell, *The Parish of Swift Current, 1885-1949*.

[95]*Census, 1901*, Vol. 1, Table X, pp. 276-279. By 1901 the Swift Current district included all or part of the census districts of Swift Current, Saskatchewan Landing, Gull Lake, Eagle Quill Lake, and Chaplin.

[96]*Ibid.*, Table IX, pp. 152-153.

[97]Walsh, *The Christian Church in Canada*, p. 271.

[98]Reverend Howell, *The Parish of Swift Current, 1885-1949*.

[99]J. H. Riddell, D.D., Ll.d., *Methodism in the Middle West* (Toronto: The Ryerson Press, 1946), p. 126.

[100]*M.H.T.*, June 25, 1903.

[101]*Census, 1884-5*, Table II, pp. 607, *Census, 1890-91*, Vol. 1, Table IV, pp. 328-329, *Census, 1901*, Vol. 1, Table X, pp. 276-279.

[102]*Ibid.*

[103]*Census, 1901*, Vol. 1, Table IX, pp. 152-153.

[104]*M.H.T.*, July 13, 1893.

[105]Walsh, *The Christian Church in Canada*, p. 275 and p. 278.

[106]*Swift Current Sun*, April 7, 1904.

[107]*Ibid.*, April 23, 1907.

[108]*History of Rural Municipality of Excelsior, No. 166*, p. 19.

[109]*Census, 1884-5*, Table XIII, p. 59.

[110]*The Sun*, 25th Birthday Number, June, 1929.

[111]*Ibid.*

[112]*Henderson's North-Western Ontario, Manitoba & Northwest Directory & Gazetteer, including the City of Winnipeg, 1887* (Winnipeg: James Henderson, Winnipeg Directory Publishing Co., 1887), pp. 461-462.

[113]*The Sun*, 25th Brithday Number, June, 1929.

[114]*M.H.T.*, July 9, 1887.

[115]*Ibid.*, July 16, 1887.

[116]*Ibid.*, August 2, 1888 and *Henderson's Gazetteer and Directory of British Columbia, North-West Territories and Manitoba, 1889*, as cited in *The Sun*, September 1, 1971, p. 1. Miss Kerr was probably a well-qualified teacher, since she was elected to this key position in the Teachers' Association in which males outnumbered females.

[117]*North-West Territories Gazette*, Regina, March 1, 1890, p. 31 and *The Sun*, 25th Birthday Number, June 1929.

[118]A.S., North-West Territories, *Report of the Board of Education for Quarter Ending December 31, 1889 to Quarter Ending June 30, 1891*, p. 52. The amount of tax revenue apparently should have been $222.89, but only $105.06 of revenue is reported.

[119]*Ibid.*

[120]*Ibid.*

[121]Interview with Alexander Oman, Swift Current, Saskatchewan June 12, 1968.

[122]Interview with Mrs. Florence Peterson (née McTaggart) Swift Current, Saskatchewan, August 8, 1968.

[123]A. S., Department of Education, North-West Territories, Secretary's Office files, 1902-1918, Part 1, *Swift Current School District No. 167*, file no. 36355.

[124]*Ibid.*, file no. 16876.

[125]*Ibid.*, file no. 22727.

[126]*Ibid.*, file no. 36511.

[127]*Ibid.*, and *M.H.T.*, April 21, 1904 and *Swift Current Sun* April 7, 1904.

[128]A.S., Department of Education, *Swift Current School District No. 167*, file no. 35647.

[129]*Ibid.*, file no. 36355.

[130]*Ibid.*, file no. 35565

[131]*Ibid.*

[132]*North-West Territories Gazette*, August 31, 1904, p. 12.

[133]A.S., Department of Education, *Swift Current School District No. 167*, file no. 6639.

[134]*Ibid.*, Cooper to Colder, March 3, 1906.

[135]*Ibid.*, file no. 13113.

[136]*Ibid.*, W. H. Field and Charles Reid to the Deputy Commissioner of Education, September 25, 1906.

[137]*Swift Current Sun*, April 23, 1907.

[138]*M.H.T.*, August 24, 1905.

[139]*History of Rural Municipality of Excelsior, No. 166*, p. 18 and p. 22.

[140]*North-West Territories Gazette*, October 15, 1904, p. 9.

[141]*Medicine Hat News*, January 24, 1907.

[142]*The Gull Lake Advance*, July 5, 1967.

CHAPTER IX
LIVING

[1]*Census, 1884-5*, Table I, pp. 2-3 and *Census, 1890-91*, Vol. 1, Table II, pp. 112-113.

[2]*S.P.*, 1906-7, No. 17a, pp. 28-31.

[3]*Census, 1901*, Vol. 1, Table XI, pp. 400-403.

[4]*S.P.*, 1906-7, No. 17a, pp. 28-31.

[5]*Census, 1884-5*, Table III, pp. 10-11 and Table IV, pp. 14-15.

[6]*Census, 1901*, Vol. 1, Table XI, pp. 400-403.

[7]*Ibid.*

[8]*Census, 1884-5*, Table I, pp. 2-3.

[9]*Census, 1890-91*, Vol. 1, Table III, pp. 220-221.

[10]*Ibid.*
[11]*Census, 1884-5,* Table V, pp. 21-24.
[12]*Ibid.,* pp. 18-33.
[13]*Ibid.,* Table VI, pp. 36-37.
[14]*Ibid.,*
[15]*Ibid.,* Table I, pp. 2-3 and Table V, pp. 18-33.
[16]*Census, 1890-91,* Vol. 1, Table III, pp. 220-221.
[17]Interview with Mr. Donald MacIntosh, December 8, 1971.
[18]During the 1880's and 1890's the local Indians remained in the district only in the winter, going south to the U.S. for the balance of the year. See: *S.P.,* 1896, No. 15, pp. 24-25. In 1896, there were seven Salteaux and nine Crees living at Swift Current. See: *S.P.,* 1897, No. 15, p. 182.
[19]Interview with Alexander Oman, June 20, 1968.
[20]*Census, 1884-5,* Table I, pp. 2-3.
[21]*Census, 1890-91,* Vol I, Table II, pp. 112-113.
[22]*Ibid.*
[23]*S.H.,* November 17, 1888.
[24]*M.H.T.,* January 21, 1889.
[25]*S.P.,* 1890, No. 13, p. 144.
[26]*M.H.T.,* July 6, and July 13, 1899.
[27]*Ibid.,* August 27, 1903.
[28]*Ibid.,* February 5, November 19, and December 3, 1903, April 5, 1906 and *Medicine Hat News,* February 7 and 21, 1907.
[29]*The Daily Times,* Medicine Hat, July 23, 1888.
[30]Mrs. James McDougald, "Cypress Hills Reminiscences", *Saskatchewan History,* Vol, XXIII, no. 1 (Saskatoon: The Saskatchewan Archives Board, 1970), p. 29.
[31]*Swift Current Sun,* April 23, 1907.
[32]*Ibid.*
[33]*Henderson's Manitoba & North-West Territories & Western Ontario Gazetteer for 1904,* p. 454.
[34]McDougald, "Cypress Hills Remininscences." p. 29.
[35]Turner, Vol. I, p. 611.
[36]*The Sun,* June 25, 1958.
[37]*S.H.,* June 23, 1883.
[38]Gregory, "Swift Current in the Early Days," p. 2.
[39]*Regina Leader,* March 29, 1883.
[40]Z. M. Hamilton and M. A. Hamilton *These are the Prairies* (Regina, School Aids and Text Book Publishing Co., Ltd., 1955), p. 24.
[41]*M.H.T.,* August 21, 1886.
[42]J. W. Morrow, *Early History of the Medicine Hat Country,* p. 55 and *The Sun,* June 13, 1951.
[43]*S.H.,* July 7, 1888.
[44]*Ibid.,* August 25, 1888.
[45]*Ibid.,* December 22, 1888.
[46]*Ibid.,* November 29, 1886.
[47]*M.H.T.,* September 11, 1890.
[48]*Ibid.,* September 6, 1906.
[49]Turner, Vol. II, p. 358.
[50]*The Sun,* 25th Birthday Number, June, 1929.
[51]*Ibid.,* July 13, 1893, March 8, 1900 and January 31, 1901.
[52]*M.H.T.,* December 6, 1894 and May 16, 1895.
[53]*Ibid.,* November 24, 1898 and July 4, 1901.
[54]*Ibid.,* July 11, 1895, July 4, 1901, July 9, 1903.
[55]*Ibid.,* December 31, 1885.
[56]*Ibid.,* February 4, 1886.
[57]*Ibid.,* and *Ibid.,* February 27, April 8, May 31, 1886.
[58]*Ibid.,* December 6, 1894.
[59]*Ibid.,* February 21, 1901.
[60]*Swift Current Sun,* April 23, 1907.

BIBLIOGRAPHY

BIBLIOGRAPHICAL NOTE

Formidable obstacles had to be overcome by the author in writing the early history of Swift Current and district. The problem has been primarily one of a lack of any single concentrated body of source material. For example, though Swift Current and other railway points in the region came into being in 1882, a local newspaper did not appear until late in 1903. To make matters more difficult, only two issues of this newspaper exist for the period up to the spring of 1907. Because of this, it was necessary to research copies of other newspapers (generally on microfilm), published during all or part of the period between 1882 and 1907 in such distant communities as Battleford, Medicine Hat, Maple Creek, Moose Jaw, Regina and Winnipeg. Frequently, numerous successive issues of these newspapers had to be meticulously scanned to find even the smallest scrap of information on the Swift Current region. Moreover, in order to find useful material, it was necessary to research special issues of still other Saskatchewan newspapers published to commemorate historic occasions. Finally, every existing issue of the *Swift Current Sun* up to 1915 was read to gain information, as were selected later issues covering many more years. This one aspect of research occupied the author for over a year.

Obviously, a satisfactory history could not be written from material found only in these newspapers or in the local histories cited in the notes, for they mainly covered a period after 1907. A search was made for diaries of pioneers, but other than the excerpt from a diary published by *The Sun* in 1909, nothing was discovered. Appeals were made through the *Swift Current Sun* for the loan of photos, documents or memorabilia of this early period, but without success. However, direct correspondence with pioneers did elicit some response. Since this history begins by describing events which occurred over a century ago and ends with happenings now sixty-eight years old, there was little opportunity to gain much first hand knowledge of past events by interviewing people who had taken part in the developments under study. Still, interviews were secured with the only two Swift Current residents (one since deceased) who had personal recollections of the region during the nineteenth century, and also with two former residents of the district (both over ninety years of age and now residing at Victoria, B.C.), who had arrived in Swift Current early in the twentieth century. An interview was also held in Victoria with the Contessa de la Feld (now deceased), niece of Sir John Lister-Kaye.

In addition to this research, a great deal of published and unpublished material was investigated. Every book or article was consulted which promised to yield some information about this region during this pioneer phase, and while most of these sources did help the author to relate regional developments to the wider scene, only those works cited in footnotes of this history will be found in the bibliography. The most helpful general sources of local information were Grant MacEwan's *Between the Red and The Rockies* and John Warkentin's *The Western Interior of Canada.* In addition, five early *Henderson's Gazetteers,* some found in the Archives of Saskatchewan, others in the Archives of British Columbia, provided valuable facts. In compiling a history of churches in the district, *The Acts and Proceedings of the General Assembly of the Presbyterian Church in Canada,* the *Historical Sketches of the Parishes of the Diocese of Gravelbourg,* as well as the booklet by Reverend Howell on *The Parish of Swift Current* were of great value. Information related to the early history of public education in the district was gathered from a variety of sources, but this research was hampered by the absence of the early minutes of the Swift Current School District. The sections of this book dealing with local government could not have been written without the pertinent municipal files of the Department of Municipal Affairs, in the Archives of Saskatchewan, and the minute books of the village and town councils of Swift Current, kept in the Swift Current City Hall.

Details of the settlement of the local Mennonites between 1904 and 1907 were found mainly in two sources — microfilmed files of the Department of the Interior, Dominion Lands Branch, and the papers of the Hon. Walter Scott, both kept in the Archives of Saskatchewan. The Sir John Lister-Kaye papers in the Department of the Interior, Dominion Lands Branch Correspondence, in the Public Archives at Ottawa, amounting to over 700 pages of material, were microfilmed on request, and were invaluable for writing that portion of this history dealing with the ''76'' ranch-farm operations. A great deal of material exists related to military actions in the Swift Current region during the 1885 Rebellion. Professor R. H. Roy of the University of Victoria consented to the examination of the Caron Papers, which he was then researching, with the result that some previously unpublished and interesting material about the Riel Rebellion was discovered and now forms part of this work. The Glenbow-Alberta Institute augmented that information by providing copies of telegrams related to the rebellion. Finally, the report of Major-General John Laurie, militia commander at Swift Current in 1885 (apparently overlooked by other historians concerned with the Riel Rebellion), proved to be an excellent source of new knowledge.

As helpful as the foregoing sources were, the most wide-ranging information about the early history of the region was found in the annual reports of the various departments of government. The Census records, the reports of the territorial, provincial and federal departments of agriculture, the extensive reports in the *Sessional Papers* of Canada from the several branches of the Department of the Interior, the reports of the Postmaster General and those of the (Royal) North-West Mounted Police, all of which covered at least the years from 1883 to 1907, and the reports of the Minister of Militia and Defence for the period 1885 to 1887, were thoroughly researched with frequently good results. Other government documents, such as government land records of townships in the region, land survey files, certain *Parliamentary Papers* of Great Britain, *Journals of the Council of the North-West Territories of Canada,* and the *North-West Territories Gazette* covering several years, supplied some facts which either resolved a conflict between other sources or provided new information not available elsewhere. Finally, various files of the Archives of Saskatchewan, related to such topics as ranching, steamboat navigation of the South Saskatchewan River, pioneer farming attempts (for example, the William Pearce Manuscript), and early maps and photos of the region helped fill out incidental features of the area.

A. PRIMARY SOURCES

I: Published
a. Public Documents and Official Reports.

The Acts and Proceedings of the Thirteenth to the Twentieth General Assemblies of the Presbyterian Church in Canada. 1887-1894. Toronto: The Presbyterian Church of Canada, 1887-1894.

Bell, Robert, "Report on the Country between Red River and the South Saskatchewan, with Notes on the Geology of the Region between Lake Superior and Red River." *Geological Survey of Canada, Report of Progress for 1873-74.* Montreal: Dawson Brothers, 1874.

Campbell, J. B., Lodge, R. W., Johnston, A. and Smoliak, S. *Range Management of Grasslands and Adjacent Parklands in the Prairie Provinces.* Canada, Department of Agriculture. Ottawa: Queen's Printer, 1966.

Canada. Department of Agriculture. *Census of Canada, 1890-91.* Ottawa: Queen's Printer, 1893.

———. *Census of the Three Provisional Districts of the North-West Territories, 1884-5.* Ottawa: MacLean, Roger and Co., 1886.

———. *Fourth Census of Canada, 1901.* Ottawa: King's Printer, 1902.

———. Research Branch, *Research Report, 1955-1960, Experimental Farm, Swift Current, Saskatchewan.* Ottawa: Queen's Printer, 1963.

———. Department of Trade and Commerce. *The Canada Year Book, 1914.* Ottawa: King's Printer, 1915.

———. Department of Trade and Commerce. *Census of the Prairie Provinces, 1916.* Ottawa: King's Printer, 1917.

———. Parliament. *Sessional Papers,* Annual Report of the Department of the Interior, 1883-1911, Ottawa: Government Printer, 1884-1912.

———. *Sessional Papers,* Annual Report of the Department of Militia and Defence, 1885-87. Ottawa: Queen's Printer, 1886-1888.

———. *Sessional Papers,* Annual Report of the Postmaster General, 1883-1907. Ottawa: Government Printer, 1884-1908.

————. *Sessional Papers,* Annual Report of the (Royal) North-West Mounted Police Force, 1883-1907. Ottawa: Government Printer, 1884-1908.

————. *Sessional Papers,* 1906-7. Census of Population and Agriculture of the Northwest Provinces, Manitoba, Saskatchewan, Alberta, 1906. Ottawa: King's Printer, 1907.

————. *Sessional Papers, 1888.* Report of the Secretary of State on All Subjects Affecting the Canadian Pacific Railway, 1887. Ottawa: Queen's Printer, 1889.

Great Britain. *Parliamentary Papers.* Emigration, Sessions 1889-91. No. 9. London: Henry Hansard and Son, 1890.

North-West Territories. Department of Agriculture. *Annual Report of the Department of Agriculture of the North-West Territories, 1900.* Regina: Government Printer, 1901.

————. Legislature. *Journals of the Council of the North-West Territories of Canada, 1887.* Regina: Government Printer, 1888.

————. *North-West Territories Gazette, for 1890, 1892, 1898, 1899, 1902, 1904, 1905.* Regina: Government Printer, 1890, 1892, 1898, 1899, 1902, 1904, 1905.

Saskatchewan. Department of Agriculture. *Annual Report of the Department of Agriculture of the Province of Saskatchewan, for 1905, 1907, 1908, 1912.* Regina: Government Printer, 1907, 1908, 1909, 1913.

b. Books and Pamphlets.

Committee of the Historical Association of Saskatoon. *Narratives of Saskatoon, 1882-1912, by Men of the City.* Saskatoon: University Book Store, n.d.

Cowie, Isaac. *The Company of Adventurers, a Narrative of Seven Years in the Service of the Hudson's Bay Company during 1867-1874 on the Great Buffalo Plains.* Toronto: William Briggs, 1913.

Davin, Nicholas Flood. *Homes for Millions, The Great North-West, Its Resources Fully Described.* Ottawa: Queen's Printer, 1891.

MacDonald, Rev. P. M. *Letters from the Canadian West.* Picton, Nova Scotia: Advocate Print, 1903.

c. Articles.

McDougald, Mrs. James. "Cypress Hills Reminiscences." *Saskatchewan History.* Vol. XXIII, No. 1. Saskatoon: The Saskatchewan Archives Board, 1970.

Murphy, George B. Diary. *Swift Current Sun* (Swift Current). April 2, 1909.

Roy, R. H. "Rifleman Forin in the Riel Rebellion." *Saskatchewan History.* Vol. XXI, No. 3, Autumn, 1968.

d. Newspapers.

The Broadview Express (Grenfell, Sask.). Golden Jubilee Edition, 1955.

The Commercial (Winnipeg). July 23, 1895.

The Daily Times (Medicine Hat, Alberta). June 23, 1888 and July 21, 1888.

The Medicine Hat News. August 31, 1888, 1894-1895, 1907.

The Medicine Hat Times. 1886-1907.

The Moose Jaw News and Qu'Appelle Record. Moose Jaw, N.W.T., 1884.

The Morning Leader (Regina). September 15, 1923.

The Ranching News and Cypress Hills Gazette (Maple Creek, Assiniboia, N.W.T.). May 19, 1904.

The Regina Leader. 1883-1885.

The Saskatchewan Herald (Battleford, N.W.T. and Sask.). 1882-1907.

The Sun (Swift Current). 25th Birthday Number, June 1929, June 13, 1951, June 22, 1955, June 25, 1958.

Swift Current Sun. April 7 and 21, 1904, April 23, 1907, April 2, June 4 and 11, 1909, June 29, 1910.

The Weekly Times (Medicine Hat, Assiniboia, N.W.T.). June 14, 1888.

e. Gazetteers.

Henderson's North-Western, Ontario, Manitoba & Northwest Directory & Gazetteer, including the City of Winnipeg for 1887. Winnipeg: James Henderson, Winnipeg Directory Publishing Co., 1887.

Henderson's Manitoba and North-West Territories Gazetteer and Directory for 1899. Winnipeg: The Henderson Publishing Co. Ltd., 1899.

Henderson's Manitoba, North-West Territories and Western Ontario Gazetteer and Directory for 1904. Winnipeg: Henderson Directories Ltd., 1904.

Henderson's Manitoba and North-West Gazetteer for 1905. Winnipeg: Henderson Directories Ltd., 1905.

Henderson's North-West Gazetteer for 1906. Winnipeg: Henderson Directories Ltd., 1906.

II. Unpublished

a. Papers.

Canada. Department of the Interior, Dominion Lands Branch, Correspondence of the Minister of the Interior. Vol. 3, File Nos. 410, 595 - 5,617880. Archives of Saskatchewan. (Microfilmed.)

———. Department of the Interior, Dominion Lands Survey Files, 1880-1934, No. 1384. Archives of Saskatchewan.

————. Department of the Interior, Dominion Lands Survey Records, Kerr File, No. 248. Archives of Saskatchewan.

————. Department of the Interior, Ranch File No. F, 170077 and 175823, Archives of Saskatchewan.

Caron Papers, Sections 1-7, pp. 1-640. Correspondence of A. P. Caron, Minister of Militia and Defence during the Riel Rebellion, 1885. Vol. 199, Public Archives of Canada.

North-West Territories. Department of Education. Report of the Board of Education for quarter ending December 31, 1889 to quarter ending June 30, 1891. Archives of Saskatchewan, Regina.

————. Department of Education. Secretary's Office files, 1902-, Part 1, *Swift Current School District No. 167.*

Papers of the Honourable Thomas Walter Scott. Archives of Saskatchewan.

Saskatchewan. Department of Agriculture, Lands Branch. Records of Township 15, Range 14, and Township 15, Range 13, and Township 13, Range 14, all west of the 3rd Meridian.

————. Department of Municipal Affairs, Administrative Services Branch, Municipal Corporation Files. Rural Municipality No. 137. Archives of Saskatchewan.

————. Administrative Services Branch, Municipal Corporation Files, Cities: Swift Current. File No. 1. Archives of Saskatchewan.

Sir John Lister-Kaye Papers. Department of the Interior, Dominion Lands Branch Correspondence: Vol. 93, File 80274, Vol. 123, File 131787, Part 1-3, Vol. 124, File 131787, Part 4. Public Archives of Canada. (Microfilmed.)

Swift Current. Town Council Minutes. 1907-1910.

————. Village Council Minutes. 1904-1907.

Telegrams Relating to the Riel Rebellion, 1885. Glenbow-Alberta Institute, Calgary.

b. Interviews.

Contessa de la Feld, Interviewed at Victoria, British Columbia, May 13, 1971.

Mr. Donald MacIntosh. Interviewed at Victoria, British Columbia, December 8, 1971.

Alexander Oman. Interviewed at Swift Current, Sask., June 20, 1968.

Mrs. Florence Peterson. Interviewed at Swift Current, Sask., August 8, 1968.

Colonel William Milwarde Yates. Interviewed at Victoria, British Columbia, May 4, 1970.

B. SECONDARY SOURCES

I. Published

   a. Books.

Belbeck, Dave and Alice (eds.). *Golden Furrows, an Historical Chronicle of Swift Current.* Swift Current: The Local Council of Women, 1954.

Berton, Pierre. *The Last Spike: The Great Railway, 1881-1885.* Toronto: McClelland and Stewart Limited, 1971.

Campbell, Marjorie Wilkins. *The Saskatchewan.* Toronto: Clarke, Irwin & Co. Ltd., 1965.

Dawson, George F. *The Municipal System of Saskatchewan.* The Department of Municipal Affairs. Regina: Government Printer, 1965.

The Farm Business in Saskatchewan, Survey of the Swift Current-Gull Lake District. Saskatoon: Department of Farm Management, College of Agriculture, University of Saskatchewan, 1931.

Fifty Years Along the Cutbank. Swift Current: Burnham Homemakers Club, Burnham, Sask., 1955.

Hamilton, Z. M. and Hamilton, M. A. *These Are The Prairies.* Regina: School Aids and Text Book Publishing Co. Ltd., 1955.

Hedges, James Blaine. *Building the Canadian West: the land and colonization policies of the Canadian Pacific Railway.* New York: Macmillan Co., 1939.

Historical Sketches of the Parishes of the Diocese of Gravelbourg, Saskatchewan, on the Occasion of its Silver Jubilee, 1930-1955. Winnipeg: The Diocese of Gravelbourg, Sask., 1956.

History of the Rural Municipality of Excelsior, No. 166, 1910-1967. Swift Current: History Committee of the Rural Municipality of Excelsior, No. 166, 1967.

Howell, Rev. Ralph E. R. *The Parish of Swift Current, Commemorating the Fiftieth Anniversary of the Dedication of Saint Stephen's Church, Swift Current, by the Right Reverend John Grisdale, D.D., Lord Bishop of Qu'Appelle, on Saint Mark's Day, April 25th, 1899.* n.p.: n.n., 1949.

Macoun, John. *Autobiography of John Macoun, M.A., 1831-1920.* Ottawa: The Ottawa Field-Naturalists' Club, 1922.

————. *Manitoba and the Great North-West.* Guelph, Ont.: The World Publishing Company, 1882.

MacEwan, Grant. *Between The Red and The Rockies.* Toronto: University of Toronto Press, 1952.

Memories of Yesteryear, Rural Municipality of Miry Creek No. 229, 1913-1963. Saskatoon: Rural Municipality of Miry Creek, 1963.

Morrow, J. W. *Early History of the Medicine Hat Country,* Medicine Hat, Alberta: *The Medicine Hat News,* 1923.

Morton, Arthur S. and Martin, Chester. *History of Prairie Settlement and "Dominion Lands" Policy.* Parts I and II, Vol. II. *Canadian Frontiers of Settlement.* Edited by W. A. Mackintosh and W. L. G. Joerg. Toronto: The Macmillan Company of Canada Limited, 1938.

Morton, Desmond and Roy, Reginald J. *Telegrams of the North-West Campaign, 1885.* Toronto: The Champlain Society, 1972.

Morton, W. L. *Manitoba, A History.* Toronto: University of Toronto Press, 1957.

Reid, J. H. Stewart, McNaught, Kenneth and Crowe, Harry S. *A Source-Book of Canadian History.* Toronto: Longmans, Green & Co., 1959.

Riddell, J. H. *Methodism in the Middle West.* Toronto: The Ryerson Press, 1946.

Stanley, George F. G. *The Birth of Western Canada: A History of the Riel Rebellions.* Toronto: University of Toronto Press, 1966.

Steele, Col. S. B. *Forty Years in Canada.* Winnipeg: Russell, Lang & Co., 1915.

The Students and Staff of the Henry Kelsey Public School in Saskatoon, *What's In a Name?* Saskatoon: Western Producer Prairie Books, 1968.

Thomson, Don W. *Men and Meridians, the History of Surveying and Mapping in Canada, 1867-1917.* 2 vols. Vol. II. Ottawa: Queen's Printer, 1967.

Turner, John Peter. *The North-West Mounted Police, 1873-1893.* 2 vols. Vols. I and II. Ottawa: King's Printer, 1950.

Walsh, H. H. *The Christian Church in Canada.* Revised; Toronto: The Ryerson Press, 1968.

Warkentin, John. *The Western Interior of Canada, A Record of Geographical Discovery, 1612-1917.* The Carleton Library, No. 15, Toronto: McClelland and Stewart, Ltd., 1964.

Woodsworth, James Shaver. *Thirty Years in the Canadian North-West.* Toronto: McClelland, Goodchild & Stewart, 1917.

b. Articles.

Clark, Archibald B. "Municipal Institutions." *Canada and Its Provinces: A History of the Canadian People and Their Institutions by One Hundred Associates.* Vol. XX. Edited by Adam Shortt and Arthur G. Doughty. Toronto: Edinburgh University Press, 1914.

Dryden, Keith. "The Historic Knoll." *The Western Producer* (Saskatoon), December 12, 1968.

Greenblatt, Jim. "Those Were the Days." *The Sun* (Swift Current). October 30, 1970.

MacEwan, J. W. G. "Matador — A Famous Ranch." *The Family Herald and Weekly Star* (Montreal). September 23, 1942.

Roe, Frank Gilbert. "An Unsolved Problem of Canadian History." *Report of the Canadian Historical Association, 1936.* Toronto: University of Toronto Press, 1936.

Rutherford, W. J. "Economic Resources of Saskatchewan." *Canada and Its Provinces: A History of the Canadian People and Their Institutions by One Hundred Associates.* Vol. XX. Edited by Adam Shortt and Arthur G. Doughty. Toronto: Edinburgh University Press, 1914.

c. Directories.

The Saskatchewan Archives Board. *Directory of Members of Parliament and Federal Elections for the Northwest Territories and Saskatchewan, 1887-1966.* Regina and Saskatoon: Government Printer, 1967.

————. *Directory of Saskatchewan Ministries, Members of the Legislative Assembly, Elections 1905-1953.* Regina and Saskatoon: Government Printer, 1954.

d. Newspapers.

The Gull Lake Advance (Gull Lake, Sask.). July 1, 1965 and July 5, 1967.

II. Unpublished

a. Theses.

Clark, S. Delbert. "Settlement in Saskatchewan with Special Reference to the Influence of Dry Farming." Unpublished M.A. thesis, University of Saskatchewan, 1931.

McPherson, Arlene Esther. "A History of the Battlefords to 1914." Unpublished M.A. thesis, University of Saskatchewan, 1966.

b. Other.

Archives of Saskatchewan. "Early Steam Vessels on the Saskatchewan River."

————. Chronological Roll of School Districts.

————. "William Pearce Manuscript." Index and Vol. I. Chapters 1-2.

Gregory, Hillyard. "Swift Current in the Early Days." Unpublished article, n.d. (Mimeographed.)

Otterson, Harry. "Thirty Years Ago on the Whitemud River, or the Last of the Open Range." Unpublished article. Eastend, Sask., n.d. (Mimeographed.)

"Souvenir Album." Swift Current Rotary Club, 1955. (Typewritten.)

INDEX

Adam, Jean-Baptiste, 140.
Agriculture,
  agricultural settlement, 79-84, 86, 91-93;
  farming methods, 63, 64, 67;
  technology, 170;
  markets, 171.
Alberta, see Galt steamers.
Alexander, Wm., 72, 73, 80, 118.
Allen, Rev. Wm. K., 144.
Andrews, D. H., 69, 74, 76, 147, 182
  (Ch. V, fn. 109).
Anglicans, *see* Religion, Church of England.
Animals, 2.
Annable, Geo. M., 133.
Argue and Cooper, 116.

Barker, Mr. and Mrs. J. T., 159.
Baroness, see Galt steamers.
Battleford, 11-56, *passim.*
Battleford-Swift Current trail, 11, 32, 33.
Bell, Major W. R., 58.
Bethania (School), 149, 150.
Beverley, 80, 149.
Bilbrough, Geo. W., 133, 178,
  (Ch. VIII, fn. 38).
Big Bear (Cree Chief), 40, 46, 138.
Blumenhof, 100.
Blumenort, 100.
Bottely, Corporal, 105.
Bracy, W. P., 103.
Brown Edward J., 124.
Buffalo,
  bone trade, 11-12, 23, 50, 51;
  hunting, 1, 2, 161-163.
Burnham, 149.

Canada Northwest Land Co., 19, 118.
Canadian Agricultural Coal and
  Colonization Co. (C.A.C.C. Co.),
  formation, 60;
  acquires livestock, 61, 64, 65;
  establishes ranch farms, 61, 63;
  recruitment of employees, 61-62;
  grain growing, 63, 64, 69;
  diversification, 69-71;
  changes management, 67;
  sheep losses, 67, 69;
  reorganization as Canadian Land and
    Ranche Co., 71.
Canadian Land and Ranche Co.
  (C.L. & R. Co.),
  formation, 71;
  consolidation, 71-72;
  land trade, 71-72;
  operations, 72-73;
  anthrax outbreak, 73-74;
  livestock loss, 73-74, 77;
  disposal of ranch farms, 76.
Canadian Pacific Railway,
  selection of route, 11-14;
  Swift Current becomes divisional point,
    14, 19;
  main line surveying, 12-14;
  branch line surveying, 55;
  Mile belt reserve, 177 (Ch. II, fn. 6);

construction of railway facilities,
  14-15;
train service, 15;
land selection, 15;
dam, 19;
experimental farms, 57-59;
facilities in 1907, 126, 128.
Canadian Red Cross Unit, 40.
Cattle ranching, *see* Ranching.
Cheadle, Dr. W. B., 178 (Ch. II, fn. 17).
Chortitiz (Chortitz), 100.
Church buildings,
  Presbyterian, 141;
  Church of England, 142;
  Mennonite Brethren, 97, 144;
  Methodist, 144;
  Roman Catholic, 140.
Churches, *see* Religion.
Clarke's Crossing, 35, 41, 45, 179
  (Ch. III, fn. 38).
Climate, 7-8.
Clinite, H. E., 103.
Clinton, Hubert Pelham, 61, 62, 68, 69, 138.
Clubs, 166.
Coons, Donald, 146, 149.
Cooper, W. W., 149.
Corbett, R. H., 114.
Councillors, (S.C. rural), 102, 103.
Cowie, Isaac, 5.
C.P.R., *see* Canadian Pacific Railway.
Crane Lake Ranch, 69, 72, 75, 76.
Crime, 137, 138.
Cruickshank, Robert, 76, 80, 108, 116.
Cunliffe, Rev. Thomas W., 142.
Curry, Alex., 21, 83, 161.
Curry, Samuel J., 21, 25, 83, 146, 161, 165.
Cutbank (School), 149.
Cypress Hills, 2-3, 5-6, 13, 39, 69, 83, 84,
  106, 138.

Davin, Nicholas Flood, M.P., 83, 132.
Dawson, Geo. M., 6.
Dawson, S. J., 5-6.
Day, A. J. ("Tony"), 86, 87.
Day, John, 86.
Demographic features,
  population and sex distribution, 1901-1906,
  see Tables 4 and 5, pp. 154-155.
Denny Land Co., 76.
Depression (economic), 118-122;
  "depression phobia", 122.
Desjarlais, Marie-Emilie, 140.
Diseases (human), *see* Health.
Dixon, John, 133.
Doctors and dentists, 124, 160.
Dodds, James T., 103, 133, 147.
Dominion Day celebrations, 127, 143, 164.
Dominion Government,
  homestead policies, 82, 96-100;
  land lease policies, 79, 80, 91, 95.
Dominion Lands Agency, 57, 58, 82, 84, 92.
Dominion Lands Surveyors,
  Hugh Kerr, 16;
  R. C. Laurie, 16, 53;
  L. A. Hamilton, 19, 20.

201